Direct Action in British Environmentalism

Direct action has become a key part of the strategy of the radical environmental movement since the early 1990s, and has been used to address issues such as road building and car culture, genetically modified foods, consumerism and global financial institutions. It has helped shape the political climate and has transformed the way people view political action, undermining the assumption that the power of politicians and big businesses cannot be contested. At the same time, it is highly controversial, often illegal, and has become increasingly militant in 1999 and 2000.

Direct Action in British Environmentalism charts and analyses the nature and impact of this new wave of direct action. The contributors approach the phenomenon from a wide variety of perspectives and disciplines and present data concerning both the quantity and type of recent environmental protest, and the sociological and organisational features of those performing it. Subjects covered include:

- the history of the movement and its influence on contemporary activism
- the identities and new tribalism of radical environmentalists
- the reaction of the mass media
- the impact of direct action on mainstream politicians and policy
- the strategies and tactical innovations which underlie direct action

Direct Action in British Environmentalism is the fullest scholarly analysis available of this phenomenon to date. It is essential reading for students of Politics and Environmental Studies as well as all those interested in the development and impact of direct action in environmentalism.

Benjamin Seel is a Research Associate in Religious Studies and the Institute for Environment, Philosophy and Public Policy at Lancaster University. **Matthew Paterson** is Senior Lecturer in International Relations at Keele University. **Brian Doherty** is Lecturer in Politics at Keele University.

Direct Action in British Environmentalism

Edited by Benjamin Seel,
Matthew Paterson and
Brian Doherty

London and New York

First published 2000
by Routledge
11 New Fetter Lane, London EC4P 4EE

Simultaneously published in the USA and Canada
by Routledge
29 West 35th Street, New York, NY 10001

Routledge is an imprint of the Taylor & Francis Group

Typeset in Baskerville by Taylor & Francis Books Ltd
Printed and bound in Great Britain by Clays Ltd, St Ives plc

British Library Cataloguing in Publication Data
A catalogue record for this book is available from the British Library

Library of Congress Cataloging in Publication Data
Direct action in British environmentalism / edited by Benjamin Seel,
Matthew Paterson and Brian Doherty.
p. cm.
Includes bibliographical references and index.
1. Environmentalism–Great Britain. 2. Direct action–Great Britain.
I. Seel, Benjamin II. Paterson, Matthew III. Doherty, Brian
GE199.G7 D57 2000
363.7'05'0941–dc21

00-032174

ISBN 0–415–24245–2 (hbk)
ISBN 0–415–24246–0 (pbk)

Contents

List of illustrations   vii
Notes on contributors   ix
Acknowledgements   xi
List of abbreviations   xiii

1 **Direct action in British environmentalism**   1
   BRIAN DOHERTY, MATTHEW PATERSON AND BENJAMIN SEEL

2 **Environmental protest in Britain 1988–1997**   25
   CHRISTOPHER ROOTES

3 **Manufactured vulnerability: protest camp tactics**   62
   BRIAN DOHERTY

4 **Snowballs, elves and skimmingtons?:**
   genealogies of environmental direct action   79
   DEREK WALL

5 **Modern millenarians?: anticonsumerism,**
   anarchism and the new urban environmentalism   93
   JONATHAN PURKIS

6 **Coming live and direct: strategies of Earth First!**   112
   BENJAMIN SEEL AND ALEX PLOWS

7 **'It's just not natural'?: queer insights on eco-action**   133
   WENDY MAPLES

8 **Swampy fever: media constructions and
direct action politics**   151
MATTHEW PATERSON

9 **Friends and allies: the role of local campaign groups**   167
GILL CATHLES

10 **The vitality of local protest: Alarm UK and the British
anti-roads protest movement**   183
WALLACE MCNEISH

11 **The politics of the car: the limits of actor-centred models of
agenda setting**   199
NICK ROBINSON

Index   218

Illustrations

Tables

2.1   The spatial distribution of environmental protests compared with
population (1988–1997 inclusive)   32
2.2   Issues and the forms of protest   41
2.3   Number of protests involving leading groups by year   42
2.4   Groups and their forms of protest   43
2.5   Groups and their issues of protest   45
2.6   The interaction between groups (environmental
and animal welfare)   46
9.1   Protest strategies   170
10.1   Socio-demographic characteristics of Alarm UK supporters   189
10.2   Political values and political activism of Alarm UK supporters   190

Figures

2.1   The network of protest: environmental groups and others   30
2.2   Environmental, animal welfare and anti-hunting protests by year   31
2.3   Issues raised in environmental protests (1988–1997)   34
2.4   Four leading kinds of environmental issues over time   35
2.5   Forms of protest over time   36
2.6   Numbers of participants in demonstrations with 500 or more
participants by year   37
8.1   'Swampy's grotto'   153

Contributors

Gill Cathles recently completed an MA in Public Order in the Scarman Centre at Leicester University.

Brian Doherty is Lecturer in Politics, Keele University.

Wallace McNeish teaches in the Department of Sociology at the University of Glasgow.

Wendy Maples is Senior Lecturer in Media Studies in Communications, London Guildhall University.

Matthew Paterson is Senior Lecturer in International Relations, Keele University.

Alex Plows is a researcher in the School of Politics, International Relations and the Environment, Keele University.

Jonathan Purkis is Lecturer in Media and Cultural Studies, Liverpool John Moores University.

Nick Robinson is Lecturer in Politics, University of Leeds.

Christopher Rootes is Reader in Political Sociology and Environmental Politics and Director, Centre for the Study of Social and Political Movements, University of Kent.

Benjamin Seel is a Research Associate in Religious Studies and the Institute for Environment, Philosophy and Public Policy, Lancaster University.

Derek Wall is a researcher in the School of Politics, International Relations and the Environment, Keele University.

Acknowledgements

The idea for this book came from a conference on the theme of direct action in British environmentalism at Keele University in October 1997, organised by Brian Doherty. The conference was intended to combine activist and academic analysis so that both could learn from each other, and this is the spirit that we wanted to retain for the book. Some of those who gave papers at the conference wrote chapters for this book, but all of those who took part in the lively debates on that day helped to encourage us to carry on the discussion, first over a curry, and ultimately in the book. Thus, we should record a particular note of thanks to Simon Festing, Nick Fiddes, Robert Garner, Steve Griggs, David Howarth, George McKay, George Monbiot and John Stewart. Jane Ardley, Tim Arnold, John Barry, Dave Durham and Pauline Weston all provided the kind of help that was really needed on the day without having to be asked.

We owe a number of other debts. The major one is to the contributors, who we think have provided us with lively, enjoyable chapters to read, comment on and edit, and without whom the book would of course not be possible. Without exception, they have provided us with well-organised contributions in decent time, and, in addition to the intellectual side of their efforts, have made the often unwieldy task of coordinating such a book a relatively painless task. Wendy Maples deserves particular mention for her help late on in the project, doing some of the editing legwork on several chapters, formatting some in the house style, and commenting on the introduction. Her enthusiasm about the quality of those chapters she read at a late stage was very welcome. We would also like to thank Caroline Wintersgill for encouraging us with the project early on in its development, for comments on the original book proposal, and for her usual enthusiasm. Thank you to Gavin Burrows for permission to reproduce his cartoon from Do or Die in Chapter 8. Thank you also to those involved in the Transformation of Environmental Activism project for allowing Ben to spend some of his time employed there to work on this book.

Brian Doherty, Matthew Paterson and Benjamin Seel

Abbreviations

ACT-UP	AIDS Coalition to Unleash Power
ALARM	All London Against the Roads Menace
BRF	British Road Federation
CJA	Criminal Justice and Public Order Act 1995
CPRE	Council for the Protection of Rural England
DBFO	Design, Build, Finance and Operate
DoE	Department of the Environment (pre-1997)
DoETR	Department of the Environment, Transport and the Regions (1997 onwards)
DoH	Department of Health
DTp	Department of Transport (pre-1997)
EF!	Earth First!
ELF	Earth Liberation Front
EMO	environmental movement organisation
FoE	Friends of the Earth
GA	Green Anarchist
GEN	Genetics Engineering Network
GMO	genetically modified organism
HSA	Hunt Saboteurs Association
IWW	International Workers of the World
LIFFE	London International Financial Futures Exchange
NGO	non-governmental organisation
NIMBY	Not in my back yard
NSM	new social movement
NVDA	non-violent direct action
RTS	Reclaim the Streets
SACTRA	Standing Advisory Committee on Trunk Roads Assessment
SSSI	Site of Special Scientific Interest
TEA	Transformation of Environmental Activism
TLIO	The Land Is Ours

1 Direct action in British environmentalism[1]

Brian Doherty, Matthew Paterson and Benjamin Seel

Introduction

The 1990s saw substantial changes in the character of British environmentalism. After a decade of increasing professionalisation of environmental organisations and increasing legitimacy of those organisations with state policy makers, environmentalism in the UK suddenly seemed to take a radical turn. In part in reaction to this professionalisation and the insider status of formerly radical groups like Friends of the Earth (FoE) and Greenpeace, a new generation of environmentalists emerged with significantly different aims, ideologies, and forms of action.

At one level, this could be seen simply as a pendulum swing, with a resurgence of radicalism in response to perceived failures or limitations of the reformist strategies adopted by mainstream groups. Radicalisation involved a significant shift in the forms of action, and increasing numbers of activists taking part in direct action. There are debates about whether these forms of direct action are in themselves new, but nevertheless in the 1990s there was a dramatic rise in the amount of direct activism (see Rootes on confrontational action, this volume).

By direct action, we refer to protest action where protesters engage in forms of action designed not only or necessarily to change government policy or to shift the climate of public opinion through the media, but to change environmental conditions around them *directly*. Direct action is almost always illegal and involves situations where participants may or may not be prepared to accept arrest. It includes, but is also broader than, civil disobedience, which, as conventionally defined, requires protesters to be prepared to accept arrest. What distinguishes the new wave of direct action is an ethos characterised by an intention to affect social and ecological conditions *directly*, even while it also (sometimes) seeks indirect influence through the mass media, changed practices of politicians and political and economic institutions.

Traditions of civil disobedience and direct action have tended to draw their power from one of two logics. In Gandhi's 'satyagraha' or 'truth-force' activists have sought to influence their opponents to change their plans by showing the moral superiority of their own perspectives through their willingness to undergo physical discomfort and other self-sacrifices. A second logic of 'bearing witness' makes it clear to the opponent that the protester believes what a government or company is doing is wrong and, despite lacking the physical or political power to stop them, they insist on witnessing the act to show that it is opposed. Both these logics apply moral pressure on opponents; the first appeals to their better nature, while the second also applies political pressure through the appeal to an audience.

The new wave of 1990s direct action draws upon aspects of these logics. Doherty (this volume) for example, shows how protesters have manufactured situations of personal vulnerability through tactical innovations, such as tunnels or treehouses, that give them the moral high ground and require their opponents to use physical power to implement their plans (see also Wall, this volume). Actions such as defending trees against destruction are not intended to show that protesters are in a majority, but to demonstrate the force of their commitment. While most 1990s environmental direct activists were sceptical about the chances of their protests causing a moral turn-about in their opponents, they did seek to apply political pressure through the force of bearing witness. However, what was original about this new wave of direct action was that it developed and propelled a new ethos and spirit of direct action. Protesters had a clearer idea that their opponents' plans and ethos were firmly embedded in the capitalist political economy. The new environmental direct action has also emphasised the direct-ness of its effect. Not content to try to influence politicians or institutions, protesters have seen direct action as disruption seeking to delay environmentally damaging projects and to escalate their costs. At many sites of direct action there was an avowed goal of actually stopping particular projects going ahead by getting in the way, damaging equipment and creating physical obstacles like tunnels, as well as building a groundswell of opinion to make the project politi-cally untenable.

If the media has become a privileged site for the battles over cultural codes, then small but dramatic protests, which attract media attention, are effective. Nevertheless it is not clear that this is why protesters take this kind of action. Those involved in non-violent direct action (NVDA) are, unsurprisingly, ambiva-lent about the media. They do not see themselves as performing only to reach an audience through the media (see, for example, chapters by Seel and Plows, and Paterson, this volume). Most would argue that action which delays destruction and increases the costs for developers is worthwhile and justified, even without the media's gaze.

There has already been much research into this development in British envi-ronmentalism, as the bibliographies to the various chapters in the book attest. This book tries to bring together and develop much of this research, to provide a broad set of accounts of the major questions concerning the nature, role and impact of direct action in British environmentalism in the 1990s. As will be obvious from the diversity of the chapters, there are a wide range of questions which could be asked in relation to this phenomenon, reflecting differences in disciplinary background or political concerns. Among these questions, perhaps seven are worth highlighting here.

One question concerns the novelty or otherwise of this development. How new is the 'new environmentalism', or 'direct action'? Does the putative novelty consist in the forms of action adopted, the forms of organisation and self-understanding of the direct action groups, or simply the scale of activity? Alternatively put, what histories can be written about the origins of contemporary direct action? Such questions are important to understand the significance of this development in terms of broad questions of social change. These questions are addressed in different ways in the chapters by Rootes, Doherty, Wall and Purkis, in particular.

A second question is a fairly general one arising out of social movement analysis. To what extent can the 'new environmentalism' be referred to legitimately as a social movement, or more specifically as a new social movement (NSM)? Such a question asks theoretical questions concerning the nature of the groups involved, their identities and ideologies. We address this question more fully later in this introductory chapter.

A third question follows on: a central debate about (new) social movements is whether they should be understood primarily in terms of instrumental, goal-seeking logics, or in terms of an expressive, identity-oriented logic (Rucht 1990: 162). This question concerning the nature of the groups and individuals involved in direct action is addressed in particular in chapters by Purkis, Seel and Plows, and Maples, while an instrumental logic is assumed by Robinson.

A fourth question, also concerning the nature of (new) social movements, concerns their social basis. From which sections of society do activists such as those involved in roads protests come? Do they follow general patterns often associated with NSMs, of being based in a 'new middle class'? One prevalent image of the roads protests has been that most local environmental campaigns have come from a rather different background – affluent, often Conservative-voting, 'Not in my back yards' (NIMBYs). McNeish's survey of the activists in local anti-roads groups contradicts this image. He shows that most activists were already members of environmental groups, particularly FoE. He also shows that there was a significant overlap between Earth First! and local anti-roads campaigns, and that most activists in Alarm UK (the national network of local anti-roads groups which evolved out of ALARM – All London Against the Roads Menace) were drawn from the new middle class and had a political identity that was leftist, but not socialist. These are important findings because they contradict the perception in media reports that local anti-roads groups were made up of wealthy country-dwellers who were either Conservatives or 'apolitical'. Instead it seems that the social profile of local anti-roads campaigners matched the typical profile of NSMs.

Fifth, are debates within the movement about tactics and strategy. What forms of action are most appropriate or effective in achieving the movement's goals? Are some forms of action (in particular violent ones) off limits? What is the relationship between the direct nature of the action and some of its inevitably mediated consequences? These questions are addressed in particular in the chapter by Seel and Plows, although the last of these questions is also discussed by Paterson. Another aspect of this sort of question is about relationships between direct action groups and others within a broader environmental movement – for example, mainstream environmental organisations and local protest groups. What are the connections between these groups? What are the tensions between them? What are the synergies between their different forms of action and organisation? The chapters by Cathles, McNeish, and Seel and Plows discuss these questions.

Sixth, in what sense should we understand developments in British environmentalism as peculiar to the UK? Are there commonalities between developments in the UK and elsewhere? What is the nature of the transnational connections between direct activists in different countries? These questions ask us to investigate the significance of direct action in environmentalism by interrogating whether it can be regarded as a generalised development in Western capitalist democracies, or particular to specific societies. This question is discussed later in this chapter, and also in the chapter by Rootes.

Finally, what impact has the rise of direct action had? In terms of conventional political science, what has its impact been on state policy-making? Robinson and McNeish both discuss this question very directly. Others discuss, more tangentially, the impacts on other environmental organisations, such as the way in which FoE and Greenpeace have been affected by the rise of direct action. But the impacts of direct action can also be read more broadly, in terms of challenges to broad cultural understandings within societies, and relationships between the state and civil society (see, for example, the chapters by Maples, and Seel and Plows). We emphasise this point in the conclusion to this introductory chapter.

These questions guide the organisation of the book's chapters. Inevitably, some receive more attention in the book than others. In the rest of the introduction, we will focus on the first, second, third and sixth questions. Taken together, the discussion of the origins of direct action, debates concerning the nature of social movements, and comparisons between Britain and other countries provide a starting point for understanding the movement. This will complement the more specific questions raised in subsequent chapters.

The evolution of direct action in British environmentalism

Several chapters in this book make links between the current environmental protest and previous traditions of protest in Britain and beyond. Purkis suggests the new wave of radical activism can be understood as the latest manifestation of the millenarian tradition. Wall examines the history of different forms of action going back to the late medieval period.

But direct action became transformed as part of the transformation of environmentalism which occurred in the late 1960s and early 1970s. The key organisations in this context became FoE (established 1969 in the USA, 1970– 1971 in the UK) and Greenpeace (1971 in Canada, 1977 in the UK). Environmental direct action was initiated in Britain by FoE, who in May 1971 made their first famous bottle-drop on the London offices of Cadbury Schweppes. Richard Sandbrook, then the Director of FoE in the UK, describes how this direct action functioned to kick-start the FoE movement in Britain:

> The early campaigns were a hotchpotch of things. But the whole thing didn't really gel until Graham [Searle] – bless his heart – stood up at the Institute of Contemporary Arts, where they were holding a public seminar about the environment, and said: 'Well I'm going to take my bottles Saturday morning over to Cadbury Schweppes'. Schweppes had just announced they weren't going to use returnable bottles for their drinks products and people had been vocal about this throughout the seminar. He said 'Anyone else who wants to do it can come along, FoE is going to organise a bottle dump on Cadbury Schweppes' ... . We got 50 yards of bottles quite closely set, it looked like a phenomenal sea of bottles. It made a terrific photograph. It went straight into the Sunday papers and that was that. People started ringing us up in the hundreds. We were away.
>
> (Sandbrook, in Lamb 1996: 38)

This action, and to a lesser extent the series of bottle-drops that followed it, attracted a large amount of newspaper coverage, although despite this no change was forced upon Schweppes. However, the interest in FoE that followed from this initial publicity allowed local groups and a membership scheme to be set up, so establishing a decentralised base that has grown and become distinctive of FoE. FoE followed these actions with the picketing of fur retailers, the sailing of inflatable whales up the Thames and, in 1979, they marshalled a Reclaim the Roads event in Trafalgar Square in which 6,000 cyclists took part to stop London traffic for half an hour. FoE's style was to combine such direct actions with a strong emphasis upon detailed and well-researched scientific reports, which were used to lobby government. They also fought nuclear public inquiries and gave evidence in parliamentary select committees.

FoE were quickly overshadowed, however, by Greenpeace's direct actions on the high seas. The *Phyllis Cormack* – Greenpeace's first ship, which was later renamed the *Rainbow Warrior* – was first used to protest about US nuclear tests in earthquake-prone Amchitka in Alaska. Greenpeace then used similar tactics of bearing witness to protest against seal culling in Newfoundland and then to confront whaling fleets. In 1978 early Greenpeace UK volunteers in London converted the 23-year-old *Sir William Hardy* from a trawler into the original *Rainbow Warrior* campaign boat. Through their early campaigns against the Orkney seal cull, Icelandic whaling and British nuclear waste and weapons – and later the famous sinking of the *Rainbow Warrior* by the French Secret Service in Auckland, 1985, while it protested against nuclear tests – Greenpeace successfully gained media coverage and established an international reputation for daring sea-borne protests. As it became more difficult to attract media attention, more risky actions were pursued:

> Public opinion and media perception of what was newsworthy had changed
> over the seventies. The Schweppes bottle dump was big news in 1971, but if
> we'd done it in 1981 it would probably have been completely ignored. Come
> the late seventies/early eighties, to get coverage of a media stunt you had to
> do something more dramatic.
>
> (FoE campaigner, Czech Conroy, in Lamb 1996: 75)

FoE consciously decided not to get involved in this logic of escalation, as they
were committed to acting within the law, and Greenpeace became a kind of
brand leader in environmental activism. It is significant that Conroy speaks here
of 'media stunts' rather than 'direct actions'. The original Greenpeace activists
included experienced journalists who were influenced by Marshall McLuhan's
ideas about the mass media; their actions were therefore especially media-
oriented (see Dale 1996). In the original Amchitka outing the crew returned to
shore with only photograph stills, but by the 1980s Greenpeace was in the business of producing its own televisual images. Whaling actions would be filmed by
activists and edited and narrated by Greenpeace before being released to the
media.

Other notable events in the 1970s were the disruption of public inquiries by
anti-roads campaigners led by John Tyme and actions against nuclear energy
such as the non-violent occupation of the site of a power station at Torness in
Scotland 1978. Yet, in comparison with most other industrialised countries,
direct action against nuclear power in Britain was sporadic and small scale. The
anti-nuclear campaign was overtaken by the growth of the peace movement
after 1979 and this produced a more significant and extensive campaign of
counter-cultural direct action based around peace camps. Although membership
of environmental movement organisations (EMOs) grew apace in the 1980s,
there was little evidence that this numerical strength would produce significant
political change.

The new wave of radicalism

Extensive media coverage of environmental issues, the 15 per cent vote for the
Green Party in the 1989 European elections and Margaret Thatcher's apparent
conversion to the environmental cause indicated in her speech to the Royal
Society in September 1988, suggested that the green movement was on the verge
of a major political breakthrough. However, by the early 1990s, many in the
British environmental movement had realised that the belief in such a breakthrough was illusory and were coming to terms with the limits to achieving
change through British political institutions. By the early 1990s the Green Party
had returned to the political margins after its shock breakthrough in the 1989
European elections, while the major political parties had developed a rhetorical
response to the growth of environmental concern that promised little for those
concerned about the ecological crisis. Subscriptions to FoE and Greenpeace
were falling and after a period of rapid organisational growth they were seeking

to improve the efficiency of their internal organisations by adopting management practices and personnel recruited from business (Rawcliffe 1998; Jordan
and Maloney 1997). The best that could be hoped for was that the government
would have to face up to the responsibilities acknowledged in the various international agreements signed in 1992 at the Earth Summit and that in the longer
term the environmental constituency might be revitalised. But there was little
confidence among politicians that the environment mattered enough to the
public for government to take even some of the measures sought by environmentalists. Above all what was missing in the environmental movement was a
passionate critique of existing social and political structures and of the dominant
assumptions about the relationship between material growth and the good life.
FoE and Greenpeace did their best, but FoE was seeking to influence government and to retain as broad a base of subscription-paying supporters as possible,
which made it less confrontational. Greenpeace, in Britain as in other countries,
concentrated on single issues that were likely to be winnable, as distinct from a
more ideological argument against the forces pushing economic growth and
exploitation.

Without a Green Party strong enough to raise these issues at the national
level, those environmentalists who saw the existing system as deeply unjust and
requiring radical change had no political voice. As well as this, the deregulation
of planning by the Conservative government and the emergence of new industry
and services had led to major new developments in infrastructure such as roads,
airports, supermarkets and housing, and quarries to provide the material for
building. Local environmental groups opposed to specific schemes were soon
confronted with the fact that they had no effective means of challenging a planning decision to accept a developer's proposal. The public inquiry, the formal
occasion when opponents of particular schemes could make their case, was too
expensive and, most importantly, too limited in its terms of reference – because
it excluded any argument that challenged government policy or the principles by
which it was justified. Local anti-roads groups soon learned that their best
chance of success was to concentrate on fighting schemes politically by building
local opposition outside the formal decision-making process. This political exclusion was the shared experience that provided the basis for ad hoc alliances
between local opponents of development schemes and the more radical direct
action groups.

The immediate provocation that ignited the new wave of direct action in
British environmentalism was the Conservative government's *Roads for Prosperity*
road-building programme. Many EMOs took up or increased their commitment
to campaigning on transport policy after they saw the 1989 *Roads for Prosperity*
White Paper (Rawcliffe 1998: 128, see also Robinson, this volume). In 1989 the
Transport Activists' Roundtable was set up to improve the co-ordination of
groups' transport campaigning. In 1990 it included nine groups – Council for the
Protection of Rural England (CPRE), the Environment Council, FoE, Greenpeace,
Ramblers' Association, Wildlife Trusts, Transport 2000, the WorldWide Fund for
Nature and the Youth Hostels Association, and by 1993, Alarm UK had also

become involved (Rawcliffe 1998: 131, 137). They published a joint response to the White Paper called 'Roads to Ruin'. All London against the roads menace (ALARM) became a UK wide group (ALARM UK) networking over 250 local anti-roads groups. This shows the strength and breadth of the opposition that *Roads for Prosperity* provoked.

Earth First! (EF!) UK was the first of the new direct action groups. They were influenced by the original EF! groups set up in 1980 in the USA by a group of whom Dave Foreman became the most well-known.[2] Chris Laughton, a physics graduate, first attempted to launch EF! in the UK in 1987. He imported fifty copies of Foreman and Haywood's *Ecodefense* and sold them to radical bookshops, adding his name and address to each copy as an EF! contact. He also approached green journals including *Green Line* and *Green Anarchist* and promoted EF! through the *Green Anarchist* network. But he failed to meet anybody who was interested (Wall 1999: 45–46). Collie, a Scots activist, had organised a Scottish EF! network prior to 1991 which organised demonstrations on peace themes, but by 1991 it had ceased to be active (Wall 1999: 46). There were a group of activists in the South West who perpetrated covert actions on JCBs and other earth-moving equipment in the summer of 1991, but they were reluctant to organise openly, to network, or to publicise their illegal actions (Wall 1999: 46).

The first open British EF! group was founded by two students, Jake Burbridge and Jason Torrance, in Hastings, East Sussex. They had participated in other green groups and were disillusioned with them. After reading a copy of the US *EF! Journal* they decided to set up an EF! movement in the UK. The first UK action was a blockade of Dungeness nuclear power station; participants were drawn from local peace and anti-nuclear networks. The Hastings EF! group consisted of only about ten people in 1991.

Burbridge and Torrance met up with George Marshall, who had previously been active in the Australian rainforest movement and who was then involved in the London Rainforest Action Group. Marshall provided an issue focus – rainforests – and through his working for the *Ecologist* managed to secure funding from the right-wing financier Sir James Goldsmith (Wall 1999: 47–49). Given for rainforest campaign action in the UK, this money was used to help fund early EF! projects, including the setting up of an Oxford rainforest group which shortly afterwards became Oxford EF!, and an EF! UK office to support the Sarawak campaign against rainforest destruction. Marshall's previous Australian experience complemented the peace and anti-nuclear repertoires drawn upon by Torrance and Burbridge (Wall 1999: 47–49).

The first EF! mass action was on 4 December 1991 when 150–200 people attempted to prevent a ship filled with rainforest timber from docking at Tilbury on the Thames Estuary. Sea Shepherd, the Greenpeace splinter group, supported this action logistically. Some Earth First!ers used rubber dinghies to impede the ship's approach, while others supported by more mainstream green groups, notably FoE, participated in a demo on the docks. March 1992 saw a similar action on Liverpool docks, involving 400 activists. This was organised to coincide with the National Green Student Network Gathering in Liverpool (leading to the formation of Manchester and Merseyside EF! groups) and the EF! roadshow. In May 1992 over 200 activists occupied a timber yard in Oxford, forcing it to close down for the day. In June 1992 there was a similar action at a Rochdale timber yard.

The first EF! national gathering was held in Brighton and attended by sixty activists in April 1992. By April 1992 there were seven EF! groups listed by the EF! *Action Update*. By 1992–1993 the early focus on rainforests was overtaken by the emergence of protests against the *Roads for Prosperity* road-building progr-amme. It was the road-building programme that fanned the flame of EF!'s initial direct actions. Proposed sites for new roads provided ideal spaces for occupa-tions. The Twyford Down M3 protest was particularly influential in launching the anti-roads movement and shaping the future of EF! over the following years. Protest at Twyford was initiated by the Donga Tribe, who named themselves after a network of ancient pathways which criss-crossed Twyford Down. They drew on the pre-existing green and traveller counter-culture and devised a new nomadic, back-to-the-land ethos, even using horse-drawn carts. The M11 protest in London was also important because it brought together lots of different groups of people – green direct activists, urban anarchists, punks, leftist groups like Class War, and local, more single-issue focused campaigners – thus helping to broaden the base of direct activism.

From about 1995–1996 onwards the targets of protest have broadened out from road building and car culture, to airport construction, quarrying, open-cast mining and, in particular, genetically modified (GM) foods. Increasingly, the focus of protest has become global capitalism itself. Protests have targeted the G8 summit in Birmingham (June 1998), City institutions in London (18 June 1999), the World Trade Organisation (WTO) meeting in Seattle (30 November 1999), and the World Economic Forum in Davos, Switzerland (27 January 2000). Working in co-operation with social movements around the world, including Indian farmers and Mexican Zapatistas, the direct action groups have become more concerned with exposing the global role of organisations such as the International Monetary Fund (IMF) and the WTO in environmental destruction and social injustice.

Social movement analysis and the new environmentalism

Is the new environmentalism a social movement?

The term social movement often tends to be used very loosely to refer to almost any political activity by groups outside political parties. One of the problems with this is that it suggests greater uniformity than is often the case empirically within the environmental movement. There is clearly considerable difference between the bureaucratic and professional structures of groups like Greenpeace, the particular commitments of local environmental campaigns and the broader radicalism of the more anarchistic direct action groups. Also, it is perhaps legitimate to ask whether individuals whose activism consists only of signing a cheque once a year can be seen as 'members' of a social movement. As Jordan and Maloney (1997) note, when membership figures are cited for environmental groups it is important to remember the limited form of participation this often represents.

A more precise definition of what a social movement is can help here. We have modified della Porta and Diani's (1999: 14–16) definition slightly to suggest that the social movement has four typical characteristics:

1   It is based upon informal networks. These may include more formal organisations, such as pressure groups, but are also broader than them.
2   Those involved must share a set of beliefs and a collective identity. This defines whom or what they see as allies and opponents, what their goals are and how they are to be reached.
3   Social movements are involved in collective challenges and may threaten their opponents with sanctions.
4   Social movements use protest and cultural practices, which may or may not be confrontational.

Concepts such as collective identity are difficult to measure empirically and critics of the social movement concept find such imprecision dissatisfying, preferring to use more general terms such as interest group. There is no clear analytical distinction between the kinds of groups dealt with in the interest group and pressure group literatures in political science and the social movement literature in political sociology. Rather, the difference tends to be one of focus. The political science literature tends to focus on the instrumental assessment of groups' involvement in policy making (as in Robinson's chapter, this volume), whereas the strength of the social movement concept is in the attention given to the cultural and sociological dimensions of collective action. For instance, a social movement analysis of local environmental groups is likely to assess the extent to which such groups develop a broader political critique of democracy and place their own campaign within a framework shared with other environmental groups. It is more likely to seek to explain this in relation to broader structural changes in society. There is also a focus on the forms and scale of action undertaken, and how social movement organisations (SMOs) mobilise support.

One example of this kind of analysis is found in the debate about NSMs. Some sociologists have argued that new kinds of social movements began to emerge in the 1970s (e.g. Melucci 1981). Where most previous movements had focused on claiming rights such as the vote or material equality, many new movements seemed to give greater attention to the development of autonomous identities. In contrast to the earlier movements, they did not seek to capture the state and their challenge was as much cultural as material. They did not believe that the revolutionary overthrow of the state would be sufficient to bring about a new society and directed their actions as much at the general public as the state.

The environmental movement, the women's movement, gay and lesbian movements and movements based on ethnicity were among the core groups included in this category. In the case of the environmental movement it was only the more radical sections of the movement that fitted the ideal type of the NSM. Empirically NSMs were said to favour informal and non-hierarchical forms of organisation and confrontational but non-violent tactics. Applied to the new environmentalism in Britain, it is clear that the direct action groups fit this ideal type very well.

The NSM concept, however, has been the subject of much criticism, particularly from within those who study social movements. This criticism is both analytical and empirical. Since all social movements develop their own identity, common values and culture, it seems unjustified to see older social movements as materialist and NSMs as concerned solely with identity. Culture and symbols were important to nationalist, fascist and workers' movements in the nineteenth and twentieth centuries. Almost all the empirical features said to be distinctive about the new movements can be found in some historical precursor (Calhoun 1995; d'Anieri *et al.* 1990). Thus, if NSMs are new, it is only in degree and can only be debated case by case.

What the theorists who defended the newness of NSMs were referring to, however, was the extent to which new movements seemed to be responding to structural changes in society. In this sense, it is not the empirically based historical comparison with precursors that matters most, but whether the new movements are responding in ways that are only possible in the new kind of society. Thus the newness of the NSMs is not based upon an empirical analysis of all the actions of all movements that call themselves women's movements or environmental movements. What counts as decisive in this debate is whether we are living in a new kind of society and whether this has led to new kinds of collective action, which can be seen in a variety of contemporary movements. Only some of the actions of the NSMs have to be of a new kind to sustain this argument (Melucci 1994).

What is held to be new by NSM theorists? Common to all NSM theory is an emphasis on the increased importance of culture and information. Melucci (1996) argues that NSMs are new, not because on an overall empirical assessment they are distinct from precursors, but because culture and symbols have now become more important as sources of power, and the actions of NSMs reflect this change. Movements such as the environmental movement challenge dominant cultural codes by rejecting instrumental arguments such as those that take for granted the need for further economic growth. Castells (1997) sees the environmental movement as engaged in a battle with the dominant political and economic forces over representations of time and space. The dominant forces (major corporations, political elites and media among others) work increasingly as networks, transcending the limits of nation-states. Environmentalists argue for the importance of local spaces against the homogeneous space of flows, based on instantaneous financial transactions and global media. Against the 'timeless time' of the 'space of flows' (Castells 1997: 124–125), environmentalists assert the importance and independence of the evolutionary dimension of nature, which Castells characterises as glacial time. Other theorists, such as Beck (1992) and Giddens (1991), have seen the new era as a further stage of modernity, but one in which individuals can no longer rely on tradition and received wisdom, because these have been undermined by increased awareness of risks and the proliferation of different cultural codes as a consequence of globalisation. In response individuals have become increasingly reflexive about their own identities. For Giddens, this means that NSMs are less concerned with social liberation than previous social movements and more concerned with transformation of the self. The scepticism about GM foods in western Europe indicates greater uncertainty about the previously accepted authority of science and the extent to which 'life politics' (Giddens 1991) based on a reflexive evaluation of competing discourses has become central.

Each of these theorists has their critics (see, for example, Bartholomew and Mayer 1992; Pickvance 1986; O'Brien *et al.* 1999) but most debate concerns their analytical definition of the new social order, an issue which is too large to be resolved here. Nevertheless, in the criticism of the NSM concept one significant claim associated with it appears to be relatively unscathed. This is the view that as sites of power become more and more plural, the significance of the nation-state as the principal target of action declines. This occurs as a consequence of processes such as economic and cultural globalisation, the proliferation of new forms of media (and the decentralisation of access to media), the erosion of state sovereignty by both globally integrating and socially fragmenting forces, and the increased power of local government in some countries. It is of course possible to overstate the extent and impact of these developments. Previous social movements have sometimes bypassed the state, as in utopian and religious communes, for example. Also, many of the contemporary NSMs continue to direct much of their activity at national governments. But the real empirical question concerning this aspect of the novelty of NSMs is whether there is activity within the movement which can explained by these developments.

One example of activity which is a product of these large-scale social forces is the global action against transnational capitalism exemplified in the protests against the WTO in Seattle, London and other major cities. In these protests, not only did global institutions and processes become the site and focus of protest, but global networking became a principal means of organisation for the movements themselves – of course ironically made possible by the technological changes (especially the emergence of the Internet) which are themselves central to globalisation.

A second example could be Reclaim the Streets (RTS) parties, discussed in more detail in Maples' chapter, this volume. In these, the focus of protest is the specific place where the party is held. The intention is to reclaim directly that place for social, cultural purposes (rather than simply as a through route for cars) and thus also to transform the people who use that place. It is simultaneously a reconstruction of place and community, reflecting fragmenting forces within nation-states. In both these examples, states only appear as agencies reinforcing a dominant social logic (economic globalisation, or car-based mobility, respectively).[3]

Another question raised by the changed focus of action brought about by globalisation and other processes is whether NSM activity should be understood in terms of instrumental logics at all. While the media has tended to focus on protesters' lifestyle at the expense of political issues, studies of social movements often treat culture and identity as secondary to overtly political goals. Rucht (1990: 161–164) divides social movements into two main types according to whether they have an *instrumental* or an *expressive* logic of action. These logics of action are based on Habermas's (1981) distinction between conflicts over 'systemic control' and conflicts over the 'life world':

> The *instrumental* logic of action implies a *power-oriented* strategy, which is concerned with the outcomes of political decision-making and/or with the distribution of political power. Successful performance in struggles over power requires, above all, instrumental reasoning.
>
> (Rucht 1990: 162)

Instrumental reasoning is means–ends reasoning, the classic type of strategic thought. In Rucht's schema social movements with an *instrumental* logic of action are strategically oriented to issues of social, political and economic power. In contrast to the instrumental logic of action, the expressive logic of action is concerned with issues of culture, lifestyle, role behaviour, and personal and collective identity.

> The *expressive* logic of action corresponds to the *identity-oriented* strategy, which focuses on cultural codes, role behavior, self-fulfilment, personal identity, authenticity, etc. Such a strategy relies mainly on expressive behavior, trying to change cultural codes by alternative lifestyles.
>
> (Rucht 1990: 162)

Kevin Hetherington's (1998) identity-oriented approach theorises expressive social movements as being the performance of personal and collective identities through tribal forms of dress, speech and ritual. He argues that these 'neo-tribes' (Maffesoli 1996; 1998) or 'communities of feeling' facilitate the construction of a personal and collective identity for participants. Hetherington follows Maffesoli in arguing that the key to understanding such 'neo-tribes' is through participants' need for affective sociality. People need a sense of fellowship, communion and belonging to groupings bigger than themselves; they want to be able to show empathy and solidarity with like-minded people. Participation in a neo-tribe gives a sense of identity as part of a collective. Through an 'ethic of aesthetics' where style, bodily dispositions and the construction of a persona are used as a means of communication about one's allegiances, participants create an individual identity as part of a collective identity.

While clearly appropriate to the 'tribal' aspects of the direct action movement, this kind of analysis of the expressive dimension of social movements should not be pushed too far. As Szerszynski argues:

> If … emblematic protests were *only* performances of the signs of membership to other movement members, then their *real* audience would be the 'integral' one of the movement itself, not the 'accidental' one of the wider public.
>
> (Szerszynski 1999: 221)

To write-off performative protest activity as merely internally oriented to other protesters would be both unfair and inaccurate. Protest is not merely a badge of membership aimed at achieving a sense of belonging and of being a member of a moral elect; we should also not neglect the instrumental aspect of the new wave of direct action (Seel 1999). We hope to have covered both aspects in this book. The chapters by Maples, Purkis and Seel and Plows all look at both the movements' sense of collective identity and their strategies to effect change. Purkis looks at the millenarian and anarchist heritage of contemporary protest, arguing that contemporary direct activists should be seen as millenarian anarchists, whether or not they themselves use that term. Maples' chapter examines the crossover between the expressive and the instrumental in the formation of collective identity in direct action groups. She suggests there may be lessons to be learnt from queer theorists' and activists' experience.

Ultimately, whether understood in instrumental or expressive terms, NSM activity is in either case fundamentally about challenging dominant cultural codes. This is partly a reflection of dominant social logics. Castells argues (1997: ch. 6) that in the 'Information Age' it is battles over the production of cultural codes that matter most. The media has become a privileged site of politics because of its crucial role in framing political codes. Continual polling, stronger emphasis on short-term popular reaction to leaders' personality and performance, has produced a particular and limited form of reflexivity. It is limited because it focuses on short-term performance on issues such as the position of states in international markets, while leaving unquestioned the rationality of neo-liberal economic growth.

For Castells (1997) and Melucci (1996), among others, movements such as the British direct action groups are important because they produce alternative cultural codes which challenge the dominant economistic ones. By arguing that other factors needed to be set against cost–benefit analyses of motorists' time saved, such as the loss of unique landscape, the contribution of increased traffic to global climate change, or by questioning the very rationale of continually striving to save time, British protesters against new roads politicised what previously had been seen as purely technical decisions that were best left to experts. By occupying a particular place, RTS activists challenge dominant cultural codes concerning urban politics, resisting not only dominant notions concerning the absolute priority of (car-based) mobility, but also reclaiming notions of community, development and progress, and the refusal to subordinate life to the dictates of work in formal employment. Perhaps, then, as Melucci has suggested (1996: 8), the debate over *the concept* of NSM has tended to obscure the extent to which *the activity* of NSMs poses a direct challenge to dominant contemporary cultural codes and socio-economic logics.

British direct action environmentalism in international context

Another set of questions that can be asked of direct action in British environmentalism are comparative ones. We ask two such questions here. The first concerns what is peculiar or distinctive about the UK in this context. The second looks more generally in comparative terms at differences and similarities between developments in environmentalism in the UK and elsewhere (we confine our comparative discussion to western Europe and occasionally North America).

British exceptionalism?

One of the most striking aspects of the new environmental protest is that where Britain was previously regarded as exceptional in the lack of environmental protest, it now appears to be exceptional in comparison with other countries in the strength of protest. Neither is it a simple case of Britain 'catching up' with other countries. The pattern is much more complex than this. First, the thesis that Britain was exceptional in the lack of protest by social movements can be challenged. Instead, it can be argued that Britain was unusual in having less environmental protest, as distinct from protest more generally. For example, the peace movement protests of the 1980s were very large and, despite the importance of the link with the Labour Party, gained support not only from the 'old left'. The opposition to the poll tax at the end of the 1980s also included socialist organisations, but went beyond them to embrace community groups, particularly in working-class areas (Bagguley 1995). Second, there was a strong green counter-culture, with an extended milieu based on political lifestyle practices (Jowers *et al.* 1999) which predated the current environmental protest movement and from which some of its participants were drawn. Because it did not mount large-scale protest, it was not necessarily visible as a social movement, but its existence was necessary for the 1990s protests and it shaped the expressive and tribal character of the movement.

Britain was unusual in European terms for two reasons, the first of which was the absence of a large-scale protest movement against nuclear energy. In most other western European countries, opposition to nuclear power provided the foundation upon which the green movement grew. Green parties in France, Germany, Italy, Sweden, Austria and Switzerland all grew out of opposition to nuclear power in the 1970s and 80s. In most cases the conflict over nuclear power became a major issue in national politics and produced significant and often violent demonstrations. The second reason why Britain is unusual is the absence of the Green Party from parliament. In both these cases, however, it was the nature of British political institutions that explained British exceptionalism. Oil, gas and coal reserves meant Britain was under less pressure to develop nuclear power than other countries and the autonomy of the government meant that they were able to be flexible in how they implemented decisions (Rüdig 1994). The Green Party was unable to win seats in the Commons because the first-past-the-post electoral system made it all but impossible for a new party to make a breakthrough. It was probably not that the British were less radical or less green, only that the potential protest constituency had not been provoked sufficiently on environmental issues.

During the late 1980s and early 1990s, groups like Greenpeace and FoE were becoming institutionalised. They were reorganised in the 1980s to become more professional organisations using direct-mailing techniques to maintain large membership levels. Rising public support for environmental issues meant that by 1989 even figures such as Margaret Thatcher – who had included groups like FoE in the early 1980s in her definition of 'the enemy within' and whom many movement activists considered their arch-enemy – were learning to adopt 'green-speak'. The doors of government and business were increasingly open to EMOs. This new openness did not often convert into actual policy influence, but EMOs faced a more favourable political opportunity structure with the rise of both national and international participation opportunities. This reached its high point in 1992 with their participation in the much-hyped Earth Summit in Rio de Janeiro and in a plethora of post-UNCED consultative bodies in the UK. Both FoE and Greenpeace had achieved 'insider' pressure group status and were fronted by 'establishment' figures for part of this period (Rawcliffe 1998: 55). Practical advice to business and government was replacing critical and confrontational campaign strategies in both organisations, even though Greenpeace, in particular, continued to use media stunts as well.

Before the 1990s the rise of a radical environmental movement was considered unlikely in Britain (Rootes 1995; Rüdig 1995). This was because it was thought that the 'bureaucratic accommodation' of environmental organisations in Britain constrained them to moderate forms of action and the pursuit of broad political alliances (Rootes 1997: 45). Academics thought that environmental activists would be drawn into environmental organisations with consultative or 'insider' status. It was reasoned that these organisations would constrain the ways in which affiliated activists could act because they did not want to risk their insider status either by arguing for highly radical change or by employing provocative tactics. For instance, on occasion even Greenpeace was forced to stand down after being sued by BP in late summer 1997. But in contrast to these expectations, from 1991 a new wave of direct action was begun in Britain by a new wave of radical activists who were crit-ical of organisations like Greenpeace, WWF and FoE, not to mention old guard conservation organisations such as the National Trust. Rather quickly, the UK seemed to have considerably more radical activism than many other countries in western Europe.

There is no obvious structural explanation as to why this happened (Doherty

1999, but cf. Rootes' chapter, this volume). Models based upon political opportunity structures suggest that factors such as the emergence of new allies within the political system, or apparent splits and weaknesses among political elites encourage protesters to take action. In Britain, however, these factors do not appear significant. The opportunities for EMOs to participate in policy making expanded during the early 1990s, which, according to the model, should have reduced the likelihood of protest. Environmental protesters had no support from any major political party and no allies within political elites. And although the Conservative governments under John Major were weakened on occasion by splits, these were not over environmental issues. Thus, there is little evidence that protest began because of the kind of changes in the political system that models of political opportunity structures suggest (see Doherty 1999). A more convincing explanation suggests that direct action began because there had been a growth of environmental consciousness in the 1980s which raised expectations that could not be met by existing EMOs; resources and repertoires for radical action were available through existing counter-cultural networks; and the provocative character of the government's road-building programme provided a basis for the coalition of direct action groups and local anti-roads groups. While the causes of this rise in protest action may be based on contingent British circumstances, Britain is no longer exceptional, except in the current vitality of its environmental protest.

Cross-national comparisons

The twin processes of institutionalisation and the emergence of grassroots protest are to some extent paralleled elsewhere. First, as Diani and Donati (1999) show, there has been a major shift across western Europe away from environmental protest and towards institutionalisation. The major EMOs have increased in size, with more supporters and income, despite stagnation for some in the mid-1990s. They also employ more staff and have larger and more specialised bureaucracies. They have more involvement with government policy makers and major corporations. Although there are national variations (Rootes 1999), the similarity of this general pattern is more or less universal in western Europe and can be extended as well to Australia (Connors and Hutton 1999) and the USA (Dowie 1995). Membership increased exponentially in the late 1980s and this provided the EMOs with new resources and legitimacy. The evidence of new environmental problems, particularly climate change and biodiversity also put new pressures on governments. As a result, the EMOs have become more significant actors within political institutions, but as van der Heijden points out (1997: 46) this does not necessarily mean that they have more political impact: 'Many environmental organisations have lost their movement character and therefore an important part of their strength. It is doubtful whether their stronger position at some negotiating tables will compensate for this.'

A second cross-national trend is the apparent growth in grassroots-type environmental protest (Rootes 1999; Diani and Donati 1999). In many countries local protest groups emerged independently of the major EMOs and sometimes, as in the USA, reacted against them. This is much more difficult to measure, however, than the institutionalisation of EMOs. Environmental protests are often local and small scale. Measuring their incidence relies on protest event data drawn from newspaper sources. Rootes' chapter reports the results of such an analysis of the *Guardian* for environmental protest in Britain 1988–97. As would be expected there is evidence of a significant rise in the coverage of environmental protest and of confrontational actions, peaking in 1995, though it should be noted that this measures the visibility of protest, rather than its actual level. Nevertheless, the *Guardian* had a single editor for the environment through the ten-year period and the *Guardian* offers the most complete environmental protest coverage of any of the national daily newspapers. While the results Rootes presents here focus on Britain, the Transformation of Environmental Activism (TEA) study is also a cross-national study of environmental protest in seven European Union countries; it aims to shed further light on the question of whether the surge in radical protest in Britain has been replicated elsewhere in Europe. Preliminary analysis suggests that there are some clear differences between developments in the UK and elsewhere.

There has been some diffusion from the ideas of British EF! groups to other parts of western Europe. Dutch and German groups were formed by activists who had spent time in Britain, and Irish groups also had strong ties with Britain. In other countries such as Sweden and Finland animal liberation activism seems to have become more important, also because of direct ties with activists in Britain. It is, however, almost impossible to trace the path of diffusion between Britain and other countries in Europe with any great confidence. The Internet, TV and press reports may have as much a part to play in explaining diffusion as direct contact between activists.

But generally, environmental protest in western Europe is stronger in Britain than in other countries at the moment. Of the largest western European countries, Germany stands out as showing no real decline in protest. In Germany, however, protests against nuclear energy remain very high, and, in contrast to almost all other countries and groups, these protests are more likely to be confrontational and carried out by groups with less formal organisation than protests on other environmental issues (Rucht and Roose 1999).

Another major difference is that the nature of policing is substantially different in other countries, affecting the nature of NVDA protest. The repertoires of site occupation tactics used in Britain depend on legal restraints on the use of force as well as the political costs of injury to protesters. Some tactics seem to work well in most countries. For example walkways in trees delay eviction as long as the evictors are concerned about the political cost of death or injury to demonstrators. In other situations, where the police are prepared to impose pain or use tools such as pepper sprays to force protesters to unlock themselves, such tactics appear less useful. In Germany the scale of the police operation to ensure the delivery of nuclear waste transports to Gorleben in 1996 and Ahaus in 1998 was massive, and unmatched by policing of demonstrations in Britain. The policing of the protests in Seattle at the

WTO meeting in November 1999 was similarly heavy-handed compared to the policing of protests in the UK.

Comparative research on policing is interesting in relation to some of the debates within the direct action movement (see especially della Porta 1998). The British police have been less militarised and more independent of politicians than police in most other 'established democracies', but the degree of difference has been reduced as the British police became tougher on violent protest and riots while police in other countries tended to become more tolerant. In countries such as Germany, Italy and Spain, the police and governments tended to view any protest by anyone as a challenge to democracy that had to be suppressed. This was partly a reflection of the newness and insecurity of democracy in these countries. But by the 1980s and 1990s this was no longer the case. There has been a major shift in attitudes to protest, in public opinion and even within the police in these countries. For instance, the German police union campaigned for greater court protection for the right to demonstrate.

Most police forces are prepared to tolerate some illegal action. But they are more sympathetic to protesters they can understand and identify with – such as strikers – than to direct action by the young, whom they see as misinformed and manipulated. They are more tolerant, even of anarchist protests, when they can establish some kind of dialogue (della Porta 1998). British police have, at times, allowed protests to go ahead in defiance of government requests – as with an anarchist rally in Trafalgar Square in 1991. The government had refused permission for the rally to be held there as it was technically government property, but the police refused to take action to prevent it or to arrest anyone. All police forces are worried about their legitimacy and sensitive to their image in the media and they are vulnerable to attack, not only from those defending civil liberties, but also from those always wanting a tougher line. Allowing the Cenotaph to be defaced – contrary to some theories – was probably a disaster for the senior officers in charge of policing the Mayday protests in London in 2000.

Conclusion: impacts of direct action

Speaking about Monsanto's failure to understand the changes taking place in society, Peter Melchett (Executive Director of Greenpeace UK) said that 'People are becoming more confident in their understanding of what is at stake and more resolute in their ability to resist. There has been an unprecedented, permanent and irreversible shift in the political landscape' (as quoted in the *Guardian* 7 October 1999). Melchett was himself arrested for his part in an action against a GM crop trial site in Norfolk earlier that year. While the major EMOs remain constrained by the need to strike a balance between protest and protection of the assets necessary to make their other work possible, the new protest movement has given them the confidence to use bolder language. Melchett spoke of widespread mistrust of the combination of big science and big business and the imbalance of power between multinational corporations and farmers in the developing world.

There is some evidence that people in Britain are more willing than they have been in previous decades to take part in protest activity (Curtice and Jowell 1995: 154; Jowell *et al.* 1997: 320). Since this evidence refers mostly to attitudes rather than actual behaviour it needs to be treated with caution. As Rootes shows in this volume, it is surprisingly difficult to measure whether actual levels of protest have increased. However, it is reasonable to argue that a loss of confidence in political parties and greater acceptance of protest is a reflection of the importance of movements such as those analysed here. As Castells argues (1997), it is now social movements (NSMs) rather than political parties whom we look to as the generators of new political ideas and values that can provide a sense of what should be done.

Conventionally, in political science, we would take the impact of protest to refer to impacts on policy makers within the state. Movements and protests would be regarded as being successful to the extent they achieved changes in policy outcomes at the levels usually of national governments. Certainly, Robinson's chapter in this volume shows persuasively that at the very least, a whole host of other factors have to be taken into account in order to explain the way in which the roads programme as originally envisaged in *Roads for Prosperity* was cut back. Robinson goes further than perhaps we would in arguing that direct action against road building was relatively unimportant in this policy change, but the importance of structural factors and of other actors, such as SACTRA, were clearly important.

This can clearly be seen in the way that opponents of schemes in some areas had more leverage than others. Those opposing the widening of the M25 were able to win the support of backbench Conservative MPs at a time when the Conservative government was very dependent upon the loyalty of those MPs. The opponents of the Manchester second runway were less fortunate. Although able to secure the support of their local borough council, they were in the constituency of a pariah MP, Neil Hamilton, and the neighbouring local authorities in Greater Manchester had a substantial economic stake in the expansion of the airport. This small example helps to illustrate Robinson's more general point. Nevertheless, backbench MPs were clearly affected by widespread disaffection with particular road schemes and the roads programme in general. Direct action helped bring the issue on to the public agenda and both EMOs and more radical activists were then successful in winning debates about transport policy. Thus, backbench Conservative MPs' pressure upon their government can itself be traced back to a shift in public mood – a shift in which direct action seems to have played a crucial part.

In general, the quote from Peter Melchett leads us towards other ways of thinking about the impact of direct action in British environmentalism. First, direct action has helped to radicalise and revitalise the more mainstream EMOs established in the early 1970s, particularly Greenpeace and FoE, who have tried to increase their ability to empower and support local activism in the late 1990s and early 2000. FoE worked hard after their initial failure to support the protests at Twyford Down, in order to re-establish their credibility with direct activists (see Seel and Plows, this volume). Greenpeace UK took a little longer to respond, but it has recently reinvigorated its relationship with its local groups so that 'active supporters' are now given support and training; as a result of this, rather than just raising funds, they can now perform protests themselves (albeit on campaigns set by Greenpeace UK). Greenpeace UK has also recently partici- pated in combined protest actions with newer direct action groups and networks like the Genetics Engineering Network (GEN) in a way that they have previously not done.

But also implied in Melchett's statement, and perhaps more important than the reorienting of the strategies of other EMOs, is the more direct radicalisation of political culture which direct action has helped to produce. Relations between civil society and the state have been in part restructured, with more people expressing beliefs that the state supports only the interests of big business and more people sceptical of the role of the police in maintaining public 'order' and the interests that order serves.[4] The way in which the law and the police have overtly been used by the state to repress protest, notably in the Criminal Justice Act 1995 and the Prevention of Terrorism Bill going through Parliament at the time of writing (January 2000), has heightened this sense.

Finally, over certain issues, direct action has helped to shift radically specific cultural codes concerning certain dominant aspects of contemporary life. Two in particular are clear. First, the relationship which people have to the car has been transformed. While it would of course be ridiculous to argue that the car culture has been overturned in the UK, the numbers of people expressing fundamental ambivalence towards the social role the car plays has risen. As a consequence, 'the need to reduce car use' has become an accepted, everyday part of normal political discourse on the subject. It cannot (yet?) be measured in direct policy impact, but it has filtered through to high level policy discourse in the UK.

Second, the cultural codes concerning food have also been transformed by direct action. There were other forms of protests and consumer movements against GM foods before direct action against GM crops occurred, but it would be reasonable to argue that the emergence of direct action helped to precipitate the change of policy by Monsanto in particular. However, the most salient point here is perhaps not so much that direct action changed the public's attitude towards GM food, but that direct action reflected, propelled and informed an increasingly critical attitude to big business and to official science, and an increased confidence to challenge the power of those two institutions directly.

In challenging these codes, direct action in British environmentalism has played an important part in transforming contemporary British politics. It remains to be seen how deep and long-lived its impacts will be on the practices of environmental movements, on popular political culture, on state–society rela- tions, and on the practice of conventional politicians. The following chapters do however attest to the depth and diversity of its contemporary significance.

Notes

1   We are extremely grateful to Wendy Maples for incisive and helpful comments on an earlier draft of this introductory chapter.
2   For more on US EF!, see Balser (1997); Bari and Kohl (1991); Ingalsbee (1996); London (1998); Taylor (1991); Wall (1999: 3–7).
3   On the reconstruction of place as part of direct action protests, see also Smith (1997). The two forms of action intersected in Birmingham, where part of the protest against the G8 summit in 1998 was a 'Reclaim the Summit' RTS action to occupy a major city centre roundabout, St Martin's Circus.
4   This development has of course been helped by public scandals surrounding the police, particularly the Stephen Lawrence affair. But direct action has increased the number of people, especially comfortable, white middle-class people, who have personally come to experience the police as an oppressive rather than comforting presence.

Bibliography

Bagguley, P. (1995) 'Protest, poverty and power: a case study of the anti-poll tax movement', *Sociological Review* 43, 4: 693–719.

Balser, D.B. (1997) 'The impact of environmental factors on factionalism and schism in social movement organizations', *Social Forces* 76, 1: 199–228.

Bari, J. and Kohl, J. (1991) 'Environmental justice: Highlander after Myles', *Social Policy* 21, 3: 71–79.

Bartholomew, A. and Mayer, M. (1992) 'Nomads of the present: Melucci's contribution to social theory', *Theory, Culture and Society* 9, 3: 141–159.

Beck, U. (1992) *Risk Society*, London: Sage.

Calhoun, C. (1995) 'New social movements of the early nineteenth century', in Traugott, M. (ed.) *Repertoires and Cycles of Collective Action*, Durham, NC: Duke University Press.

Castells, M. (1997) *The Information Age: Economy, Society and Culture. Volume II: The Power of Identity*, Oxford: Blackwell.

Connors, L. and Hutton, D. (1999) *A History of the Australian Environmental Movement*, Cambridge: Cambridge University Press.

Curtice, J. and Jowell, R. (1995) 'The sceptical electorate', in D. Ahrendt, L. Brook, J. Curtice, R. Jowell, and A. Park (eds) *British Social Attitudes: The 12th Report*, Aldershot: Dartmouth.

Dale, S. (1996) *McLuhan's Children: The Greenpeace Message and the Media*, Toronto: Between the Lines.

D'Anieri, P., Ernst, C. and Kier, E. (1990) 'New social movements in historical perspective', *Comparative Politics* 22, 3: 445–458.

Della Porta, D. (ed.) (1998) *Protest Policing*, London: UCL Press.

Della Porta, D. and Diani, M. (1999) *Social Movements: An Introduction*, Oxford: Blackwell.

Diani, M. and Donati, P. R. (1999) 'Organisational change in western European environmental groups: a framework for analysis', *Environmental Politics* 8, 1: 13–34.

Doherty, B. (1999) 'Paving the way: the rise of direct action against road-building and the changing character of British environmentalism', *Political Studies* 47(2): 275–291.

Dowie, M. (1995) *Losing Ground: American Environmentalism at the Close of the Twentieth Century*, Cambridge MA: MIT Press.

Giddens, A. (1991) *Beyond Left and Right: The Future of Radical Politics*, Cambridge: Polity.

Habermas, J. (1981) 'New social movements', *Telos* 49: 33–37.

Hetherington, K. (1998) *Expressions of Identity: Space, Performance and the Politics of Identity*, London: Sage.

Ingalsbee, T. (1996) 'Earth First! activism: ecological postmodern praxis in radical environmentalist identities', *Sociological Perspectives* 39, 2: 263–276.

Jordan, G. and Maloney, W. (1997) *The Protest Business? Mobilizing Campaign Groups*, Manchester: Manchester University Press.

Jowell, R., Curtice, J., Park, A. and Thomson, K. (eds) (1997) *British Social Attitudes: The 14th Report*, Aldershot: Ashgate.

Jowers, P., Dürrschmidt, J., O'Doherty, R. and Purdue, D. (1999) 'Affective and aesthetic dimensions of contemporary social movements in South West England', *Innovation* 12, 1: 99–118.

Lamb, R. (1996) *Promising the Earth*, London: Routledge.

London, J.K. (1998) 'Common roots and entangled limbs: Earth First! and the growth of post-wilderness environmentalism on California's north coast', *Antipode* 30, 2: 155–176.

Maffesoli, M. (1988) 'Jeux de Masques: postmodern tribalism', *Design Issues* 4, 1–2: 141–151.

—— (1996) *The Time of the Tribes*, London: Sage.

Melucci, A. (1981) 'Ten hypotheses for the analysis of new movements', in D. Pinto (ed.) *Contemporary Italian Sociology*, Cambridge: Cambridge University Press.

—— (1994) 'A strange kind of newness: what's "new" in NSMs?', in E. Larana, H. Johnston and J.R. Gusfield (eds) *New Social Movements: From Ideology to Identity*, Philadelphia: Temple University Press.

—— (1996) *Challenging Codes: Collective Action in the Information Age*, Cambridge: Cambridge University Press.

O'Brien, M., Penna, S. and Hay, C. (1999) *Theorising Modernity: Reflexivity, Environment and Identity in Giddens' Social Theory*, London: Longman.

Pickvance, C. (1986) 'Concepts, contexts and comparison in the study of urban movements: a reply to Manuel Castells', *Society and Space* 4, 2: 221–231.

Rawcliffe, P. (1998) *Environmental Pressure Groups in Transition*, Manchester: Manchester University Press.

Rootes, C. (1995) 'Britain: Greens in a cold climate', in D. Richardson and C. Rootes (eds) *The Green Challenge: the Development of Green Parties in Europe*, London: Routledge.

—— (1997) 'The transformation of environmental activism', in N. Russell (ed.) *Technology, the Environment and Us* (Proceedings of the Sixth IRNES Conference), London GSE: Imperial College (pp. 40–49).

—— (ed.) (1999) *Environmental Movements: Local, National and Global*, London and Portland, OR: Frank Cass.

Rucht, D. (1990) 'The strategies and action repertoires of new movements', in R.J. Dalton and M. Kuechler (eds) *Challenging the Political Order: New Social and Political Movements in Western Democracies*, Cambridge: Polity Press (pp.156–175).

Rucht, D. and Roose, J. (1999) 'The German environmental movement at a crossroads?', *Environmental Politics* 8, 1: 59–80.

Rüdig, W. (1994) 'Maintaining a low profile: the anti-nuclear movement and the British state', in H. Flam (ed.) *States and Anti-Nuclear Movements*, Edinburgh: Edinburgh University Press.

—— (1995) 'Between moderation and marginalisation: environmental radicalism in Britain', in B. Taylor (ed.) *Ecological Resistance Movements: The Global Emergence of Radical and Popular Environmentalism*, Albany: State University of New York Press.

Seel, B. (1999) *Strategic Identities, Strategy, Culture and Consciousness in the New Age and Road Protest Movements*, PhD thesis, Keele University.

Smith, M. (1997) 'Against the enclosure of the ethical commons: radical environmentalism as an "Ethics of Place" ', *Environmental Ethics*, 19, 4: 339–353.

Szerszynski, B. (1999) 'Performing politics: the dramatics of environmental protest', in L. Ray and A. Sayer (eds) *Culture and Economy After the Cultural Turn*, London: Sage.

Taylor, B. (1991) 'The religion and politics of Earth First!' *The Ecologist*, 21, 6: 258–266.

Van der Heijden, H.A. (1997) 'Political opportunity structure and the institutionalisation of the environmental movement', *Environmental Politics* 6, 4: 25–50.

Wall, D. (1999) *Earth First! and the Anti-Roads Movement*, London: Routledge.

2 Environmental protest in Britain 1988–1997[1]

Christopher Rootes

Environmentalism is changing, but how it is changing is a matter of debate. The tale most often told about the recent evolution of the environmental movement in Europe is that it has become so institutionalised that it no longer captures the imagination or commands the support of any large part of the public. In this version of events, institutionalisation is accompanied by demobilisation, protest is in decline and the prognosis for the movement is uncertain (van der Heijden 1997; Diani and Donati 1999).

The other frequently told tale, in Britain and the United States if not in continental Europe, is that of the rising threat of 'eco-terrorism' as radical environmental activists give up on a non-violent movement that seems insufficiently effective to meet the increasingly urgent challenges of securing redress of environmental grievances and achieving a measure of environmental justice. A less excited version of this story is that, as increasingly established environmental movement organisations (EMOs) vacate the streets in favour of the negotiating table and the boardroom, so protest is joined by new, more radical groups employing unfamiliar tactics and raising new issues (Rootes 1999b; Wall 1999a, b).

Both tales are told with conviction but the evidence to support them is largely anecdotal. The purpose of this chapter is to attempt to get some perspective on these claims by examining the pattern of environmental protest events from 1988 to 1997. This period includes the upsurge of environmental concern that was reflected in the unprecedented good result of the Green Party in the 1989 elections for the European Parliament; it was also a time of alleged stagnation of the environmental movement during the early 1990s, and the resurgence since 1992 of environmental protest associated with the rise of anti-roads protests, together with a new generation of environmental protest groups focused on direct action, which continued into the first year of the Labour government elected in May 1997.

How did the claims advanced by environmental protesters change during those ten years and how did the forms of environmental protest evolve? In order to answer those and related questions, and to explore similarities and differences from one European country to another, we have examined the public record of environmental protest as revealed in leading 'quality' newspapers in each of eight nations (Rootes 1999d, 2000). This chapter presents a preliminary analysis of the results for Britain.

Press reports of environmental protest: problems and potential

In Britain as elsewhere in the industrialised world, although EMOs are unprecedentedly well-resourced (Jordan and Maloney 1997; Rawcliffe 1998), in terms of the material resources essential to influence policy making and policy implementation successfully, they remain minnows by comparison with the governments and corporations whose initiatives they challenge.[2] Public opinion remains EMOs' greatest resource, and it is generally only by means of coverage in an often uncomprehending if not overtly hostile mass media that the public can be addressed.[3]

Reports carried by mass media provide not only a record of environmental movement activity but much of the material out of which public and elite perceptions of the environmental movement are constructed. But if press reports provide useful data, impressions formed on the basis of a casual reading of them may be misleading. Even knowledgeable observers believed that the incidence of environmental protest in Germany had, in aggregate, declined since the late 1980s, but preliminary results from the systematic study of protest events (PRODAT) for the early 1990s suggest that the incidence of protest as reported in leading newspapers had actually *increased* (Rucht and Roose 1999). It appears not so much that protest had declined as that, with the decline in the novelty of protest, its salience for unsystematic observers had declined. What these German findings most clearly demonstrate is the need for systematic collection and analysis of data on the incidence and forms of protest to correct the often false impressions created by casual empiricism.

Newspaper reports have often been described as 'history's first draft', but this is perhaps a generous way of describing the cumulative account that can be derived from such sources. There is, after all, abundant evidence that media reports of political action are selective and biased in various ways. But that does not mean that media reports have no evidential value at all. By recognising the limitations, biases and selectivity of media reports and applying our knowledge of media routines and the sources and consequences of selection and bias, we are able critically to evaluate the picture we can assemble from media reports. We cannot hope, even by the most sophisticated analysis of data derived from media reports, closely to approach an unmediated record of events, but we can reasonably hope to give as comprehensive and balanced an account of events as it is possible to assemble from public sources.

This part of our research is based upon the methodology of protest event analysis.[4] This methodology is a systematic means of documenting protest events, but it has important limitations. It is a complement to, but no substitute for, careful and detailed ethnographies of protest that might better get at the dynamics of protest and the submerged linkages that are so important to the maintenance and proliferation of campaigns and that very often go unremarked in even the more scrupulous and thoughtful journalistic accounts. However, although such case studies are invaluable to understanding both the particulars and processes of a small number of instances, the extent to which they are representative is always open to question and, in their focus on groups and processes of manageably small size, they are often unable to illuminate the bigger picture. Similarly, although it may well be possible to piece together from their own archives and from extended interviews with their activists better accounts of the actions of a number of groups than can be garnered from press reports, such sources are notoriously inconsistent, both over time and from one group to another. Limited resources mean that any single researcher or project is most unlikely to be able to look at more than a small number of groups in such a detailed way. What we should gain by looking closely at a few groups would have to be balanced against what we should miss, and, adopting such a research strategy, we should miss the whole range of small and evanescent groups and the large number of environmental protests that involve organised groups only peripherally or not at all.[5]

Because it is – for reasons of economy – focused upon events, protest event methodology does not encompass the many news reports and feature articles on environmental issues that do not report protest events, but which nevertheless have an impact upon public and elite knowledge of and opinion about environmental activists. Moreover, because it is limited to reported events, protest event analysis omits the many small and local protests that escape the attention of national newspaper journalists or which are deemed insufficiently newsworthy by their editors. No less importantly, however, it cannot cover the many activities of environmental organisations and activists that go on behind closed doors and which, as large parts of the environmental movement become at least semi-institutionalised, are an increasingly important means of advancing environmentalist agenda.

However, what people do not see or read about, they do not usually know about; and what they do not know about is unlikely to inform their attitudes. In defence of protest event methodology it can reasonably be claimed that it is by the employment of these means that we are most likely to get as close as resources permit to a systematic knowledge of those protests that have done most to shape public opinion and to inform elite policy preferences.

Ideally, in order to document fully the media output that has influenced public opinion, elite attitudes and public policy in relation to environmental activism, we should assemble an account from the whole output of the print and electronic media. In practice, it would be impossibly expensive and labour intensive to do so for any extended period such as the ten years covered here. In the absence of a comprehensive and easily searchable full text-and-graphics archive of even the 'quality' broadsheet newspapers, we have had to limit ourselves to an analysis of all the reports in a single newspaper.

The *Guardian* was chosen because it was published continuously through the years 1988 to 1997, has enjoyed a relatively high degree of continuity of editorial policy and of journalistic personnel throughout the period, and, from a preliminary comparison of reportage from several sample months spread over the decade, it appeared that the *Guardian* was on average more inclusive in its reporting of environmental action than the *Independent*.[6]

The discussion that follows is based on a preliminary analysis of the results of our examination of all the environmental protests reported in the *Guardian* in the ten years 1988 to 1997. For each of these years, all possibly relevant sections of every issue of the *Guardian* were read and every identifiable report of protest involving the explicit expression of environmental and animal welfare concerns was copied. Every protest event contained in those reports was then coded according to a common schedule and entered into an SPSS file.[7]

Altogether we collected data on 2,756 protest events. However, of these, 1,433 events were identified from summary reports – reports that give minimal information about a large number of (sometimes geographically dispersed) events, often (but not invariably) occurring over an extended period of time.[8] Although the coding rules we employed are designed to yield conservative estimates of events from such reports, their inclusion more than doubles the number of events reported during the ten years and may be considered to give a distorted picture of the incidence of protest and, especially, of the publicly visible volume of protest.

The amount and quality of information we are able to abstract from summary reports is limited,[9] but to disregard them entirely would be to ignore important information about the extent and character of environmental protest. Summary reports amplify the impact of protest by giving the reader the impression that the events reported in greater detail are but the tip of an iceberg. As such they are a shaft of light shone upon the large number of protests too small or localised to attract the attention of the national press. Unfortunately, however, it is unlikely that the protests illuminated by summary reports are simply a random sample of all such small or localised protests; it is much more likely that summary reports exaggerate the relative frequency of protests that are part of protracted campaigns, particularly campaigns orchestrated by national organisations.[10] For this reason, data derived exclusively from summary reports must be treated with special caution, and they have been omitted from the analyses that follow.

Defining the environmental movement

Because this research is part of a cross-nationally comparative project, we adopted a common and inclusive definition of environmental protest. However, the character and significance of apparently similar issues varies from one European country to another. This presents particular problems in the case of animal welfare and hunting issues. In most European countries these are generally regarded relatively unproblematically as a part, albeit usually a minor one, of the broad agenda of the environmental movement. In Britain, however, the anti-hunting movement has a long and particular history, as does the animal welfare movement. Although there are some overlaps of personnel and concerns, there are a number of instances in which the concerns of each are at variance with the mainstream of the environmental movement.[11]

Many people who identify themselves as members or supporters of the environmental movement in Britain do not regard that movement as including either campaigners against hunting or animal welfare campaigners. Although vegetarianism is part of the culture of the British Green Party (Faucher 1997, 1999) and many members of British EMOs are vegetarian, as a matter of policy, if not necessarily as a basis of individual choice, their vegetarianism is sometimes on ecological rather than animal welfare grounds. Some self-proclaimed conservationists are pro-hunting on the grounds that the preservation of hunting encourages landowners to retain traditional landscape features which on strictly commercial criteria might be removed, such as hedges and copses that act as refuges for hunted animals and, because they are also sanctuaries for other native wildlife and for many species of endangered flora, are considered essential to the preservation of biodiversity. This is one strand of the pro-hunting Countryside Alliance, the umbrella organisation which in 1998 organised one of the biggest street demonstrations London has seen.

It seems, then, that if we were to include animal welfare and anti-hunting protests we might be conflating two, or even three, quite separate movements. Following Diani (1992), I have elsewhere (Rootes 1997c) defined the environmental movement as: a loose, non-institutionalised network that includes, as well as individuals and groups who have no organisational affiliation, organisations of varying degrees of formality and even parties, especially Green parties; that is engaged in collective action motivated by shared environmental concern, of which the forms and intensity of both action and concern may vary considerably from place to place and from time to time. The environmental movement in Britain is large and organisationally diverse, and within it there is a variety of groups whose concerns and issue foci are more or less distinct and specialised. The extent to which they are sufficiently networked one to another and to which they have shared a common identity is problematic, especially during those periods in which competition between environmental groups has been most intense.

Our data permit us to determine the extent to which the various issues and groups, that from a European perspective might be considered part of the environmental movement, do in fact in Britain form part of a single network, at least in the limited sense of their being reported as having been present in the same protest events. Of the 321 environmental protests in which two issues were reported to have been involved, in only seventeen cases (5 per cent) was animal welfare at issue alongside an environmental issue.

When we look at the frequency with which each of the dozen most frequently named groups was involved in protests about various issues, a very clear pattern emerges. Of the 329 protests in which one or more of the seven most frequently mentioned EMOs was reported to have been involved, in only one was an animal welfare or hunting issue reported as having been raised. Similarly, of the 110 protests reported to have involved one or more of the five most frequently mentioned animal welfare or anti-hunting groups, only three were reported to have involved any issue other than animal welfare or hunting. Although there is, as we shall see, a degree of specialisation in the issue concerns of EMOs, there is no evidence of the shared concern among EMOs and animal welfare and anti-hunting groups that might justify considering them to be part of a single social movement.

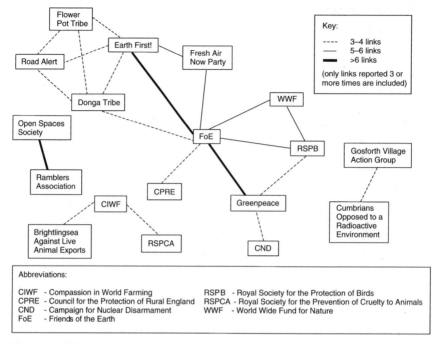

Figure 2.1   The network of protest: environmental groups and others

The picture is no less clear if we examine the pattern of interaction among the various groups. In only a relatively small number of cases were two or more groups named as having been involved in the same protest, but whereas the interactions among the EMOs varied, in not a single case was one of the seven leading EMOs mentioned as having participated in a protest with one of the five most mentioned animal welfare or anti-hunting groups. If the environmental movement is a network (see Figure 2.1), then the animal welfare and anti-hunting groups are at best distant outliers to it, and no more closely connected to it than the Labour or Liberal Democrat parties or several charities not normally considered to be part of the environmental movement.[12]

Thus it appears that animal welfare and anti-hunting groups are better considered as distinct from, rather than as part of, the environmental movement in Britain. The following discussion is therefore based principally upon the data on the 967 unambiguously environmental protests on which we have data, but we shall from time to time refer to our data on animal welfare and anti-hunting protests for comparative purposes.

The incidence of environmental protest

Figure 2.2 shows the total number of protest events involving each of environmental, animal welfare and anti-hunting issues by year, excluding those reported

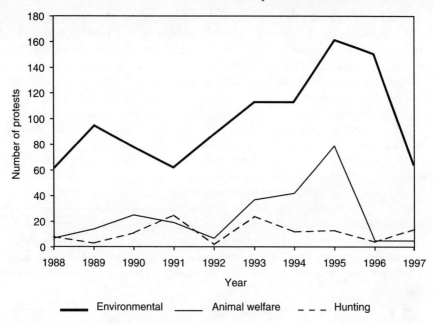

Figure 2.2   Environmental, animal welfare and anti-hunting protests by year

only in summary reports.[13] The pattern of environmental protest is much as expected: there was a marked increase (from 62 to 95) in the number of reported events from 1988 to 1989, the year which we suppose, on the basis of other information, marked the peak of the first stage of increased environmental movement activity in Britain. Thereafter the number of environmental protests settled back to the 1988 level before rising strongly from 1992 to a new peak (113) in 1993 and 1994 and thence to a still higher one (162) in 1995 – almost twice as high as that of 1989. A modest decline in 1996 was followed by a much steeper one in 1997 with the result that, in terms of numbers of reported protests, the environmental movement ended the decade where it had begun.

Animal welfare and anti-hunting protests had their own trajectories and, although there were some parallels, particularly between the courses of environmental and animal welfare protests, the effect of aggregating them with environmental protests is to moderate the downturns apparent in the trajectory of environmental protest and significantly to exaggerate the 1995 peak.[14]

It should be emphasised that our data represent the numbers of events *reported* in one national newspaper, and not the actual numbers of events. In the absence of other information, we simply do not know how many environmental and cognate protests may have gone unreported, but we can reasonably surmise that it is a great many and that the extent of under-reporting will not have been constant over time. Fillieule (1996, 1997) has ably demonstrated the extent of the bias and incompleteness of national newspaper reports of protest in France by comparison with police records and local press reports. Of these sources of data, police records were the most complete, but whilst up to 95 per cent of protest events recorded by the police were also reported in the local press, the percentage reported in the national press was very much lower. Reports in *Le Monde* under-reported events which occurred outside a 'cycle' of protest, but they also under-reported events which occurred outside the Paris region.

It seemed probable that a similar pattern of under-reporting by the London-based national press might also exist in Britain, although the fact that the *Guardian* was historically a Manchester-based paper and is still published in both London and Manchester might make it more likely to be regionally balanced in its coverage than other national newspapers. In fact, the geographical distribution of protests reported in the *Guardian* was wider than we might have expected (see Table 2.1). Just over half (52 per cent) of all environmental protests of which the location was reported occurred in London and the south-east of England, regions that together account for just under one-third (31 per cent) of the British population. The most over-represented region was London (12 per cent of population, but 30 per cent of reported environmental protest), but this is scarcely surprising.

Table 2.1 The spatial distribution of environmental protests compared with population (1988–1997 inclusive)

	% of protest events	% of population[a]	Index of representation[b]
London	29.9	11.9	2.51
South East	22.1	18.7	1.18
South West	12.2	8.2	1.48
East Anglia	1.8	3.6	0.49
East Midlands	3.2	7.0	0.45
West Midlands	2.5	9.1	0.28
Yorks and Humberside	5.9	8.6	0.69
North West	8.0	11.0	0.73
North	4.1	5.3	0.77
Wales	3.8	5.0	0.77
Scotland	6.3	8.8	0.71
Northern Ireland	0.2	2.8	0.08
Total N	910	58,394,600	

Notes:
[a] Population figures for 1994 from the Office for National Statistics, General Register Office for Scotland and Northern Ireland Statistics and Research Agency.
[b] 'Index of Representation' is a figure obtained by dividing the number of protests by the number of protests expected from the ratio of the total number of events to the total population; values above one indicate over-representation of an area in the data set, and values below one an under-representation.

In a country as politically and culturally centralised as Britain, a disproportionate share of protest action is likely to take place in the national capital, especially when such action is undertaken or co-ordinated by national organisations, is allied to lobbying activities, or is designed to put issues on national or international political agenda. London protests were little more than half as likely as the national average to be mobilised on a purely local level (22 per cent compared with 38 per cent), and they were more likely to be part of national mobilisations (58 per cent compared with 46 per cent for the UK as a whole). The disproportionate share (62 per cent) of protests involving issues whose scope is international and which took place in London is especially striking.

London apart, it was the south-west of England which was the most over-represented region: 12 per cent of reported protest was located in the South West, compared with just over 8 per cent of the population. This over-representation is consistent with a very modest geographical concentration of electoral support for the Green Party and with claims that the South West is the centre of a 'DIY' counterculture (Jowers *et al.* 1996) of which environmentalism is a key component.[15]

After allowances are made for the tendency of national protests to be concentrated in the national capital, this pattern of reported protest does not differ radically from the picture of the spatial distribution of membership of EMOs reported in earlier studies. Both Cowell and Jehlicka's (1995) mapping of the spatial distribution of membership of major environmental organisations and Rüdig, Bennie and Franklin's (1991) survey of members of the Green Party show that greens and environmentalists are disproportionately concentrated in the south of England *outside* London.

Thus although the geographical distribution of reported protest is skewed toward London and the South, the extent of that skewing is not so great that it is an implausible reflection of the probable pattern of *actual* protest.

The issues of protest

The broad pattern of environmental protest revealed in Figure 2.2 aggregates a variety of campaigns about a variety of issues conducted by a diversity of actors and employing a variety of means.

During these ten years, four major sets of environmental issues can be identified in reports of protest: transport, including railways, roads and airports (involved in 38 per cent of environmental protests); nature conservation (28 per cent); a broad spectrum of pollution, urban and industrial issues (27 per cent); and energy, including nuclear energy and nuclear waste (11 per cent). Land rights (10 per cent) and issues surrounding alternative production and technology (5 per cent) account for most of the remainder.[16] These and the main components of each of these categories are represented in Figure 2.3.

Figure 2.4 shows the trends over time in each of the four leading categories of issues. In each of the ten years there were at least ten protests concerning nature conservation, with both the number and the proportion of all protests rising

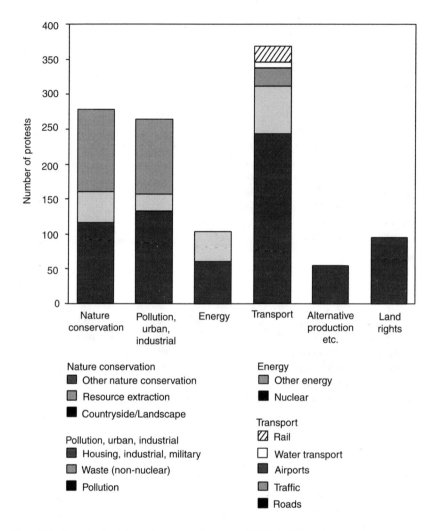

Figure 2.3   Issues raised in environmental protests (1988–1997)

sharply from 1992 to 1995 before falling back. Pollution, urban and industrial claims had two peaks – 1990 and 1995 – and only in 1997 did they fall to single figures. Energy issues – over 70 per cent of them concerning nuclear power or waste – were raised relatively infrequently and showed no clear trend. Protests concerning transport showed a modest 1989 peak associated with the many local protests against the Channel Tunnel and the proposed high speed rail link thereto, and began to rise again from 1992 to a sharp peak in 1996 associated mainly with the development of anti-roads protests. Land rights, principally concerned with ramblers' demands for the right to roam freely through privately

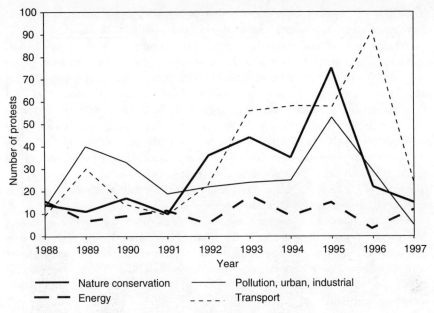

Figure 2.4   Four leading kinds of environmental issues over time

owned or tenanted land in the countryside and, to a lesser extent, to the demands for access by New Age travellers, was a recurrent issue of protest albeit that, because protest mainly took the form of Ramblers Association days of action, it gave rise to relatively few protest events outside summary reports. Protests explicitly advocating environmentally friendly activities such as alternative technology or environmentally friendly agriculture were rare and showed no clear trend.

The most strongly emergent issue of contention during this period was transport: the fifth ranking issue in 1988 and 1991, it ranked first or second in every year thereafter; indeed, protests concerned with transport were more numerous than those concerned with all other pollution, urban, industrial and energy issues combined.

The forms of protest: toward more confrontational protest?

For present purposes, we have categorised the forms of protest as: conventional (comprising procedural claims such as demands for judicial review, actions such as collective representations to officials or elected politicians, public meetings, leafleting and the collection of signatures on petitions); demonstrative actions (including street marches, rallies and vigils); confrontational actions (including occupations and physical obstruction); minor attacks on property (which stop short of posing a threat to human life, but including theft); and violence (consisting of attacks on persons whether or not they cause actual injury, and including attacks on property which might be potentially life-threatening).

What is most striking about the picture of environmental protest that emerges from newspaper reports (see Figure 2.5) is its relative moderation throughout the ten years. Conventional forms of action and demonstrations were involved in 39 and 34 per cent respectively of all reported protests during the ten years, and their incidence varied relatively little over time. In absolute numbers, conventional forms of action peaked in 1989, but then, after falling back in 1990, rose modestly until 1995; relatively, however, conventional forms of action, and especially procedural claims, have been mentioned in a declining proportion of all reported protests. The pattern of demonstrations has more closely followed the trajectory of protests as a whole, peaking first in 1989 and then, more sharply, in 1995 before falling steeply thereafter.

The total number of demonstrations was significantly higher in the second half of our decade than it was in the first (194 compared with 137). Yet it is frequently claimed by commentators on social movements that the age of mass demonstrations is over. Very large demonstrations (involving 500 or more participants) are most unlikely to go unreported, so it is worth examining their incidence over time.

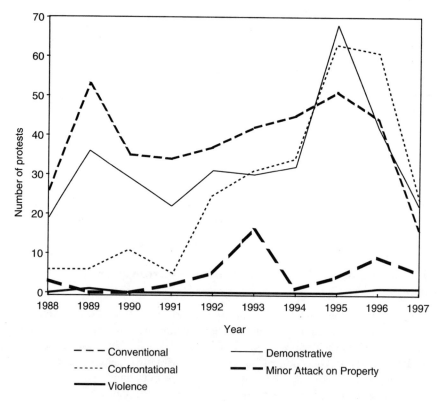

Figure 2.5   Forms of protest over time

The number of such large demonstrations about environmental issues exceeded four in only two years – 1989 (nine) and 1995 (six), and in two years – 1990 and 1997 – there was only one large demonstration reported. In all, there were 20 large demonstrations in the years 1988–1992 and 17 between 1993 and 1997. Overall, then, there was only a modest decline in the number of large demonstrations.[17]

This needs to be seen, however, in the context of the overall increase in the total number of reported protest events in the second half of our ten years: over 60 per cent of reported protests occurred after 1992. Large demonstrations may have declined only modestly in absolute numbers, but as a proportion of all protest events they have declined more markedly.

Estimated numbers of participants were given for only one-third of the events reported, and we might suppose that such estimates will more often be given in the case of large protests. From Figure 2.6 it is apparent that the total numbers of participants in demonstrations involving at least 500 people declined sharply after the 1989 peak and that it did not rise substantially again until the year following the 1995 peak in the total number of environmental protests.[18]

However we measure it, there was a marked decline in the mean and median numbers of participants in the second half of the decade as compared with the first half. Thus, the median number of participants in large demonstrations (over 500 participants) fell from 2,000 in 1988–1992 to 750 in 1993–1997, the median number of participants in *all* demonstrations fell from 250 to 100, and the median number of participants in all demonstrations and confrontations taken together fell from 200 to 56.[19] Clearly, the increased number of demonstrations and other forms of protest was the product of an absolute and relative increase in the number of reported actions involving smaller numbers of people.

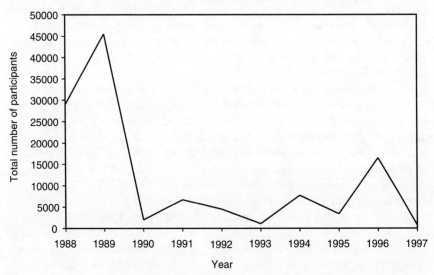

Figure 2.6   Numbers of participants in demonstrations with 500 or more participants by year

Confrontation was present in 27 per cent of protests, but there were considerable changes in its incidence over time. Uncommon at the beginning of the period, confrontation increased almost monotonically from 1992 onwards until by the mid-1990s it was reported as being involved in more than 30 per cent of environmental protests. This is a significant development.

Minor attacks on property amounted to less than 5 per cent of all environmental protests. Rare in the first half of our decade, they peaked (at 16) in 1993 when they were involved in one in eight of all reported environmental protests, but otherwise they have remained relatively infrequent and, given the very small numbers, it would be unwarranted to purport to detect a trend. Nearly half of these attacks on property were associated with transport-related protests; most of the remainder were symbolic actions such as the 'theft' of rainforest timbers from DIY stores.

Violent action has been notable by its absence; in only three reported protests about an environmental issue during the whole ten years were protests reported to have been violent in form: in 1989 a McDonald's restaurant was bombed in protest against the destruction of rainforest; in 1996 anti-roads protesters at Newbury fired catapults at construction equipment and injured a security guard; and in 1997, on the first anniversary of the commencement of construction of the Newbury by-pass, protesters occupied the site and set fire to construction equipment. In only thirteen protests in ten years were environmental protesters reported to have used force, and on eleven of those occasions (and on 57 other occasions), force was also used by the police. In only seven protests were protesters reported to have caused injuries, and in five of those protests (and in ten others) injuries were also attributed to the police. Most significantly, in view of the alarm bells that have recently been rung about the rise of eco-terrorism and the need for extraordinary measures to deal with it, there is no clear evidence of a trend towards more violent forms of environmental protest.

A major problem in interpreting the figures on the changing forms of protest derives from the media's perennial interest in novelty and spectacle. This leads to a high likelihood that the most thematically and tactically innovative and the most confrontational protests will be reported. It follows that, especially when there are novel and/or confrontational events to be reported, moderate and less innovative actions are likely to be under-reported. Because a great deal of the activity associated with the environmental movement is local, routine and seldom confrontational, it is largely unreported in the national press. The more confrontational actions of animal rights demonstrators are more likely to be considered to have news value, and so the relative importance of them may be exaggerated by the relatively greater frequency with which they are reported.

To the extent that they were in this period both novel and confrontational, anti-roads protests were especially likely to be reported and their impact amplified by comparison with that of other forms of environmental movement activity. However, the strict application of our coding guidelines tends to understate the extent of media coverage of these protests; a site occupation – the characteristic form of anti-roads protests – may last for many months and be covered by newspapers almost daily and yet give rise to as few as two codeable 'events', one at the start of the protest and another at the point of the protesters' eviction from the site.[20]

Journalists themselves testify to the declining news value of routine protest towards the end of this period. According to Paul Brown, the *Guardian*'s environment correspondent, by 1992–1993 there was an enormous fatigue about protest on the part of the news desk.[21] Whereas previously the experience of simply being on a Greenpeace boat was something a journalist could write about, by 1992–1993 such a report would only be considered newsworthy if there was a high element of danger. Thus, while the increased incidence of reported events involving confrontation almost certainly reflects a real increase in the frequency of such action, the contemporaneous relative decline in the reported incidence of moderate actions may well reflect a decline in the *reporting* of such actions rather than an actual decline in their relative frequency. To some extent this is simply a matter of the ecology of news. Confrontational or violent events will, especially when they are novel, be relatively likely to be reported. To the extent that the frequency of such events increases, so, in the competition for limited news space, reports of them are likely to drive out the less spectacular reports of more moderate actions.

The increasing volume of environmental news of all kinds also has an impact upon the extent of the reporting of environmental protests. As the number of stories offered increases so environmental journalists are forced to be, in the interests of their own survival, less accessible and to be more selective in their following up of stories.[22] Paul Brown reports that whereas in 1990 he would never take his phone off the hook, now he does so most days, relies increasingly upon contacts, and is increasingly fearful of missing an important story. He reports that he is now offered some twenty stories a day, perhaps ten of which might be considered newsworthy, and he has to whittle these down to three, two or, some days, just one report. By no means all of these stories are of protests or other forms of environmental action, but the implication is that the increasing abundance of environmental news means that the chances of any particular story actually being carried in the press have declined. The likelihood is that the usual principles of news value will select against the moderate and the unspectacular in favour of the confrontational and, where it occurs, the violent.[23]

This tendency is likely to be exacerbated by the changes that have taken place in the character of British 'quality' newspapers during the past decade. Increasingly, print media have taken on the news values of television; pictures and/or graphics are increasingly considered essential to a story, many stories now appearing only as captions to photographs. Although the *Guardian* was not in the vanguard of these changes, it has not been immune from them, and it is likely that the greater news value of stories associated with pictures of confrontation has tended further to drive out stories of more moderate and less photogenic action. Another aspect of these changes, and one in which the *Guardian* has been no laggard, is the increased requirement of 'colour' even in news stories; it is deemed important that a story should invoke the feelings of the reader, and 'human interest' is a more important criterion of news value than once it was. One consequence of this is the increasing tendency to personalise stories about protest and even to transform protesters into media celebrities. Thus, to his intense embarrassment, the anti-roads tunneller, 'Swampy', became an icon of the new wave of environmental protest (see Paterson's chapter in this volume).

We should therefore be very cautious in drawing inferences about the changing repertoire of environmental protest from data such as these. Although we are able to show that the number and proportion of *reported* protests which involve confrontation has increased, we cannot say with complete confidence that environmental protests that are confrontational have increased as a propor-tion of all the environmental protest *that has actually occurred* in Britain during these years. What we can infer, however, is that the public visibility of confronta-tional protest associated with environmental issues has increased and that it has increased relative to that of moderate protest.

Such is the news value of violence that it is most unlikely that any violent action would, if it occurred, go unreported. For this reason, we can say with some confidence that there has been no trend toward more frequent resort to violence in environmental protests.

Forms and issues

Particular forms of action appear to be associated with different kinds of issues (see Table 2.2). Only 20 per cent of protests regarding pollution, urban and industrial issues were reported to have involved forms of action more radical than demonstrations; almost half employed the most moderate forms of all – appeals and procedural claims – and conventional forms of action were predom-inant (present in 48 per cent), followed by demonstrations (occurring in 34 per cent of protests). Protests concerning energy issues were scarcely less moderate. Although land rights protests were distinctive in the extent to which they involved demonstrations (45 per cent), 27 per cent involved more radical actions. The action repertoire associated with nature protection was broader, with 37 per cent involving confrontation or, occasionally, attacks on property; nevertheless, most protests about nature protection involved forms of action at the moderate end of the spectrum, conventional forms of action and demonstrations being involved in 39 and 34 per cent of protests respectively.[24] Transport protests were rather more confrontational, just under half involving confrontation or attacks on property; confrontation (40 per cent) was the modal form of action. This, however, conceals a considerable change over time, transport issues being associ-ated especially with conventional appeals in the earlier years and with confrontation from 1992–1996. Although the trend toward more confrontation is especially evident in the case of transport-related protests, it is apparent across the broad range of environmental issues. [25]

If attacks on property and, especially, violent actions have been exceedingly rare in environmental protests, the same cannot be said about animal rights protests.

Table 2.2 Issues and the forms of protest (percentage of events involving each issue by form of action)

(Row %)	Conventional	Demonstrative	Confrontational	Minor attacks on property	Violence	N
Nature conservation	39.4	33.7	30.1	6.5	0.4	279
Pollution, urban, industrial	47.5	33.5	18.6	1.5	0.0	263
Energy	43.8	26.7	19.0	1.9	0.0	105
Transport	30.7	29.6	39.6	5.7	0.5	371
Alternative production, etc.	49.0	29.4	7.8	3.9	0.0	51
Land rights	37.9	45.3	25.3	2.1	0.0	95
N (all environmental)	383	331	264	45	3	
Animal Welfare	14.2	37.5	14.2	12.5	30.0	240
Hunting	19.0	21.6	44.0	3.4	8.6	116
N (all protests)	431	437	349	79	83	

Note: Percentages do not sum to 100 because for each protest up to two issues and four forms could be recorded.

The distribution of animal welfare protests was bimodal, with demonstrations (38 per cent) and violence (30 per cent) the most common forms of action.[26] Anti-hunting protests showed a different pattern, with confrontation the modal form of action (44 per cent). A clear majority of both hunting and animal welfare protests involved forms of action more radical than demonstrations, but it is with respect to violence that they are most distinctive (and distinct one from the other). Animal rights protests stand out starkly; whereas even attacks on property were rare in relation to other issues, they were involved in 13 per cent of animal welfare protests. More extreme forms of violence against property or persons were present in 30 per cent of animal rights protests and 9 per cent of anti-hunting protests.[27]

Organisational specialisation?

The frequency with which reported actions are associated with a particular organisation varied over time, but the numbers of organisations named in each year corresponded very closely to the number of protests reported. A total of 239 organisations were named in connection with one or more of the 967 environmental protests, but only a few were mentioned more than a dozen times.

Table 2.3 displays the number of protests involving the seven organisations most often mentioned in reported environmental protests for each year. The two organisations mentioned most frequently – Greenpeace and FoE – are also the ones most stably represented over time. Remarkably, with the exception of the 1995 surge in which both participated at least proportionately, their reported involvement in protests was relatively unrelated to the total numbers of protest events in a year. The Green Party was most mentioned in the immediate after-math of its successes in the 1989 local and European elections, but scarcely at all thereafter. The Ramblers Association was reported to be involved in protests in every year but 1993, but a marked period of heightened activity in 1995 appears only if data from summary reports are added.

Earth First! emerged strongly in 1992–1993 but its reported involvement in protest declined both relatively and absolutely after 1995. Since other evidence does not suggest a decline in Earth First!'s activity, this finding may seem surprising; it is perhaps explained by EF!'s very loose form of organisation and the consequence that Earth Firsters did not necessarily use EF!'s name but some-times protested using the names of other similarly structured but more thematically focused organisations such as Road Alert! and Reclaim the Streets, or as part of single-issue campaign coalitions such as the anti-roads group, Alarm UK (see McNeish's chapter, this volume).

The pattern of groups' reported involvement in protest appears to confirm the importance of organisation and resources to a group's ability to remain in view of the public through media reports. Greenpeace and FoE, in particular, are able to use their resources to offer relatively secure and stable employment to their research and public relations staff, who are in turn able to accumulate expertise and cultivate contacts. By regularly issuing press releases they are some-times able to keep issues on the agenda and their names in the news even in the absence of protest, something that for less well-resourced groups is virtually impossible. The temporal pattern of groups' reported involvement in protest also

Table 2.3 Number of protests involving leading groups by year

	1988	1989	1990	1991	1992	1993	1994	1995	1996	1997	N
Greenpeace	14	6	11	10	10	10	9	19	6	12	107
FoE	5	9	7	2	10	6	7	26	12	3	87
Earth First!	0	0	0	1	7	15	6	13	1	1	44
WWF	1	0	3	2	0	3	2	1	2	3	17
RSPB	0	1	4	2	0	1	2	1	2	1	14
Green Party	0	2	8	1	0	1	0	1	0	0	13
Ramblers Association	3	6	9	7	2	0	3	8	8	1	47
Total N of events	62	95	78	62	88	113	113	162	151	64	

suggests the importance of campaigns as a lens through which media attention is focused on protesting organisations.

If there is clear evidence that the issues and the forms of protest are quite closely coupled, it is no less clear that there is specialisation among groups and organisations with respect to the forms of action with which they are associated (see Table 2.4).

Greenpeace, the organisation most frequently mentioned, appears to have had the broadest tactical repertoire of these groups, with a fairly even spread across the conventional, demonstrative and confrontational forms. By comparison, FoE, although it too appears to have employed a broad tactical repertoire, was more firmly anchored in the moderate and non-confrontational: fewer than one in six of FoE's reported actions involved confrontation, and more than half involved no action beyond the appeals and procedural claims that together comprise conventional action. If FoE has in recent years been anxious to repair its links with more radical and grassroots activists, this was not reflected in its own reported repertoire of action. Not surprisingly, the small number of reported actions involving the WWF were skewed strongly to the most moderate forms of action, as were those involving the RSPB.

Earth First!'s reported repertoire was concentrated around confrontation, followed by demonstrations and minor attacks on property.[28] The Green Party also appears tactically specialised: two-thirds of its reported actions were demonstrations. Scarcely less specialised, and again focused on demonstrations, was the Ramblers Association (RA).[29]

We should be cautious in our interpretations of these figures. These are the *reported* forms of action of the groups listed, and it may well be that journalists have sometimes wrongly described actions or have wrongly attributed an action

Table 2.4 Groups and their forms of protest (number of events)

	Conventional	Demonstrative	Confrontational	Minor attacks on property	Violence	Other	N
Greenpeace	38	33	35	2	0	10	107
FoE	47	31	13	0	0	3	87
Earth First!	4	13	26	10	0	5	44
WWF	14	1	0	0	0	2	17
RSPB	11	3	0	0	0	0	14
Green Party	2	9	2	0	0	0	13
Ramblers Association	19	32	0	0	0	0	47
Total N of events	383	331	264	45	3	66	

to a particular group. It is, however, even more likely that many of these groups' other actions have gone unreported. The effects of the normal routines and selection biases of mass media are likely to be reflected here. First, the most dramatic, confrontational and violent actions are those most likely to be reported and, as a result, the groups associated with such actions have a greater likelihood of being mentioned. Second, the larger, better organised and better resourced groups will be better able to mount and secure publicity for the full range of their activities, and especially for their less disruptive actions. Nevertheless, the picture painted by these figures is likely to form the basis of the image that the better informed members of the public have of the groups comprising the environmental movement.

If there is specialisation among environmental groups with respect to the forms of their action, it is greater still when it comes to the issues with which they deal (see Table 2.5). The most specialised was the Ramblers Association, three-quarters of whose actions involved land rights, a claim scarcely ever reported as being an issue in the protests involving other groups. If the other environmental organisations appear less specialised, there are nevertheless substantial differences among them. Although both WWF and the RSPB were primarily mentioned in reports of protests about nature protection, both were also reported as being involved in a small number of other protests, especially those concerning transport issues. The Green Party was mentioned principally in relation to protests about pollution, urban and industrial issues. Earth First! had a broader claims repertoire and was mentioned most in relation to transport and nature protection protests, with pollution and urban industrial issues a distant third. FoE's claims profile was similar to but rather less specialised than that of Earth First!, while that of Greenpeace was quite distinctive. Little involved in transport issues, Greenpeace was strongly focused upon pollution, urban and industrial issues, these accounting for half the protests in which Greenpeace was named, but it was its involvement in energy issues that most marks it out; 40 per cent of Greenpeace's reported action involved energy, and over half of all the protests over energy in which a group was named were protests by or involving Greenpeace.

Despite the evident fragmentation and specialisation of the environmental movement, throughout the period with which we are particularly concerned, there have been well-documented instances of collaboration between groups whose relationships one might suppose to be generally competitive. Thus in 1990 Greenpeace, FoE and WWF collaborated in the 'Dirty Man of Europe' campaign to undermine the credibility of the British Conservative government's environmental policy (Statham 1997). At various points in the anti-roads campaigns, Earth First! activists collaborated with FoE, first and abortively at Twyford Down (Wall 1999a, b) but later at Newbury. If Greenpeace is now resented by activists in some smaller groups, it is because it is perceived as having let down smaller, more specialised groups which it once encouraged with pump-priming funds but has more recently failed to support.

There is considerable evidence that activists ranging from Earth First! 'green

Table 2.5 Groups and their issues of protest (number of events)

	Nature conservation	*Pollution, urban, industrial*	*Energy*	*Transport*	*Alternative production, etc.*	*Land rights*	*Other*	*N*
Greenpeace	17	54	43	5	5	0	4	107
FoE	37	23	5	35	6	1	4	87
Earth First!	22	10	1	23	1	1	1	44
WWF	11	3	1	5	2	0	2	17
RSPB	11	1	0	6	0	0	1	14
Green Party	1	9	1	3	1	1	1	13
Ramblers Association	4	1	0	0	0	36	8	47
Total N of events	279	263	105	371	51	95	53	

anarchists' to the moderate and increasingly professionalised campaigners of FoE, WWF and other nature protection organisations do regard themselves as belonging to the same broad environmental movement. The conference held at Keele University in October 1997 on 'Direct Action and British Environmentalism' (out of which this book arises), which brought together activists from FoE as well as the newer, less institutionalised groups, was notable for its lack of rancour. The FoE speaker made a forthright presentation of what the movement could and could not expect of FoE, constrained as it was by its vulnerability to legal action, whilst a speaker identified with Earth First! spoke of a broad movement embracing environmental reformists and radical activists alike. In focus groups we conducted in London in late 1998, representatives of Greenpeace, Transport 2000, the Women's Environmental Network and an anti-roads protester were happy to regard themselves as all part of the same movement but practising a specialised division of labour.

Despite the fact that some groups, most conspicuously Greenpeace, appeared to show a marked preference for protesting on their own (see Table 2.6), we found confirmation of the existence of a network of EMOs in the patterning of reports of action in which two or more groups were named (see also Figure 2.1). The networks of hunt saboteurs and animal rights campaigners, by contrast, do not appear to be integrated into the network of the environmental movement, and for that reason we argued earlier that they are not fruitfully treated as part of the same movement.

Certainly, anti-hunting and animal rights protests are in Britain quite distinct in incidence and form from those concerned with environmental issues. Nevertheless, protests associated with animal rights and opposition to hunting

Table 2.6 The interaction between groups (environmental and animal welfare)

	Greenpeace	FoE	Earth First!	WWF	RSPB	Green Party	Ramblers	LACS	CIWF	ALF	Justice Dept
Greenpeace	**93**										
FoE	8	**25**									
Earth First!	0	8	**25**								
WWF	2	6	0	**5**							
RSPB	3	6	0	6	**3**						
Green Party	0	1	1	0	0	**10**					
Ramblers	0	0	0	1	2	0	**35**				
LACS	0	0	0	0	0	0	0	**12**			
CIWF	0	0	0	0	0	0	0	0	**19**		
ALF	0	0	0	0	0	0	0	0	0	**37**	
Justice Dept	0	0	0	0	0	0	0	0	0	0	**17**
Others	.19	49	27	15	12	8	12	7	6	0	0
N	**107**	**87**	**44**	**17**	**14**	**14a**	**47**	**17**	**25**	**37**	**17**

Notes:

Numbers in bold along the diagonal indicate protests in which only the named group was reported as being involved.
[a]   The only frequently mentioned environmental group named in an animal welfare protest was the Green Party.

are part of the political environment within which more strictly environmental organisations operate and it may well be that the actions of the former have exemplary value for the environmental movement. They might, however, also have cautionary value, especially insofar as the more extreme forms of action are seen to justify an intrusive and repressive response from the authorities.[30]

However, even in the case of animal rights, the incidence of violence has been sporadic and there is no evidence of any trend toward increased violence or attacks upon property.[31] Animal rights and anti-hunting protests have, if anything, become less rather than more violent. Nevertheless, if members of the newspaper-reading public associate animal rights and anti-hunting protests with the environmental movement, then, because of the heightened profile of animal rights protests and the relatively high incidence of violence it has in the past involved, it is likely that the image such people hold will be of an environmental movement that is not only more confrontational than it was a decade ago, but one that is more violent than is warranted by a close examination of environmental protests alone. Whether observers are, as a result, more or less likely to approve of the movement is another question. What is clear, however, is that there is no evidence in the public record of environmental protest to support claims about the rise of 'eco-terrorism' or to justify the extension of the ambit of the Prevention of Terrorism Act to include environmental groups.

Explaining the pattern

Notwithstanding all the caveats, it appears that in the ten years from 1988 there was a considerable increase in environmental protest in Britain, at least until the 1995 peak. Indeed, because of the declining news value of routine environmental protest, the likelihood is that the magnitude of that increase is very considerably understated, especially for the second half of the period, with the possible partial exception of the 1995 peak itself.

The most economical general explanation of the varying incidence of environmental protests over the decade is the changing balance of opportunities for political action of various kinds – increasingly, if misleadingly, referred to as 'political opportunity structures'.[32]

The wave of environmental protest that crested in 1989 began to rise soon after the re-election in 1987 of the Thatcher government, which was committed to an agenda of economic growth. Renewed economic growth brought with it a substantial increase in the number of motor vehicles on the roads and, especially in already highly populated southern England, a development boom that markedly increased pressure upon the environment. Development projects such as the high-speed rail link from London to the Channel Tunnel provoked well-publicised protests, and in towns and villages throughout the South there were conflicts between residents concerned to protect the quality of their environment and the proponents of housing, office and road developments.

Margaret Thatcher did much to legitimise environmental concerns when, in September 1988, she ended her speech to the annual dinner of the Royal Society with a declaration of commitment to preserving the balance of nature. Conservative leaders were surprised at the response to Mrs Thatcher's speech and taken aback by the number of environmentalist motions presented to the Party conference a month later (Flynn and Lowe 1992: 25–28). The Prime Minister rose to the occasion, telling the conference that 'no generation has a freehold' upon the planet but merely 'a life tenancy with a full repairing lease'. Whether Mrs Thatcher's speeches were a cynical and opportunistic attempt to leap aboard the already rolling bandwagon of increasing anxiety about the environment detected by opinion pollsters, or whether, as insider accounts suggest, they represented a genuine if belated acceptance by the first scientifically educated prime minister and her advisers that the balance of scientific evidence about the state of the global environment had tipped in favour of the alarmists, their effect was dramatically to heighten the prominence of environmental issues and to give unprecedented respectability to their articulation.

In the wake of the Prime Minister's speeches, media reporting of the environmental crisis reached a crescendo. The more radical environmentalist organisations were immediate beneficiaries: in 1988–1989 Friends of the Earth grew from 31,000 to 125,000 paid-up members, and Greenpeace's supporters went from 150,000 to 281,000 (Frankland 1990: 13).

The second and more sustained wave of environmental protest began its rise soon after the 1992 general election. Environmental issues did not figure prominently in that election and the Green Party, which had done so well in the 1989 European elections, failed dismally. More importantly, the election, which had been the most closely fought since the 1970s, had resulted in the re-election of the Conservative government, no less committed than before to economic development projects, especially road building.

With the government apparently deaf to criticism of the environmental effects of its development policies, and no immediate likelihood of a change of government, the stage was set for the rise of environmental protest. The absence of any prospect that conventional politics and reasoned argument might change policy encouraged the adoption of alternative tactics. A particular stimulus to the adoption of direct action tactics was the vigour and ultimate success of the campaign against the poll tax introduced in Scotland in 1989 and in England in 1990. Although the anti-poll tax campaign was principally co-ordinated by left-wing activists and, in general, had no close connection with the environmental movement, it, the demise of Mrs Thatcher and the government's subsequent abandonment of the tax were represented as evidence of what could be achieved by direct action. The example appealed especially to younger people impressed by the urgency of environmental concerns but dismayed by the apparent quiescence of established environmental groups. In some cases, the connection between the anti-poll tax and anti-roads protests was quite direct, as it was, for example, in the Pollok district of Glasgow where a community that had mobilised to resist the poll tax later did much to sustain the Pollok Free State protest camp in its opposition to the proposal to drive a motorway extension through a neighbouring public park (Seel 1997a; McNeish 2000). Thus the closure of political opportunities represented by the re-election of an unresponsive government was conjoined with a proximate example of an apparently successful campaign of direct action.

Nevertheless, as Robinson's chapter in this volume suggests, it was not direct action on its own that was successful in changing government policy on road building. As in the case of the poll tax, the rise of direct action against roads was paralleled by a significant shift of public opinion against government policy and by increasing conventional opposition from government MPs and local party branches in the constituencies most affected. In these circumstances, it is extremely difficult to assess the impact of direct action. It is probable that outbursts of direct action were more the symptom than the cause of widespread public discontent with a government and its policies, and that the reporting of direct action served to dramatise and amplify shifts in public opinion by keeping the roads issue more generally in the news than would have been the case if it had depended upon the pronouncements of MPs or the more conventional and localised protests of affected residents. The novelty of the alliances forged between local campaigners and eco-activists at Twyford and Newbury, and the evident public sympathy for anti-roads protesters, encouraged media coverage that accorded unprecedented legitimacy to direct action and may have contributed to its spread.

The greater radicalism of environmental protest after 1992 compared with that of the 1980s is explicable in terms of the changed political conjuncture. In 1988, Margaret Thatcher's speeches had legitimated environmentalists' concerns and had raised expectations that the policies of her government failed to meet. In 1989 the political calendar provided the opportunity to large numbers of people to register a protest by the simple act of voting for a Green candidate in the elections for the European Parliament. In 1992–1993 no such opportunity existed, and the environment had in any case slipped from the top of the public agenda. As a result, local campaigners whose concerns were as urgent as ever were pushed into the arms of the direct activists, resulting in the extraordinary sights of middle-class housewives and pensioners carrying tea and biscuits to dreadlocked tree-sitters, tunnellers and protest campers. Likewise, the wide-ranging campaign against the Criminal Justice Act (1994) – a piece of portmanteau legislation that, amongst other things, criminalised trespass – extended the networks of direct activists just at the time that Shell and the French government were providing new reasons to protest and animal welfare campaigners were stepping up their action. The 1995 peak of environmental protest, although it was directly related to only some of these campaigns, was part of a general effervescence of protest in that year. The decline of protest from 1996 may in part be attributed to the Major government's retreat from road building and its proclaimed commitment to the introduction of more effective measures to protect the environment, as well as to the imminent opportunity to change the government by electoral means.

If only because of its magnitude, the apparent decline in protest in 1997 is unlikely to have been simply a product of the declining news value of environmental protest in the wake of the 1995 peak. Notwithstanding the largely unreported continuation of some anti-roads protests and other protest camps and the recent spate of direct action to disrupt field trials of genetically modified crops, it is widely accepted by environmental activists that since 1997 environmental protest has been relatively subdued.[33]

The obvious explanation for the decline of environmental protest in (and since) 1997 is the anticipation, and then the fact, of the general election and the change of government. If the Labour Party appeared to promise little by way of environmental reform whilst in opposition, in office it has done better than almost anyone expected. As Secretary of State for the sprawling Department of Environment, Transport and the Regions, John Prescott has proved to be surprisingly environmentally aware, globally as well as nationally; his Minister for the Environment, Michael Meacher, has been one of the stars of the Blair government and has won respect both within the environmental movement and beyond.

The Blair government is, as its debacle over genetically modified foods showed,[34] very far from being regarded as a panacea by environmental activists, but so far it has done enough – and has continued to hold out enough hope of better yet to come – to have given few pretexts for large-scale environmental mobilisation. Indeed, it has thus far shown itself to be adept at defusing environmental issues just as they seem about to erupt (as they did with the 'housing developments on greenfield sites' issue at the beginning of 1998, with the 'right to roam' in 1999, and with the decision in 1999 to defer licensing genetically modified crops until extensive trials have shown them to pose no threat to humans or wildlife). Environmental promises now figure larger in the government's agenda than they did before the election.[35] However, the responsibilities of office are bound to produce compromises and unpopular decisions that may yet provoke a new round of environmental protest. Social changes, the hazards of affluence and the imperatives of the capitalist economy are producing new pressures for large-scale house building, the construction of new roads, railways and airports, and large-scale waste management facilities, any one of which could be the basis of a substantial revival of environmental protest.

Conclusion

It should be emphasised that what our investigations demonstrate is that there was, during the early to mid-1990s, a considerable increase in the number of reported environmental protest *events*. It is not clear that there was an increase, much less a proportionate increase, in the number of people who directly participated in environmental protests. Thus, although it is clear that tales of the demise of environmental protest are at best premature, it remains possible that the increase in the number of protest events is consistent with the demobilisation of the environmental movement in the sense of its capacity to mobilise large numbers of people for direct participation in protest.

The strong emergence of transport as an issue may be taken to mark an important development in the movement away from simple countryside and nature protection and towards issues reflecting the collision between the development of the capitalist economy and the preservation of valued habitat, as well as towards environmental justice issues.

Whether or not the apparent increase in confrontational protests reflects a real increase in confrontation relative to other forms of protest, it has clearly changed the publicly visible profile of environmental protest. What remains largely invisible here is the large number of local, allegedly 'NIMBY' protests. We know from other investigations that protests over the siting of waste management facilities such as landfill and incinerators have increased in recent years,[36] but there is scarcely any mention of them in the national press. The same is true of the many other local planning disputes that tend to make it into national news only when they conjoin to spark a political crisis or when they are picked up, usually by feature writers rather than news journalists, for their 'human interest'. Although such protests are by no means novel, it is likely that they have become more common, if only because, as more general surveys of political participation and social attitudes show, British society has become more directly participatory and less deferential.[37] That, however, is not something we are able to demonstrate from the data analysed in this chapter.

It is possible that in this decade we witnessed the rise of a new generation of environmental protesters with no loyalty to established EMOs. Yet there is little evidence of a sharp generational cleavage within the environmental movement; it may be younger protesters who take the more physically audacious forms of action, but they do so with the active support of older protesters.[38] However, although campaign organisations like Alarm UK bring together members and supporters of a broad range of EMOs, it is younger protesters who make up the numbers of the new, more radical groups (McNeish 2000). Some observers argue that recent anti-roads protests and other local developments may betoken the development of an environmental counter-culture on a scale not seen previously (Fiddes 1997). Similarly, whilst some see the protests against the extension of the M77 motorway across Pollok Park in Glasgow as a continuation of protest by local working-class people first mobilised by opposition to the poll tax, others see them as the work of radical eco-activists for whom Pollok is simply a battle in the long war against capitalist consumerism.[39]

Such developments pose serious problems for hitherto radical campaigning EMOs such as FoE and Greenpeace, which, as a result, experience difficulties in balancing the need to retain the support of an environmentalist constituency, some elements of which appear increasingly disposed to activism, against their own interests in deepening constructive links with governments and businesses. They create uncertainties too for environmental policy makers who fear they can no longer rely on organisations such as FoE and Greenpeace either to act as barometers of activist environmental sentiment or as negotiators on behalf of environmental interests (Rootes 1999b, 2000). Nevertheless, the experience of the 1990s shows that fruitful collaboration can be achieved between protesters and the more institutionalised EMOs (Rawcliffe 1998), and that the 'radical flank effect' produced by the existence of direct action has increased the leverage of more institutionalised EMOs such as FoE. The tactical repertoires of the several parts of the environmental movement may be different, but they may be, and often have been, employed in ways that are mutually reinforcing rather than merely competitive and so enhance the influence and impact of the environmental movement as a whole.

Preliminary examination of data from other European countries collected as part of the TEA project (Rootes 2000) suggests that the pattern of environmental protest in Britain during the decade was quite distinctive in three respects. First, Britain was the only country in which there was a dramatic surge of environmental protest. Second, only in Britain was transport the leading issue involved with environmental protest. Third, only in Britain was there a clear shift toward more confrontational forms of environmental protest; in the 1990s reported environmental protest in Britain was more confrontational than in any of the other European states for which we have systematic data. Although it is very difficult to quantify or to make reliable cross-national comparisons, it appears too that environmental protest in Britain was especially tactically innovative during this period; 'manufactured vulnerability' (Doherty 1999b) may have borrowed rather liberally from the experience of environmental protest in such other countries as Australia and the United States, but the scale of its use and the level of risk taken by the participants does appear to have been qualitatively different from anything previously seen in environmental protests in Britain.

These developments, as well as the formation of new groups that seriously attempt to develop new and more flexible forms of organisation, the persistence of more established groups such as Greenpeace and FoE, and the broadening of the agenda of the older environmental organisations such as WWF, RSPB and CPRE, all testify to the vitality of the environmental movement in Britain during the 1990s. As argued earlier, the pattern of protest appears to be explained best in terms of the pattern of opportunities presented by the electoral cycle and the policies and attitudes of governments. Nowhere else in the European Union was a government so determinedly committed to a large-scale programme of rapid road building, so resistant to hostile public opinion, or so imaginatively confronted by so heterogeneous an environmental movement.

If the peak of environmental protest mobilisation may thus be represented as a distinctive achievement of an obdurate Conservative government as much as of the activists who opposed it, it would be a mistake to suppose that the movement has lapsed quietly into repose with the election of a government that has proved to be more sensitive both to environmental concerns and to public opinion. The continued ability of environmental groups to mount campaigns (most notably over housing on greenfield sites and genetically modified organisms), the high levels of public support they have attracted, and the speed with which the Blair government has reacted, all suggest that, even if protest has declined since 1996, the environmental movement itself is very far from being dead or even in abeyance.

The future of environmental protest cannot easily be predicted, because, as always, it will depend upon the interaction of government, other political actors, commercial interests and environmental activists themselves. But it is unlikely that the environmental movement will be simply or comfortably institutionalised.

It may be that it is not other European countries but the United States that offers the closest parallels with the development of the environmental movement in Britain. The recent development of the environmental movement in the United States has been marked by the radicalisation of EMOs, the development of new groupings such as Earth First! in reaction to what came to be perceived as toothless mainstream EMOs (such as the Sierra Club and the Audubon Society), and the proliferation of the 'environmental justice movement' and local environmental protests unco-ordinated by any established EMO (Carmin 1999; Schlosberg 1999).

Environmentalism in the United States has been characterised by repeated waves of innovation. EMOs that emerge from one protest or wave of protest may become increasingly institutionalised but even the suggestion that institutionalised groups are insufficiently responsive to new concerns is enough to stimulate the formation of new *ad hoc* groups which often, in their turn, become institutionalised. If, as Michels (1959 [1912]) is usually represented as saying, there is an 'iron law of oligarchy', there is, as Alvin Gouldner (1955) observed, a correlative 'iron law of democracy'.

The institutionalisation of environmental activism in Britain has indeed proceeded apace, particularly in response to new opportunities created by political elites at international, European and national levels. Diani and Donati (1999) are undoubtedly right when they observe that there has been a general shift in Europe away from mass protest and towards public interest lobbies and professionalised protest organisations. Yet, as recent British experience shows, there are significant strands of environmental concern and activism that resist institutionalisation. Indeed, the new wave of radical environmental groups such as Earth First! deliberately resist forms of organisation that are susceptible to institutionalisation. It remains to be seen whether the rise of a radical environmentalist counter-culture will prove durable, or to what extent it is, in Europe, a peculiarly British phenomenon.[40]

APPENDIX A

The TEA (Transformation of Environmental Activism) Project

EC (DG XII) contract no. ENV4-CT97–0514

This major EC-funded project commenced in March 1998 and will be completed during 2001. The partners in the project are:

- University of Kent at Canterbury – GB – Christopher Rootes (co-ordinator)
- Wissenschaftszentrum Berlin für Sozialforschung – DE – Dieter Rucht
- University of Aalborg – DK – Andrew Jamison
- Juan March Institute, Madrid – ES – Manuel Jiménez and Andrew Richards
- Universidad del Pais Vasco – ES – Iñaki Barcena and Pedro Ibarra
- Fondation Nationale des Sciences Politiques, Paris – FR – Olivier Fillieule
- University of Crete – GR – Maria Kousis
- University of Florence – I – Donatella della Porta
- University of Strathclyde – GB – Mario Diani

The project aims to examine the various forms of environmental activism, changes in their relative incidence over the past decade and from one EU member state to another, changes in environmental movement organisations (EMOs) and their relationships with other actors within and outside the wider environmental movement, to advance explanations for the patterns of variation, and to examine their implications for policy making at the European level.

The project will undertake a systematic comparison of the incidence and forms of environmental activism and its relationship with EMOs in Germany, Britain, Italy, France, Spain, Greece, Sweden and the Basque Country as well as at the level of the EU itself.

The investigation embraces three complementary strategies:

- the quantitative and qualitative study of protest events about environmental issues by means of the analysis of reports published in mass media and environmental movement publications;
- literature-, document- and interview-based examinations of EMOs and their relations with other actors;
- observation and interviews at local level of current cases of environmental contention, and exploration, principally by means of analysis of local media reports and informant interviews, of the incidence and forms of environmental action in selected localities.

Further information on the project is posted on the WWW at: http://www.ukc.ac.uk/sociology/TEA.html

Notes

1   This chapter is based on research conducted as part of an eight nation comparative investigation: the TEA (Transformation of Environmental Activism) Project, funded by contract no.: ENV4-CT97–0514 from the EC DG XII (Science, Research and Development) (see Appendix A). I am indebted to Ben Seel and Debbie Adams for research assistance and for helpful comments on earlier drafts of this chapter, and especially to Sandy Miller who not only shared the reading and coding of newspaper reports but also coerced SPSS and Excel into producing readable tables and graphs.

2   It is the limitations of the resources at the disposal of even established EMOs such as FoE which best explain their relatively peripheral involvement in most local environmental campaigns and why local campaigners do not rely more heavily upon established EMOs. Local campaigners who do approach a local EMO group for assistance usually discover that the chief resources of such groups are the energies of one or a handful of part-time activists supplemented, on a restricted range of issues, by access to a variably reliable network of information. In the absence of well-resourced local EMOs, local campaigners are obliged to rely largely upon their own resources and, to the extent that they develop effective campaign groups, they may themselves become sources of organisational and tactical innovation within the broader environmental movement. This is one of the findings of my current EC-funded research on the political contention surrounding the siting of waste management facilities (Rootes 1997b).

3   The problematic nature of relations between campaigners and the mass media is increasingly well-recognised. The best single discussion of the issues involved in movement–media interactions is still probably Gitlin (1980), but specifically on environmental issues, see Hansen (1993) and Anderson (1997).

4   See Rucht *et al.* (1998) for an up-to-date review of the method and its applications.

5   Subsequent stages of the TEA Project will complement this research on media reports of environmental protest by examining, by means of surveys, analysis of liter-

ature and documents and interviews, EMOs, environmental activism at the local level, and interactions among environmentalists and their interlocutors at the European level (see Appendix A).

6 The *Independent*'s coverage was, however, greater in some months, and the surprisingly limited overlap between its coverage and that of the *Guardian* suggests that it would have been advantageous to have covered both papers. To have done that for every day over ten years would have been far beyond our resources, and we judged it preferable to select our data from each day's output of the one more inclusive and editorially stable source rather than to sample the coverage of two papers on alternate days.

The *Daily Telegraph* was not readily available to us in full text form, but unsystematic scrutiny, confirmed by conversation with a *Telegraph* journalist interested in environmental issues, suggests that its coverage of environmental protests is much less inclusive than that of either the *Guardian* or the *Independent*, albeit because of its libertarian interest in individuals' struggles against bureaucracy, it sometimes reports 'NIMBY' protests that the other papers miss.

7 A protest event is defined as a collective, public action by non-state actors, involving at least three people, and with the expressed purpose of critique or dissent together with societal and/or political demands (Rucht 1998).

8 Summary reports are those in which

(a) one group is reported to have performed a number of distinct protests over a considerable time span (for example, 'every Sunday for the last two years'), or

(b) a number of groups are reported to have performed a certain number of protests over a considerable time span, or

(c) a number of groups are reported each to have performed one protest on the same issue or claim on the same day or weekend, usually each group acting in a different location.

9 For example, of events derived from summary reports, 45 per cent could not be located even to a region of the UK; excluding summary reports, only 9 per cent of events were 'location unknown'.

10 If we aggregate environmental and animal welfare protests, just four campaigns – that against the export of live animals which commenced in 1990 and peaked in 1995, the 1995 Ramblers Association campaign for the 'right to roam', the 1995 Greenpeace-initiated campaign against the sea-dumping of the Brent Spar oil-drilling platform, and the 1997 campaign against deer hunting in the New Forest – account for almost half of all the 1,433 protest events derived from summary reports; excluding summary reports, the same four campaigns yielded just 85 protest events. The extreme case was the campaign against deer hunting in the New Forest; although this campaign gave rise to only a single event reported other than in summary reports, when summary reports are included it accounted for a clear majority of all the protest events reported for 1997.

11 Hunt saboteurs, in particular, have been prone to see hunting as a class issue whereas the supporters of most EMOs are typically middle class and tend to see environmental issues as inclusive and cross-class. Some hunt saboteurs are self-consciously anarchist in the manner of the strident anarchist periodical *Class War*.

12 If, in order to eliminate chance coincidences, we limit the depiction of the network to groups among which there are three or more links (as in Figure 2.1), the animal rights groups appear entirely detached from the network of environmental organisations. I am indebted to Mario Diani for advice on the network analyses and, especially, to Sandy Miller for constructing the diagram.

It should be admitted that protest event methodology, dependent as it is upon media reports, is not well suited to the identification of personal networks or of subterranean or clandestine networks that may exist among groups that do not engage in common public action. The next stage of our research, focused upon surveys, interviews and more detailed studies of EMOs, should shed more light on these less publicly visible network linkages, but a very preliminary analysis of the first round of a survey we conducted among 86 British environmental groups in 1999 does nothing to contradict the picture painted here.

13 We also examined the incidence of protest by month and by quarter but found no clear seasonal pattern save for the fact that there was, in most years, least environmental protest in December and November.

14 The inclusion of data from summary reports would also have the effect of exaggerating the 1995 peak. Including summary reports, 1995, with 441 protests, accounts for 29 per cent of all protests for the decade compared with 16 per cent if summary reports are excluded. Interestingly, the inclusion of summary reports also has the effect of increasing the number of protests in the earlier peak year (1989) by over 40 per cent (from 95 to 139).

The number of summary reports of environmental, animal welfare and anti-hunting protests varied from year to year; in low single figures up to 1994, it rose to 27 in 1995 before falling back to single figures. The proportion of all protest events reported only in summary reports has also varied, but it has shown a general tendency to rise (from roughly one in four in 1988–1990 to over 40 per cent from 1992). However in 1995 over 72 per cent of identifiable events were contained in summary reports. This pattern of variation may reflect a long-term change in journalistic practices, but it most probably results from the efforts of journalists to find means adequately to cover the widespread surges of protest associated with the peaks of protest waves.

It is also possible that at the peak of a wave of protest, a journalist, having employed the device of the summary report on several occasions in a short space of time, may become hypersensitive to instances of protest that would not normally be reported and may, by becoming more heavily reliant on the device of the summary report, exaggerate the salience of the peak of the protest wave. In other words, at the peak of the 'issue attention cycle' (Downs 1972), a smaller proportion of events may go unreported than at other times. It is noteworthy that reports of Ramblers Association actions in 1995, almost all of them derived from summary reports, referred to 103 events, more than twice as many as in any previous year.

The 1995 peak in particular was remarkable for the near coincidence of a number of campaigns: to prevent the dumping at sea of the Brent Spar drilling platform, against Shell's operations in the Niger delta, against French nuclear tests in the south Pacific, Reclaim the Streets and Critical Mass demonstrations against road traffic, as well as various new or continuing anti-roads protests and 'right to roam' protests by the Ramblers Association. Also peaking in 1995 were protests against the export of live animals. The proportion of events reported in summary reports was markedly higher in each of the three years (1989, 1993 and 1995) which appear as peaks in the waves of protest – even when excluding summary reports – than they were in the immediately preceding years. Summary reports thus appear to enhance the salience of what from more detailed reports appear to be the peaks of protest.

15 If data from summary reports is included, the over-representation of London is reduced and that of the rest of the South East is markedly increased, but both the impact of a few large campaigns and the high proportion of missing data suggest caution in the interpretation of this data.

16 Because our coding guidelines permitted the coding of up to two issues per protest event, these percentages sum to more than 100.

17 The same is also broadly true of other forms of action (such as petitions) involving large numbers of people. In only two years – 1989 and 1995 – did the number of all large protests exceed fourteen and only in 1997 was just one large protest action

reported. In all, there were 61 large actions in the years 1988–1992 and 54 in 1993–1997.

18 Environmental activists were, however, among the participants in the demonstrations, some of them large, that were mounted against the proposed Criminal Justice Act in 1994–1995. Because these protests did not directly make explicit environmental claims, they have not been included in our data set.

19 The same pattern holds if all forms of action involving 500 or more participants are compared: the median for 1988–1992 was 3,000 compared with 1,575 for 1993–1997; the median for all protests of whatever size fell from 300 to 100.

20 For this reason, we have coded as a separate protest event every distinct identifiable action – such as a mass trespass or demonstrative gathering – reported as having occurred at such sites.

21 Interview with Paul Brown conducted by Debbie Adams, 22 March 1999.

22 This is partly compensated for by the fact that other journalists are now much more alert to environmental issues and so may include them in their reports.

23 One thing that may work to counter this tendency is environmental journalists' increasing reliance upon contacts and the quality of their contacts with established EMOs such as FoE and Greenpeace, both of which are highly media-aware and very active in producing press releases. When interviewed, Paul Brown asserted that he was equally accessible to the newer, more radical groups such as Earth First!, especially since they were adept in the use of new communications technologies. Nevertheless, Brown reports that an average of three press releases a day land on his desk from Greenpeace alone, and it is very likely that, over the decade in which he has been the *Guardian*'s environmental correspondent, a symbiotic relationship has developed between him and Greenpeace and FoE; they feed him stories which he believes he can trust and so he is more likely to run their stories and has less incentive to seek out other environmental movement sources.

The more spectacular actions of less established groups may be reported, but not necessarily with sympathy or understanding. At the time of the Pollok Park protests in Glasgow, there was much resentment among Earth First! and allied protesters at what they regarded as the unsympathetic and misleading reporting of their protest by the *Guardian*.

24 One reason for this surprisingly high incidence of confrontation in nature conservation protests – the aspect of environmentalism conventionally considered most conservative – is the frequency with which nature protection issues were raised in the course of anti-roads protests. Our coding procedures allowed for the coding of up to two claims per protest event; in the case of reports of anti-roads protests in particular it was often difficult to decide which was the principal issue of protest and so two claims were often recorded for one event.

25 This is in marked contrast to animal welfare protests which have not become noticeably more confrontational but of which a higher proportion were confrontational to begin with.

26 This reflects the presence within this category of two quite distinct tendencies: an overwhelmingly demonstrative animal welfare campaign focusing especially on animal rights in respect of the export of live animals; and an animal rights campaign focused especially upon opposition to fur farming and experiments on animals, some strands of which have been relatively uninhibited about the use of violence.

27 If data from summary reports are included, the main effects are to emphasise the association of land rights protests with demonstrations, and to reduce the salience of violence in both animal welfare and anti-hunting protests (in favour of demonstrative and confrontational actions respectively). This serves as a useful reminder that, distinctive though animal welfare protests were in the extent of their resort to violence, the great majority of the large number of individual protests that were

mounted in the course of long-running and geographically dispersed campaigns were non-violent.

28 Of these ten attacks on property, three involved substantial damage to equipment operated by commercial enterprises against whom Earth First! was campaigning, but three were the symbolic 'theft' of tropical hardwood from stores.

29 The inclusion of data from summary reports emphasises the specialisation of the RA around demonstrations.

30 Equally, the actions of other groups not included in our survey may have either cautionary or exemplary value for the environmental movement.

31 Minor attacks on property were reported in 13 per cent of animal rights protests, but there is no clear pattern to the incidence of such attacks; they were scarcely more frequent in the second half of the decade than in the first, and as a proportion of all animal rights protests, they declined markedly. Thirty per cent of protests involving animal welfare were at least partly violent in form, but of those 72 events involving violence, 40 occurred in 1993–1994; in subsequent years protests involving violence fell back, both in absolute numbers and as a proportion (13 per cent) of all animal rights protests, to the very low levels of 1988–1989.

32 See Rootes (1997a, 1999c) for a discussion and critique of this concept.

33 However, McNeish (2000) asserts that the wave of protest continued at a high level at least into the summer of 1998.

34 Even when it was clear that public opinion had moved decisively against GM foods, the government seemed more anxious to maintain Britain's position as a major player in the biotechnology industry than to assuage public anxieties or environmentalists' concerns.

35 Rawcliffe (1998: 222) observes that in its last years in opposition the Labour Party was much influenced by personal links between its current leading figures and the environmental movement. The language of Labour's 1997 election manifesto ('concern for the environment at the heart of policy-making so that it is not an add-on extra but informs the whole of government policies designed to combine environmental sustainability with social and economic progress') is in fact entirely consistent with the pronouncements of Labour in government.

36 The PEM project – Policy-making and Environmental Movements: the case of waste management. This project, funded by the European Commission (EC contract no.: ENV4-CT96–0239), is part of a Spanish–British comparison conducted in partnership between Enrique Laraña (Universidad Complutense de Madrid) and Chris Rootes (University of Kent at Canterbury). A brief description of the project is posted at: www.ukc.ac.uk/sociology/polsoc.html.

37 The British have become steadily more likely to approve of recourse to unconventional protest in response to proposed legislation they considered unjust or harmful even if it means breaking the law, and more likely to say they would themselves take such action in response to an unjust law. The proportion saying they would go on a demonstration rose from 8 per cent in 1983 to 17 per cent in 1994; indeed, in 1994, 8.9 per cent said they *had* gone on a demonstration in such circumstances (Curtice and Jowell 1995: 154). In response to a differently worded question in 1996, 31 per cent said they 'definitely' or 'probably' would go on a protest march or demonstration, and 5.5 per cent said they had done so in the previous five years (Jowell *et al.* 1997: 320). This latter figure compares with the 5.1 per cent who in 1984–1985 said they had gone on a demonstration during the previous five years (Parry, Moyser and Day 1992: 44).

However, the 1993 ISSP survey found that although relatively high proportions of the British said they had in the previous five years given money to an environmental group (30 per cent compared with 19 per cent in Germany) or had signed a petition about an environmental issue (37 per cent compared with 31 per cent in Germany), only 3 per cent said they had participated in an environmentalist demonstration, a lower proportion than in Germany (8 per cent), Italy, Spain or the Netherlands (Dalton and Rohrschneider 1998: 111). It should be noted that this survey predates the peak of the 1990s surge of environmental protest in Britain, and we do not know whether the rate of participation in demonstrations has increased as a result of that surge.

38 This is well documented in the case of protests against the Newbury bypass ('The Battle of Rickety Bridge', Channel 4 TV, December 1996) but it was also apparent amongst the increasingly numerous audiences at public meetings organised by FoE during 1996–1997 (cf . Fiddes 1997: 41; Doherty 1999a).

39 See, for example, Seel (1997a). Wall (1999a, b) points to the central role played in these protests by activists identifying themselves with Earth First!, a notably loose network rather than a tight-knit formal EMO (Seel 1997b; McNeish 1997, 2000). See also North (1998).

40 As Faucher (1997, 1999) has shown, the counter-culturalism of British Greens finds no echo among the supporters of *Les Verts* in France.

Bibliography

Anderson, A. (1997) *Media, Culture and the Environment*, London: UCL Press.

Carmin, J. (1999) 'Local activism, national organisations and the environmental movement in the United States', *Environmental Politics* 8, 1: 101–121; reprinted in Rootes (1999a).

Cowell, R. and Jehlicka, P. (1995) 'Backyard and biosphere: the spatial distribution of support for English and Welsh environmental organisations', *Area* 27, 2: 110–117.

Curtice, J. and Jowell, R. (1995) 'The sceptical electorate', in R. Jowell, J. Curtice, A. Park, L. Brook and D. Ahrendt (eds) *British Social Attitudes: The 12th Report*, Aldershot: Dartmouth: 141–172.

Dalton, R. and Rohrschneider, R. (1998) 'The greening of Europe', in R. Jowell, J. Curtice, A. Park, L. Brook, K. Thomson and C. Bryson (eds) *British Social Attitudes: The 15th Report*, Aldershot: Ashgate: 101–121.

Diani, M. (1992) 'The concept of social movement', *Sociological Review* 40, 1: 1–25.

Diani, M. and Donati, P. (1999) 'Organisational change in western European environmental groups: a framework for analysis', *Environmental Politics*, 8, 1: 13–34, reprinted in Rootes (1999a).

Doherty, B. (1999a) 'Paving the way: the rise of direct action against road building and the changing character of British environmentalism', *Political Studies* 47, 2: 275–291.

—— (1999b) 'Manufactured vulnerability: eco-activist tactics in Britain', *Mobilization* 4, 1: 75–89.

Downs, A. (1972) 'Up and down with ecology: the "issue attention cycle"', *The Public Interest* 28: 38–50.

Faucher, F. (1997) ' "Think globally, act locally": paradox in *Les Verts* and the Green Party', paper presented at the workshop on 'Environmental movements', European Consortium for Political Research Joint Sessions, Bern, February.

—— (1999) *Les Habits Verts de la Politique*, Paris: Presses de Sciences Po.

Fiddes, N. (1997) 'The march of the earth dragon: a new radical challenge to traditional land rights in Britain', in P. Milbourne (ed.) *Revealing Rural 'Others'*, London: Cassell, pp. 35–54.

Fillieule, O. (1996) 'Police records and the national press in France: issues in the methodology of data-collections from newspapers', *EUI Working Papers*, RSC No. 96/25.

—— (1997) *Stratégies de la Rue: les manifestations en France*, Paris: Presses de Sciences Po.

Flynn, A. and Lowe, P. (1992) 'The greening of the Tories: the Conservative Party and the environment', in W. Rüdig (ed.) *Green Politics Two*, Edinburgh: Edinburgh University Press, pp. 9–36.

Frankland, E.G. (1990) 'Does Green politics have a future in Britain?', in W. Rüdig (ed.) *Green Politics One*, Edinburgh: Edinburgh University Press: 7–28.

Gitlin, T. (1980) *The Whole World is Watching: The Mass Media in the Making and Unmaking of the New Left*, Berkeley CA and London: University of California Press.

Gouldner, A. (1955) 'Metaphysical pathos and the theory of bureaucracy', *American Political Science Review* 49, 2: 496–507.

Hansen, A. (ed.) (1993) *The Mass Media and Environmental Issues*, Leicester: Leicester University Press.

Jordan, G. and Maloney, W. (1997) *The Protest Business? Mobilizing Campaign Groups*, Manchester and New York: Manchester University Press.

Jowell, R., Curtice, J., Park, A., Brook, L., Thomson, K. and Bryson, C. (eds) (1997) *British Social Attitudes: The 14th Report*, Aldershot: Ashgate.

Jowers, P., Dürrschmidt, J., Purdue, D. and O'Doherty, R. (1996) 'DIY culture in SW England', paper presented at the Second European Conference on Social Movements, Vitoria-Gasteiz, 2–5 October.

McNeish, W. (1997) 'Resisting colonisation: the politics of anti-roads protesting', paper presented at British Sociological Association annual conference, York, 7–10 April.

—— (2000) *The Anti-Roads Protests in Nineties Britain: A Sociological Interpretation*, PhD thesis, University of Glasgow, Department of Sociology.

Michels, R. (1959 [original 1912]) *Political Parties: A Sociological Study of the Oligarchical Tendencies of Modern Democracy*, New York: Dover.

North, P. (1998) ' "Save our Solsbury!": the anatomy of an anti-roads protest', *Environmental Politics* 7, 3: 1–25.

Parry, G., Moyser, G. and Day, N. (1992) *Political Participation in Britain*, Cambridge: Cambridge University Press.

Rawcliffe, P. (1998) *Environmental Pressure Groups in Transition*, Manchester: Manchester University Press.

Rootes, C.A. (1997a) 'Shaping collective action: structure, contingency and knowledge', in R. Edmondson (ed.) *The Political Context of Collective Action*, London and New York: Routledge: 81–104.

—— (1997b) 'From resistance to empowerment: the struggle over waste management and its implications for environmental education', in N. Russell *et al.* (eds) *Technology, the Environment and Us*, London: IRNES/Graduate School of the Environment, Imperial College, pp. 30–39.

—— (1997c) 'Environmental movements and Green parties in western and eastern Europe', in M. Redclift and G. Woodgate (eds) *International Handbook of Environmental Sociology*, Cheltenham and Northampton MA: Edward Elgar: 319–348.

—— (ed.) (1999a) *Environmental Movements: Local, National and Global*, London and Portland, OR: Frank Cass.

—— (1999b) 'The transformation of environmental activism: activists, organisations and policy-making', *Innovation: The European Journal of Social Sciences* 12, 2: 153–173. Also available at: http://www.ukc.ac.uk/sociology/TEA.html

—— (1999c) ' "Political opportunity structures": promise, problems and prospects', *La Lettre de la Maison Française d'Oxford*, 10: 75–97. Also available at: http://www.ukc. ac.uk/sociology/staff/chrisR.html

—— (1999d) *Environmental Protest in Seven European Union States*, interim report to European Commission DG XII on contract ENV4-CT97-0514, Canterbury: Centre for the Study of Social and Political Movements, University of Kent at Canterbury.

—— (2000) 'The Europeanisation of Environmentalism', in R. Balme, D. Chabanet and V. Wright (eds), *L'Europe des intérêts: lobbying, mobilisations et espace européen*, Paris: Presses de Science Po.

Rucht, D. (1998)*Transformation of Environmental Activism (Work package 1: Environmental Protests): Codebook and Practical Guide*, Canterbury: Centre for the Study of Social and Political Movements, University of Kent.

Rucht, D. and Roose, J. (1999) 'The German environmental movement at a crossroads?', *Environmental Politics* 8, 1: 59–80; reprinted in Rootes (1999a).

Rucht, D., Koopmans, R. and Neidhardt, F. (eds) (1998) *Acts of Dissent: New Developments in the Study of Protest*, Berlin: Sigma.

Rüdig, W., Bennie, L. and Franklin, M. (1991) *Green Party Members: A Profile*, Glasgow: Delta.

Schlosberg, D. (1999) 'Networks and mobile arrangements: organisational innovation in the US environmental justice movement', *Environmental Politics*, 8, 1: 122–148; reprinted in Rootes (1999a).

Seel, B. (1997a) 'Strategies of resistance at the Pollok Free State road protest camp', *Environmental Politics* 6, 3: 108–139.

—— (1997b) ' "If not you, then who?" Earth First! in the UK', *Environmental Politics* 6, 3: 172–179.

Statham, P. (1997) 'Telling tales: constructing and using political opportunities through media discourse', paper presented at the workshop on 'Environmental movements', European Consortium for Political Research Joint Sessions, Bern, February.

Van der Heijden, H.-A. (1997) 'Political opportunity structure and the institutionalisation of the environmental movement', *Environmental Politics* 6, 4: 25–50.

Wall, D. (1999a) *Earth First! and the Origins of the Anti-Roads Movement*, London and New York: Routledge.

—— (1999b) 'Mobilising Earth First! in Britain', *Environmental Politics* 8, 1: 81–100; reprinted in Rootes (1999a).

3 Manufactured vulnerability

Protest camp tactics[1]

Brian Doherty

An important factor in the impact of the new environmental protests has been the use of effective and imaginative tactics to prolong the occupation of sites of new developments. By prolonging evictions and creating a confrontation with the authorities, which can last for weeks or even months rather than the few hours duration of most protest actions, eco-activists have captured significant amounts of public attention. Although their aim is to disrupt construction directly, and they deny that media attention is an end in itself, one of their clearest successes has been in making and sustaining a dramatic news story. At most sites eco-activists have been able to rely on the support of more conventional local campaign groups. Where the latter had tended to pursue procedural measures, eco-activists mainly concentrated on attempting to prevent construction on schemes that had already been officially approved.

Continuities with earlier campaigns of non-violent direct action (NVDA) are evident in particular in the development of protest camps as sites for mobilising opposition and expressing alternative values. In using this tactic protesters were drawing on the example set by the peace camps of the 1980s. Camp culture was important in shaping both kinds of movement. However, where the peace camps were established to express opposition from outside the perimeter of military bases, the environmental camps were more defensive and focused on the aim of resisting eviction.

Theoretical perspectives on how forms of protest develop

As a case study the British eco-activists provide much material relevant to the debates about the development of protest repertoires. First, to the degree that NVDA is an established repertoire of contention (Rucht 1990), they point to the importance of learned and shared toolkits of protest emphasised by Charles Tilly (1995). In emphasising the concept of 'repertoire', Tilly points to the fact that most protesters draw on the examples provided by previous protest campaigns. As a result, the kinds of actions that they are likely to choose are limited by history, by the shared understandings of how to protest and by the values and ethos of the movement. Nevertheless, even if repertoires are limited, innovation is possible, which means that the analysis of any action repertoire implicitly raises the question of the balance between continuity and change.

Second, since they draw on examples provided by other recent NVDA movements in Britain and other countries and have, in turn, inspired movements in other countries, they provide a case for the use of Doug McAdam's (1995) model of initiator and spin-off movements. McAdam aims to show that while changes in political opportunities tend to shape the emergence of initiator movements, subsequent spin-off movements are less dependent on such openings and can take advantage of new opportunities created by initiator movements. Spin-off movements are more likely to emerge as a result of cognitive or cultural factors and usually develop within the networks of earlier movements and draw upon their frames. The eco-activists can be defined loosely as a spin-off movement of the green and peace movements, but they did not draw on opportunities provided by earlier protest. Rather they emerged at a time when protest had died down and the main peace and green organisations had become more institutionalised (Byrne 1997, 1998: 424; Doherty 1998: 374–376). Nor was their emergence the result of any opening in the political opportunity structure (see Doherty 1999). Rather, the initiative came from young activists dissatisfied with the limits of the bureaucratic strategies favoured by the established movement organisations. In choosing direct action they mixed existing British forms of action such as protest camps with new tactics developed by radical environmentalists in Australia.

Third, these protests support the view that when new forms emerge they do so as a result of interaction between movements and their opponents. Tilly argues that the forms of action chosen by movements will reflect the strategies of their opponents. In his study of the civil rights movement in the USA, McAdam (1983, 1996) suggests that much of its impact could be explained by its successes in developing new tactics just as the Southern authorities learned to cope with old ones. Thus, bus boycotts, lunch counter sit-ins, Freedom Rides and community-wide campaigns, such as those in Birmingham and Selma, each introduced a new element into the campaign and maintained the sense of crisis and confrontation upon which the movement depended. When a new tactic was introduced, movement activity as a whole rose, not simply actions involving the use of the new tactic, but once the authorities learned how to respond to the innovation a further innovation was needed. A similar dynamic characterises the eco-protests discussed below.

Fourth, it is more difficult to judge the relevance to this case of the claim that innovation and diffusion are most likely to occur during a protest wave or cycle (Tarrow 1995: 91; McAdam 1995: 235). According to Sidney Tarrow innovations are most likely to occur in what Zolberg has termed the 'moments of madness' at the beginnings of protest cycles when to protesters all seems possible. Tarrow says that innovations do not transform the whole repertoire all at once, rather they are tested, amended and diffused through larger cycles of mobilisation:

It is within these larger cycles, that new forms of contention combine with old ones, the expressive encounters the instrumental, traditional social actors adopt tactics from new arrivals, and newly invented forms of collective action become what I call 'modular'. Cycles of protest are the crucible in which moments of madness are tempered into the permanent tools of a society's repertoire of contention.

(Tarrow 1995: 92)

For Tarrow a cycle of protest is characterised by heightened conflict across the social spectrum, geographical and sectoral diffusion (from centre to periphery); increased involvement of social movement organisations (SMOs); new frames of meaning and expanding repertoires of contention. A different definition of 'protest waves' advanced by Kriesi *et al.* (1995: 113) is based on four criteria: the strong expansion and contraction of the magnitude of protest; that protest extends over a long period of time; that it encompasses large parts of the social movement sector; that it affects most of the national territory. While it is difficult to show that Britain has been in a cycle of protest which meets either definition exactly, it does seem that protest has become more socially acceptable and that groups that would not usually be seen as typical protesters have taken part. Opposition to the poll tax spread beyond the protests of the far Left to a widespread campaign of non-payment in 1990 which was particularly broad in Scotland. Since then commentators have also been taken by surprise by the intensity of support given to protest against live cattle exports by local people in Shoreham and Brightlingsea in 1995 (McLeod 1998). In 1997 and 1998 there were two large demonstrations by the Countryside Movement,[2] primarily to oppose a ban on hunting but also framed as a call to urban dwellers to stop interfering in the countryside. Less visible at a national level, and more difficult to measure, is the spread of locally based environmental protests against new developments such as roads, housing, supermarkets and waste incinerators. Overall then, there is evidence suggestive of a rise in protest (for more detail, see Rootes, this volume).

Yet there has certainly been no 'moment of madness' of the kind that occurred in Italy in 1968. What appears new in the 1990s is the spread of protests involving groups that do not have previous experience of protest and the locally based nature of much of this protest. The analysis by Rootes (this volume) of the public record of protest shows a rise in non-violent confrontational protest on environmental issues. Taken together this means that there has certainly been a series of protests that have captured public attention and made protest appear more acceptable in British political culture. Moreover, many of the features of a protest cycle are evident: there are protests in most parts of the country, including urban and rural areas, and embracing a broader range of social groups than perhaps ever before in Britain. In most cases these protests begin outside established SMOs, but the latter tend to recover their position to become involved later.[3] There has also been some diffusion of tactics from innovators to other social groups, but cultural and practical barriers mean that some forms of action remain the preserve of eco-activists.

The dynamic of protest and the evolution of tactics

Protests at road and other construction sites are a form of siege warfare. Protesters occupy a site and build defences in trees, houses or underground tunnels. The besiegers outnumber the occupiers, and have greater resources. One of the principal weapons of the besiegers is the cherry-picker crane, which can hoist bailiffs to pluck protesters from trees, rooftops or rope walkways at heights of up to 200 feet. Successive protests have produced new techniques for resisting the besiegers to the extent that, when the time comes for an eviction, great hopes are invested by protesters in the effectiveness of specific forms of obstructing eviction. Yet, while the eviction represents the culmination of the campaign, it is not the only event of significance. Aside from the considerable amount of work invested in building site defences, there are also forays into the territory of their opponents. Contractors' offices are occupied and sometimes damaged and shareholders' meetings are disrupted. Also, since 1995 the campaign has been taken into city streets with surprise actions to reclaim urban space from traffic.

Three factors have influenced the development of tactics by protesters. First, situational factors such as the terrain and also the nature of the local community shape the choices available and influence the values appealed to. Open chalk downland such as at Twyford Down (Hampshire) provided fewer opportunities to defenders than the woods at the M65 in Preston (Lancashire). The destruction of designated Areas of Outstanding Natural Beauty and wildlife habitats was emphasised at Newbury and other rural sites, while the social destruction of an east London community, bisected by a road intended to bring commuters from outside into central London more quickly, was the main issue for those opposing the M11 link.

Second, the values of protesters also influenced tactical choices. At Twyford, the Dongas Tribe (who named themselves after the medieval trackways that crossed the Down) used dragon symbols, and drew boundary circles, invoking the power of magic to defend their site. It was argued by some in this group that rediscovering indigenous Celtic and earth-based spirituality would help to restore the balance of nature. Adopting a tribal identity, and in the case of the Dongas, even a nomadic way of life, was also a means of situating themselves in the global struggles of indigenous peoples against ecological destruction. After their eviction from Twyford, some of the Dongas lived in mobile camps of benders (tents made of hazel branches and tarpaulins), carrying possessions on carts and donkeys along old trackways, so minimising their contamination by modernity.

In the first years of the protests some activists expressed anti-urban sentiments. For example, some contributors to *Do or Die* (the discussion journal for Earth First! (UK)) emphasised the need to escape from the spiritual desolation of cities. This influenced the choice of tactics. In the M11 campaign some of those squatting houses in Leytonstone could not understand the 'hippies'' obsession

with sitting in trees'. The squatters believed that 'it made far more sense tactically to occupy houses than trees'. Furthermore, 'once there were other rural
campaigns to go to (first Bath, later Preston) the "tree people" tended to move
away from the urban wilderness of east London, particularly once the "bender
site" had been destroyed in July 1994' (from an email interview with an activist
in Reclaim the Streets – RTS). Trees also had an expressive role. They were
given personalities, and some at Preston (M65) left before the eviction rather
than see their tree destroyed. Tree sits have been a feature of environmental
direct action in Australasia and North America since at least the late 1970s, but
even the most recent New World manuals for eco-activists do not include tree
houses, as distinct from platforms (DAM Collective 1998). Tree houses had
considerable defensive value. It is difficult to be caught by surprise action by
evictors in a tree house. They also provide a base for storing supplies and can
provide a platform for defences. These became more sophisticated as the protests
developed.[4] The eviction of the tree houses at Newbury and Manchester saw
desperate and emotional confrontations in which protesters used flour, urine and
disinfectant, as well as staves with rubber hoses, designed to impede chainsaws,
to hamper the actions of bailiffs.

In contrast, the adoption of the street party as a tactic by RTS (on which, see
also Wall and Maples, this volume) drew on a mix of sources from dance culture
of rave parties to anarchist traditions of popular participatory revolts in which
the politics of urban space and community were more central than the natural
environment:

> The privatisation of public space in the form of the car continues the
> erosion of neighbourhood and community that defines the metropolis. Road
> schemes, business 'parks', shopping developments – all add to the disintegra-
> tion of community and the flattening of locality … . To rescue what is left of
> the public arena, to enlarge and transform that arena from a selling and
> increasingly sold space – from controlled locality to local control – is funda-
> mental to the vision of reclaiming the streets.
>
> (Anon. 1997e: 4–5)

For RTS the street became a metaphor for the communal sphere embracing
'dwellings, people and interaction' in contrast to the sterile tarmac of roads.
Pointing to the danger that the street party as a festival might become a caricature of
itself, RTS argues that the street party could develop into a regular political space:

> The participatory 'party' or 'street' meeting could be a real objective for the
> future street party. For an event that goes beyond temporarily celebrating its
> autonomy to laying the ground for permanent social freedom. Discussion
> areas, decision-making bodies, delegates mandated to attend other parties;
> in short the formation of a 'body politic', could all happen within the
> broader arena of the street party.
>
> (Anon. 1997d: 5)

For RTS 'the street party of street parties' is therefore an anarchism which poses a direct challenge to the state and capitalism. It is not simply roads and cars but the system that produces them that must be opposed and the street party is a means of doing this appropriate to the modern era.

The third factor that shaped the development of tactics was the ability of opponents to adapt to earlier tactics. The main initial successes at Twyford Down in 1992 and 1993 were in disrupting construction work through surprise invasions of the site. Under safety at work legislation the builders were forced to stop work and on many days protesters were successful in climbing on bulldozers and chaining themselves onto vital machinery. These tactics could be countered by increasing the number of security guards, but by increasing the level of security required protesters were increasing the costs of developers. A bigger blow was the criminalisation of action that disrupted work in the Criminal Justice Act (CJA) 1995.

In response activists occupied buildings and trees.[5] New defences at such sites meant that even the use of overwhelming numbers by the authorities did not guarantee easy success. The eviction of Claremont Road, the last main squatted site on the path of the M11 (London), in November and December 1994 was carried out by 700 police, 400 security guards and 200 bailiffs. Nevertheless, the eviction took 4 days during which the 500 occupiers were able to make themselves a major news story and score tactical successes, such as maintaining power supplies to the occupiers through a secret tunnel beyond police lines.[6] A scaffolding tower constructed on the rooftop of one house allowed one protester to delay the evictions single-handedly for a further day.

Whereas, by the time of the evictions at Claremont Road protesters had accepted that the houses would be demolished, when evictions began at Newbury in January 1996 there was greater optimism that skilled defences would delay the progress of road building long enough for procedural measures to halt construction. The evictions of the 31 camps at Newbury took eleven weeks and became a regular feature on TV news. In one sense this was a success, since the theatre of direct action forced awareness of the depth of feeling expressed by the protesters, and protesters themselves were conscious of this effect of their action. One M11 protester said: 'Direct action is a theatre. The media like that … . Direct action is totally direct: it's real and not just mediated politics. The agreement on non-violence is ritualised. It's like a performance' (Carey 1995: 22), but in other respects the dramatic quality of the evictions reinforced the viewers' sense of distance. The medieval character of the battle, with massed lines of security guards with bright tunics moving through the mist, cherry pickers like siege engines manoeuvring slowly towards their goal, and a phalanx of security guards and knights in the form of police on horseback, suggested dislocation from everyday life. While more conventional groups of locals were often portrayed acting in support of the eco-activists (see Cathles, this volume on this), they were usually on the fringes, reinforcing the image that eco-protest had become a technically skilled form of action which not only required a difficult lifestyle but also a degree of professionalism that should not be attempted by amateurs. Other evictions of the trees and tunnels at Fairmile in Devon in January 1997, Crystal Palace in 1999 and Manchester Airport in May 1997 and September 1999 were all represented as a battle between specialists. Moreover, the authorities were able to reduce some of the visual impact of the eviction by establishing cordons around sites which meant that neither supporters nor reporters were able to see much of the drama of the eviction.

The Government also tried to harass road protesters through the courts but initially this back-fired badly. Attempts to sue protesters at Twyford Down for the costs of the police action were unsuccessful and when several Twyford protesters were sent to jail for breaking injunctions against protesting they received significant supportive media coverage and a visit from the European Environment Commissioner, Carlo Ripa de Meana. Compensation payments for wrongful arrest provided resources for the movement. However, protest also provided opportunities to justify repressive legislation. The CJA (1995) introduced new restrictions on the right to protest which made it possible for the police to prosecute protesters for trespass as a criminal offence. Probably the most effective legal measure used by the authorities was the regular use of injunctions to stay away from the site of roads as a part of bail conditions. This kept hundreds of protesters, once arrested, off site.

Surveillance also played an increasing role as protests developed. From 1992 onwards the Government employed a private detective agency to gather evidence about protesters. Since the information gathered was not often used in prosecutions protesters assumed that the presence of camcorders and surveillance teams was intended mainly to intimidate. The same was true of the raid on the offices of RTS in London in August 1996. Rather than try to arrest the 7,000 who joined in the previous month's street party on the M41, the police waited to target the main organisers. They took away a computer from the group's office and threatened an activist with conspiracy charges. In March 1996 the Association of Chief Police Officers announced that they would use anti-terrorist squads to step up surveillance of environmental activists. Despite the lack of any serious violent incidents at any road protests the spectre of environmental terrorism was being used to justify the need for domestic intelligence spending.[7]

Technical interaction

The clearest examples of innovation were in the development of techniques for resisting and delaying eviction. Some of these techniques or similar variants had previously been used by eco-activists in Australia and the USA, but they were novel in Britain. The further evolution of these techniques was also affected by the ability of the authorities to react and adapt. The most successful of the technical devices used by protesters were lock-ons, walkways and tripods. To 'lock-on' protesters placed their hand in a tube wide enough only for their arm and clipped their wrist onto a metal bar at the other end of the tube. When the bar and tube were embedded in concrete it became very difficult to move them.

At Claremont Road (M11, East London), for instance, people who appeared to be lying on mattresses in the road were actually locked-on to concrete in the road itself and were able to delay the advance of cherry-picker cranes for several hours. Lock-ons could even be used in trees. An empty oil barrel was hoisted into the tree and then filled with concrete and lashed down with a tube inserted to allow the protester to lock-on. Pneumatic drills had to be used to extract the tube. However, whereas at first this often took hours, as bailiffs became more experienced and prepared they were able to break lock-ons more quickly. In response, protesters adapted their own tactic, adding rubber, metal and glass to hamper the drills.

Walkways were ropes strung at a height between trees or houses to allow protesters to move around above ground level. Once an eviction began, some protesters would move onto the walkways and climb up and down, sometimes without harnesses, to avoid being plucked from them. There were many cases when the ropes were cut with protesters still on them and on several occasions protesters fell. However, the most effective counter to walkways and tree climbers was the introduction of a specialist team of paid climbers by the bailiffs. The recruitment of climbers caused considerable controversy in climbing clubs, but the Sheffield-based group were used regularly after the evictions at Stanworth Woods near Preston in 1995. The battles in the tree tops at Newbury were dangerous and on some occasions violent, as protesters, who included some famous in climbing circles themselves, were chased across trees until eventually removed.

Tripods were scaffolding poles of around 10 metre length, formed into a tripod and clipped together, from which protesters could be suspended. To move them risked causing the protester serious injury. They were first used to block bulldozers by rainforest campaigners in Australia in the early 1980s. In Britain, their first use was by the urban-based group RTS to block traffic in the rush hour in Greenwich (south-east London) in 1995. Tripods became a regular feature of RTS's actions across the country because they provided a portable and rapidly erected barricade.

The final and probably the most effective general technical innovation was the use of tunnels. These do not appear to have been used by protesters elsewhere prior to their use in Britain. The first extensive network of tunnels was at Allercombe, Trollheim and Fairmile in Devon in the route of the A30. The effectiveness of the tunnels depended in part on the nature of the ground. By locking-on underground, protesters hoped to make it impossible for the evictors to bring up heavy machinery, based on the risk of the tunnels collapsing. At previous evictions at Newbury tunnels were seized before protesters could get into them, and at Trollheim in December 1996 protesters were evicted from tunnels within hours, but the evictors had taken considerable safety risks, cutting off air and communication for several hours and moving heavy machinery close to the tunnels, which protesters were able to exploit for publicity. The network at Fairmile was more extensive and sophisticated than elsewhere, and three protesters remained in the tunnel in January 1997 for almost seven days. In later evictions at Manchester Airport in May 1997 and September 1999, and Crystal Palace in 1999, evictions lasted more than two weeks. In some cases little effort was made to evict those in tunnels, with bailiffs prepared to wait until boredom, lack of food or claustrophobia drove the protesters out.

The main limitation of tunnels is the same as that of other methods used by this movement: their success depends upon the risks taken by the protester and the care taken by evictors to avoid causing injury. As experience of evictions developed, the bailiffs and police became less cautious in using force and more skilled at overcoming the defences relied on by protesters. Whereas earlier the technical devices developed by protesters had created confusion and secured delay, by the end of the decade the authorities were able to take them into account in their planning. Moreover, each new device has required protesters to take new risks. Only the most committed activist would take the deliberate risk of locking-on within a home-made tunnel. Although to some protesters such risks are too great, because the campaign has no rules banning excessive risks, the level of risk is an individual's choice. But to some this also has the effect of concentrating attention on the heroic actions of individuals and further distancing the movement from potential new activists.

One way of defining the novelty of the tactics used by eco-activists is to point to the manufactured character of their vulnerability. The deliberate use of vulnerability has been central to the moral force of all NVDA, but the eco-activists were not in themselves vulnerable to any major violence from opponents or the authorities, nor could they hope to provoke or expose it. Blockaders in liberal democracies in the past have usually been removed quickly by police and such tactics have become too routine to be effective, particularly when carried out by familiar protest groups. Eco-activists have attempted to create their own new form of vulnerability. If the authorities are not going to use violence on a scale sufficient to shock the public, how can protesters resist in a way that maximises their effectiveness but also exposes the contrast between the force used by the authorities and protesters' moral superiority? Eco-activists in Britain and elsewhere have used technical devices to manufacture their own dangers in order to make their bodies vulnerable. The use of tools is therefore more than simply a technical game; it is essential to the dual aims of making power visible by prolonging its exposure and attempting to change government policy directly. In Britain these tactics allowed protesters to achieve success in two ways. They could delay evictions for days and even weeks, in contrast to the few hours that it usually takes to remove a sit-down blockade, substantially increasing the economic and political costs of road building, and they were able to carry out a sustained performance of their own moral commitment for a media and public captured by the epic quality of the confrontation.

Some of the forms of actions adopted by the British eco-activists are less new and more inclusive than others. In particular, the actions that take place away from the defence of a site for development have allowed for wider participation. Critical mass bicycle rides which slow down urban traffic by filling the roads with bikes have a long tradition internationally, but became widespread for the first time in British cities in the 1990s because of initiatives taken by the eco-activist groups. The actions oriented to reclaiming urban streets do not at first sight appear novel because they are a variation on the tradition of barricades (Traugott 1995), but this is misleading because the tripods used are a very new form of barricade. Whereas previously barricades provided protection for protesters, now the tripod exposes the vulnerability of the protester. It does not oppose force with force, but places the responsibility for the protester's safety in the hands of the authorities. One of the effects of street parties and some of the other urban actions was that larger numbers of people were able to join in protest actions than at sites being defended against evictions, without relying on the prior mass mobilisation sought for traditional demonstrations.

By the end of the 1990s there were signs that the protest camp was no longer the dominant tactic for the direct action groups. Numerous camps remained, but they attracted fewer activists and their eviction was not covered in the same depth by the media. For instance, the second eviction of camps at Manchester Airport in 1999 took longer than that in 1997 but attracted much less coverage. Activists were well aware that the 'arms race' between them and opponents could not continue indefinitely (Anon. 1999a). Many criticisms were made of the limits of camps. The intensity of living on a site meant that camps tended to be chauvinistic. They saw their own campaign as the priority and because of the concentration on eviction there was little discussion of strategy. Camps were also seen as encouraging spectacularisation by taking too uncritical a view of the media. The cultural politics of camps were also seen as limiting. At a time when the movement was seeking more ties with wider social groups some camps were seen as alienating in their 'aggressively countercultural vibe' (Anon. 1999a: 155). The intensity of camps meant that strong solidarity and friendships were achieved quickly, but the experience of continual eviction also led to fatigue. Nor was the solidarity always perfect. As one account said:

> Sites are often also home to various hierarchies based upon gender, expertise and sub-cultural credibility. If you don't know how to climb trees, have a job, look fairly straight or are female, then the chances are that you will be made to feel that you can't do much to help, and, what you can do will involve you playing a supportive role for those who are doing the real work.
>
> (Anon. 1999b: 157)

The declining value and attraction of camps is perhaps also related to the strategic shift towards more offensive action (see Plows and Seel, this volume). When all efforts are focused on defending a site it is difficult to justify using resources for other kinds of action. However, as the movement focused on new targets such as GM foods and global trade, it sought new tactics (see Wall this volume). Nevertheless, despite their limitations, camps were crucial in shaping the nature of the direct action movement. Instrumentally, they provided activists with permanent and accessible centres of activism, and the tactics that evolved meant that activists knew that they were costing their opponents large amounts of money. Culturally, their spectacular form attracted attention and significant support, albeit through the problematic frames presented by the media (see Paterson this volume).

Continuity, diffusion and change

In Britain the tactics used by eco-activists appeared innovative, but new repertoires do not emerge spontaneously. In this case prior British traditions of protest and techniques borrowed and adapted from other eco-activist movements were important factors as well as genuine tactical innovations such as tunnels. As we would expect, there are inherited elements in the frames, organisations and forms of action adopted by the contemporary eco-activists. As research by Derek Wall (1999) has shown, the founders of the Earth First! (EF!) network all had prior political experience in green or peace movement groups. Those with previous experience of NVDA from the peace movement played an important role in passing on lessons to the younger founders of EF! But this is a two-way process. After a lull in the early 1990s, direct action at military bases, weapons factories and arms fairs has revived in recent years partly because of the involvement of eco-activists. The GenetiX Snowball campaign against genetically modified food also revived an earlier Snowball campaign by the peace movement in the 1980s which was intended to fill the courts with civil protest cases (see Wall, this volume: 82-85).

The eco-protest camps are in some respects a continuation of the peace camps of the 1980s (one peace camp at Faslane in Scotland has been in continuous existence since the early 1980s). The women's peace camp at Greenham Common became the best known of the women-only and mixed camps. Aspects of the ethos that Sasha Roseneil (1995) describes in her analysis of Greenham can also be said to be dominant in the 1990s eco-protest movement, particularly the individualist character of protesters, notable especially in the strong emphasis on autonomy and taking personal responsibility for action. Peace camps provided crucial lessons about occupying space and using that space to create an alternative community. There are also, of course, important differences between the 1980s peace camps and the 1990s eco-activists not least of which was the importance of women organising autonomously at Greenham. The lack of attention given to gender issues among eco-activists has been noted by commentators (Hunt 1995; McKay 1998: 49–50), and activists have pointed to occasions when women left camps because of the men's patriarchal attitudes and behaviour (Anon. 1997a, 1998; Donga 1996).[8] Attitudes to non-violence also appear to be somewhat different. There seems to be less concern with non-violence as an end in itself among eco-activists and a clear consensus that damaging property can be justified. In general, the rejection of violence appears to be strategic and many eco-activists resist what they perceive to be the more dogmatic elements of the philosophy of non-violence. Another difference arises over the question of accountability. There is stronger loyalty among peace activists to taking public responsibility for direct action to the extent that many pledge not to evade arrest. This is a position taken by some eco-activists, such as those involved in GenetiX Snowball, but most eco-activists prefer to avoid arrest. A common justification for this is that the criminal justice system is deliberately designed to prevent protest through its use of injunctions, fines and jail and they do not want to put themselves at its mercy. Evading arrests is the best way to carry on protesting.[9]

Indigenous British networks and cultural examples clearly provided important resources for eco-activists, but activists 'adapted and interpreted' (McAdam 1995: 229) this heritage. In this sense they fit McAdam's description of a spin-off movement. However, it is also important to stress that the height of peace move-ment activism was in the early and mid-1980s. While peace movement NVDA continued after this time, from the accounts given by activists and because of their youth – most are in their twenties – it seems probable that most did not have personal experience of direct action prior to their involvement in eco-protests.

This suggests that the category of spin-off movement may need to take into account not only the influence of visible initiators of a protest cycle but also longer-term and less visible influence from apparently latent networks of activists. In this case the eco-activists drew on the counter-cultural networks and traditions of NVDA that had become established in the early 1980s and remained in existence despite the decline in NVDA in the late 1980s and early 1990s (Maguire 1992). It was these activists who assisted in the revitalisation of NVDA in the early 1990s and the counter-culture that they had maintained provided the anarchistic frames which made sense of their actions.

McAdam (1995; McAdam and Rucht 1993) also notes that the example of diffusion from the US to the German New Left suggests that spin-off movements can arise through cross-national diffusion. The second major feature of this repertoire is its transnational character. As noted, some of the technical devices used by British protesters such as tripods were previously used in Australia. The nature of the lock-on also seems to have developed over time. The suffragettes are still remembered for chaining themselves to railings, but until the invention of the bicycle D-lock bolt cutters proved effective in removing chains quickly. In the USA and Australia eco-activists used the new bicycle D-locks to chain them-selves to machines, but this tactic was only effective on mobile actions and when contractors did not have hydraulic bolt croppers. Concrete lock-ons have become common for eco-activists in Britain and the New World. The exchange of tactics is so rapid that it is difficult to trace a clear path. Whereas in the late 1980s technical manuals such as US EF!'s *Ecodefense* reflected the emphasis of its activists on sabotage, the *Earth First! (USA) Direct Action Manual* and the Australian *Inter-Continental Deluxe Guide to Blockading* and the British *Road Raging* overlap considerably and make reference to each other's tactics. Nevertheless tactics remain easier to diffuse than identities. There are points in common between eco-activists in all three countries, such as the rejection of formal organisation, and a common (but not universal within any one country) interest in paganism. But British activists have concentrated more on public protests and relatively less on covert sabotage, and are less concerned with the defence of wilderness, or with issues of deep ecological philosophy. Anti-capitalist global political economy is more important in the discourse of British activists,[10] while there is much less debate about issues of race and gender than in North America and Australia. In that sense, though inspired by overseas examples, British activists remain different from their New World counterparts.

The high media profile of British eco-protests and the ease of travel within Europe has assisted the diffusion of the eco-activist repertoire directly through activist networks to other countries in Europe and beyond. British activists have been visited by German, Scandinavian, Dutch, Belgian, Spanish, Italian, Polish, American and Canadian activists keen to take part in the British protest and to learn the techniques of tunnelling, lock-ons and tree defences. German radical ecology activists set up groups inspired by British EF! in 1994 and anti-roads tree camps in Freiburg and Thüringen in 1996.[11] A Dutch EF! group was formed in 1997 under the title Groen Front! by activists who had been at British protest camps who then formed a protest camp against the building of a new harbour outside Amsterdam.[12] In the same year Irish EF! groups established camps using techniques borrowed from Britain. There have been RTS parties in Amsterdam, Berlin, Dublin, Helsinki and Sydney, and Polish police were said to be non-plussed by lock-ons and tree houses used to obstruct a new road in 1998. *Do or Die!* devotes considerable space to news from 'other islands' and British activists clearly present themselves as part of an international direct action movement. There is also evidence of organised efforts to diffuse this knowledge. In October 1997 an anti-roads conference in Lyon brought together 65 activists from 21 countries who shared tactics and carried out a Reclaim the Streets action. While the British eco-activists now appear to be at the centre of this tactical innovation, they in turn owe much to Australian activists and admit that they can learn from the experience of German anti-nuclear protesters in stopping convoys.

The tactical repertoire of eco-activists is therefore a complex process of diffusion both within national counter-cultural networks and cross-nationally. This repertoire appears to have spread because manufactured vulnerability can be useful wherever the police, developers and authorities are constrained by public opinion in their use of force against eco-activists. Like the sit-in in the 1960s, the use of technically manufactured vulnerability to prolong a site occupation seems to have become the signature form of action for eco-activists cross-nationally.

Conclusion

In Britain the tactics defined here as manufactured vulnerability were at first unexpected and caused confusion but have now become part of the cultural fabric, and the authorities have learned how to deal with them more effectively. In this sense, it can be argued that manufactured vulnerability has elements of modularity (Tarrow 1994). However, the tactics used by eco-activists are seen as the property of a specialised sub-culture and it seems likely that this will remain the case, particularly in the case of protest camps. These have become part of a NVDA tradition but are unlikely to be appropriate to other groups, first because they are so situationally specific – as a means of establishing as permanent as possible an occupation of a space – and, second, because the skills and time that they demand are too difficult for most older people and those with family and work commitments to take up. Although most forms of high risk and confrontational NVDA are mainly carried out by the young and able-bodied, this is not always the case. For instance, in other campaigns, die-ins, blockades of military bases or animal exports attracted wider social groups. These are short-term protests of a few hours and older people or those with major commitments outside the campaign have taken part in many blockades or other demonstrative actions in other campaigns, such as those of the peace and animal rights movements. Protest camp tactics, dependent as they are on maintaining a full-time presence, technical skills which take time to master and are learnt by living on site, and high levels of personal discomfort and risk, all seem unlikely to be used by other groups in society. In that sense, there is a professionalism inherent in manufactured vulnerability which demands full-time activists.

However, that does not mean that there has been no tactical diffusion to other groups. In August 1997 *Earth First! Action Update* reported: 'Increasing numbers of community groups and local residents are ringing local EF! activists asking them for help with campaigns. Rather than parachuting in a small, already over-stretched rentamob, we need to be able to pass on our skills and experience to other groups.' Opponents of a housing development in Yorkshire were advised by a local eco-activist on how to get legal recognition for a site occupation forcing the developer to take court action to evict them.[13] Local groups have occasionally set up their own camps. This happened on the route of the M77 in Corkerhill, Glasgow (Seel 1999) and on the site of a supermarket in Golden Hill (Bristol), where locals had seen the squat of an empty Safeways supermarket by South Somerset EF! shortly before.[14] Protest camps have also tried to make links with local supporters by holding open days and encouraging people to join in with actions when possible (see Cathles, this volume). Activists also undertook direct action with groups of sacked workers, most notably the Liverpool dockers, using their climbing skills to occupy gantries and office roofs. Thus, even if the more technically demanding tactics remain the preserve of a specialised group, eco-activists can still play a role in diffusing other tactics to new groups. And, as we have seen, the other notable aspect of the diffusion of this repertoire is its international character. British activists learned from US EF! and Australian rainforest campaigners, and the tactics developed in Britain have been used subsequently in other parts of Europe.

It may be that tactics assume a larger role in this movement than in others because by living at a protest camp in what is more or less a permanent and public state of confrontation so much of what protesters choose to do is related to tactical choices. In his account of the Newbury protests, Merrick (1997) described continuous camp fire conversations about tactics, and saw the inability to talk about anything else as one of the signs of 'losing it'. This campaign might therefore be argued to be unusually tactically obsessive, but also unusually tactically creative.

Notes

1 An earlier version of this article appeared in *Mobilization*, 1999, 4, 1: 75–89. I would like to thank Ben Seel and Chris Rootes for their advice.
2 The second of these in March 1998 attracted 250,000 people, a figure not matched since a peace movement demonstration of 1983.
3 This is most clear in the case of Friends of the Earth (FoE). Having been taken by surprise by the growth of environmental direct action, FoE began to make contact with eco-activists and to transfer resources into supporting local grassroots campaigning from around 1994. Compassion in World Farming assisted the protest against live exports (McLeod 1998) and its success in mobilising media coverage and protests at docks and airports in 1994 undoubtedly helped to frame the issues for the local protesters who blockaded trucks at Shoreham and Brightlingsea in 1995. Nevertheless, even Compassion in World Farming was taken by surprise by the largely spontaneous participation of a high proportion of the local population.
4 For a description of the technical rationale for more sophisticated tree house defences, capable of dealing with improved eviction techniques, see the account of the building and eviction of the Battle Star Galactica at Manchester Airport, Anon. 1997a.
5 Tree houses were (probably) first used at Jesmond Dene in Newcastle in 1993.
6 One activist commented proudly: 'The phenomenal thing is, Amsterdam was the longest eviction before this one at two and a half days and they had AK47s and Kalashnikovs, so the fact that we held out with ingenuity and non-violence – that was the beauty of it' (quoted in Carey 1995: 18).
7 A detailed review of police surveillance and intelligence gathering tactics is given in a recent issue of the EF! journal *Do or Die* (Anon. 1997c).
8 As one woman activist commented: 'protest camps can be one of the most chauvinistic, domineering and belittling experiences for a woman to be in. Maybe it's the extremely unbalanced ratio of men to women on site that makes the leering fire-lit eyes of the cider-induced hippy a very bothersome experience. For starters there seems to be this assumption that women can't climb, can't put up walkways and that their tree houses need the stern eye of the more experienced male cast upon them before anyone would dream of having a smoke in them' (Anon. 1998).
9 Similar debates have occurred among Australian eco-activists dividing those loyal to traditional forms of NVDA and those taking a more militant line (Doyle 1994).
10 An extract from an RTS leaflet can illustrate this: 'The struggle for car free space must not be separated from the struggle against global capitalism, the streets are as full of capitalism as of cars and the pollution of capitalism is much more insidious.'
11 A German activist estimated the numbers involved in the radical ecology network at around 500, but spoke of obstacles to building the movement because of the tendency of left-wing greens to see radical ecology as potentially ecofascist (Anon. 1997b).
12 An account of the formation of this group includes the following passages: 'It all began over a year ago when the Dutch direct action movement Groen Front! started, based upon the ideas of the British Earth First! Several Dutch activists had been over to the action camps at Newbury, Fairmile and Manchester to learn from their British counterparts ... in April 1997 the group went on tour with visiting British Earth First! activists to different cities in the Netherlands' (Anon. 1998: 97).
13 Activists at the N11 anti-road building camp in Ireland have been contacted by local groups in Bray and Santry wanting to know how to prevent new housing. In general, however, the reports that suggest that other groups are about to take up eco-activist

tactics tend to mean only the kind of tactics that can be used quickly and which have often been used by other NVDA groups. For instance, in May 1997 the Pensioners' Rights Campaign blocked traffic on Leicester's main street and in September the same group blocked the Humber Bridge and Women's Institute members in North Yorkshire planned to take direct action against plans to erect new electricity pylons. But while they intended to set up a telephone tree a spokeswoman 'insisted that members would not be embracing true eco-warrior behaviour by digging tunnels or building tree houses' (Hall 1998). The campaign to preserve hunting with hounds provides another example. Its spokesman, Lord Apsley, was reported as 'threatening to adopt the same direct action tactics of eco-warriors like Swampy and Animal if Parliament bans hunting. "When it comes down to it I believe [we] would be prepared to go out and protest by blocking roads. There are a lot of us, and we are a very well disciplined bunch. I believe we would be prepared to follow orders. A well-disciplined force is a lot more frightening than a rabble ... We have all seen the French burning things and blocking roads, and naturally there was talk of these things"' ('Hunt Peer Sees Fear Campaign' *Guardian* July 18 1997). However, blocking roads is not the same as occupying a site and transforming it into a defended encampment. It is difficult to imagine hunters being able to sustain such a presence and even more so, as well as incongruous, to imagine them using the form of vulnerability expressed in the tactics developed by eco-protesters. Rather, in drawing from the example of French farmers, and stressing the disciplinary strength of his followers Lord Apsley seems to be looking for traditional models of how to express the anger of rural areas.

14 I am grateful to Ben Seel for drawing this to my attention. On this, see also Wall (this volume:79-81).

Bibliography

Anon. (1997a) 'Life on the Battle Star: a personal account', *Do or Die: Voices from Earth First!* 6: 82–86.

—— (1997b) 'What's on in Germany: from Autonomen to Zeitgeist', *Do or Die: Voices from Earth First!* 6: 109–110.

—— (1997c) 'The empire strikes back', *Do or Die: Voices from Earth First!* 6: 136–142.

—— (1997d) 'Why Reclaim the Streets and the Liverpool Dockers?', *Do or Die: Voices from Earth First!* 6: 10–11.

—— (1997e) 'Reclaim the streets!', *Do or Die: Voices from Earth First!* 6: 1–6.

—— (1998) 'Green Fort versus Mean Port', *Do or Die: Voices from Earth First!* 7: 97–99.

—— (1999a) 'Camps are not enough', *Do or Die: Voices from the Ecological Resistance* 8: 155–156.

—— (1999b) 'It's shite on site!', *Do Or Die: Voices from the Ecological Resistance* 8: 157.

Byrne, Paul (1997) *Social Movements in Britain*, London: Routledge.

—— (1998) 'Nuclear weapons and CND', *Parliamentary Affairs* 51, 3: 424–434.

Carey, Jim (1995) 'Towers of strength', *Squall* 9: 18–22.

DAM Collective (1998) Earth First! Direct Action Manual, SWEF: Eugene, OR.

Doherty, Brian (1998) 'Opposition to road-building', *Parliamentary Affairs* 51, 3: 370–383.

—— (1999) 'Paving the way: the rise of direct action against road-building and the changing character of British environmentalism', *Political Studies* 47, 2: 275–291.

Donga, Alex (1996) 'The rise (and fall?!) of the eco-warrior', *Do or Die: Voices from Earth First!* 5: 88–89.

Doyle, Timothy (1994) 'Direct action in environmental conflict in Australia: a re-examination of non-violent action', *Regional Journal of Social Issues* 28: 1–13.

Hall, Sarah (1998) 'WI members transform into eco-warriors to fight blot on the landscape', *Guardian*, November 24.

Hunt, Heather (1995) 'Balancing act: personal politics and anti-roads campaigning', *Soundings* 1: 123–138.

Kriesi, Hans Peter, Koopmans, Ruud, Duyvendak, Jan W. and Giugni, Marco G. (1995) *New Social Movements in Western Europe: A Comparative Analysis*, London: UCL Press.

McAdam, Doug (1983) 'Tactical innovation and the pace of insurgency', *American Sociological Review* 48: 735–754.

—— (1995) ' "Initiator" and "spin-off movements": diffusion processes in protest cycles', in Mark Traugott (ed.) *Repertoires and Cycles of Collective Action*, Durham, NC: Duke University Press.

—— (1996) 'The framing function of movement tactics', in Doug McAdam, John McCarthy, and Mayer Zald (eds) *Comparative Perspectives on Social Movements*, Cambridge: Cambridge University Press.

McAdam, Doug and Rucht, Dieter (1993) 'The cross-national diffusion of movement ideas', *Annals of the American Academy of Political and Social Science* 528: 56–74.

McKay, George (1998) 'DiY culture: notes towards an intro', in George McKay, (ed.) *DiY Culture: Party and Protest in Nineties Britain*, London: Verso.

McLeod, Rhoda (1998) 'Calf exports at Brightlingsea', *Parliamentary Affairs* 51, 3: 345–357.

Maguire, Diarmuid (1992) 'When the streets begin to empty', *West European Politics* 15, 4: 75–94.

Merrick (1997) *Battle for the Trees*, Leeds: Godhaven Ink.

Roseneil, Sasha (1995) *Disarming Patriarchy: Feminism and Political Action at Greenham*, Buckingham: Open University Press.

Rucht, Dieter (1990) 'The strategies and action repertoires of new movements', in Russell Dalton and Manfred Kuechler (eds) *Challenging the Political Order*, Cambridge: Polity.

Seel, Ben (1999) 'Strategic identities: strategy, culture and consciousness in the new age and road protest movements', PhD thesis, Keele University.

Tarrow, Sidney (1994) *Power in Movement*, Cambridge: Cambridge University Press.

—— (1995) 'Cycles of collective action', in Mark Traugott (ed.) *Repertoires and Cycles of Collective Action*, Durham, NC: Duke University Press.

Tilly, Charles (1995) 'Contentious repertoires in Great Britain, 1758–1834', in Mark Traugott (ed.) *Repertoires and Cycles of Collective Action*, Durham, NC: Duke University Press.

Traugott, Mark (1995) 'Barricades as repertoire', in Mark Traugott (ed.) *Repertoires and Cycles of Collective Action*, Durham, NC: Duke University Press.

Wall, Derek (1999) *Earth First! and the Origins of the Anti-Roads Movement*, London: Routledge.

4 Snowballs, elves and skimmingtons?

Genealogies of environmental direct action

Derek Wall

Britain during the 1990s has seen nearly a decade of sustained environmental direct action that has mobilised thousands of individuals. Such direct action of the 1990s must have seemed to those outside, including many academics, journalists and members of the public, to have come from nowhere. Even to those of us active in the green movement during the 1970s and 1980s the landscape appeared to have changed.

I remember sitting up a tree in May 1992, albeit a small tree and for a very short time, as part of an anti-supermarket protest at Golden Hill in Bristol. At Golden Hill between 1992 and 1993, hundreds of local residents took part in direct action to prevent Tesco constructing a new store on a field cherished by dogs, walkers and children. The Golden Hill Residents Association (GHRA), having exhausted legal means, had phoned many local green activists, including green anarchists and Green Party members, looking for support when the contractors were due to come in with their chainsaws. So I went along. In 1992, it seemed new. We seemed to be doing something for a change. So much of my political activity in the Green Party seemed wholly discursive with so many policy platforms, worthy statements and internal disputes. Personally for me, Earth First! (EF!), the anti-roads movement and wider environmental direct action seemed to be a new way of doing green politics. Rather than letter writing, petitioning or electioneering we were using direct action to contest environmental ills such as road building, rainforest destruction and global warming.

Yet of course it wasn't new or at least not entirely. Social movement theorists argue that it is rare for protest to emerge from nowhere. Typically mobilisations draw upon pre-existing networks which may be latent or almost invisible (Diani 1994; Melucci 1996). In turn, apparently novel tactics are often borrowed from earlier waves of protest before being adapted. The idea that a set of tactics, variously described as 'repertoires of contention', 'modular collective action' or 'repertoires of action' can be learnt, adapted and used to resource movement activity has been widely applied to social movements (Kriesi *et al.* 1995: 119; Roseneil 1995: 99–100; Tarrow 1994: 31–47).

Repertoires of action were first described by Tilly as 'the whole set of means [a group] has for making claims … on different individuals or groups' (1986: 2). Repertoires are historically located (Roseneil 1995: 99) and 'at once a structural and a cultural concept' (Tarrow 1994: 31) made up of tactics already familiar to activists, derived from existing movements and seen as part of more extensive cultural toolkits (Swidler 1986). They may be transformed by changing political opportunities and creative adaptation. While such change is often perceived to be 'glacial' (Tarrow 1994: 31), it has been argued that a degree of activist reflexivity allows an element of choice and adaptation within the context of a repertoire (Roseneil 1995: 99).

To map the diffusion and mutation of particular repertoires, I have provided a broad narrative of environmental direct action during the 1990s, and examined antecedents in the 1980s and 1970s. My focus is on three forms of criminal damage. While much environmental direct action uses repertoires that do not damage property, I am fascinated by findings that indicate that such acts of criminal damage may be inspired by varied political assumptions. Thus, as we shall see, an individual may enter a field and pull up genetically modified crops as part of a Snowball group, an Earth Liberation Front (ELF) cell or within a festive situation resembling a skimmington. Snowball actions were developed in the 1980s within the peace movement. They involve symbolic damage with activists perhaps cutting a single strand of wire around a site before giving themselves up to the police. ELF actions involved covert criminal damage similar to that practised by the Animal Liberation Front (ALF) since the 1970s (Lee 1983). Skimmingtons are riotous ritual processions, festivals accompanied by music and assaults on physical targets. A seventeenth-century skimmington parade might be targeted against enclosures and accompanied by the removal of fences (Underdown 1985).

Criminal damage, which might be seen as that most spontaneous and unmediated of direct action, seems to be a cultural product which is learnt and practised with recourse to particular genealogies. I have also tended to focus on the campaigns against genetic modification because this is very much the principal issue focus of environmental protest in the last year of the millennium and relatively little has been published by researchers in this area.

Environmental action during the 1990s

1990 and 1991 saw the initial actions against supermarket expansion. At Stroud in Gloucestershire activists sat in trees to prevent them being cut down to make way for an approach road to Tescos. When built, the road curved around the trees. A Friends of the Earth (FoE) report noted:

> When Tesco applied to build a store at Golden Hill in 1990, 16,664 people objected in writing. ... Planning permission was granted by the Secretary of State. During construction protesters first blockaded the gate and then occupied the site, and also occupied the Tesco HQ and held national days of action. Eventually the store was built in 1993.
>
> (FOE 1998: 2)

The campaign failed to stop the devastation of Golden Hill in Bristol but may have contributed to a change in Government policy. Golden Hill was paralleled by similar but more immediately successful protest at Wyndham Hill in Somerset. Direct action was used at other proposed supermarket sites throughout the 1990s; for example, the land reform group The Land is Ours built an eco-village in Wandsworth, London in 1996 to oppose a Safeway store.

Earth First! (EF!), initially a controversial US environmental network, was launched in the UK in 1991. By 1992 EF! was carrying out occupations of timber yards and ship blockades as part of a global campaign against rainforest destruction. For example, several hundred protesters occupied Timbmet's timber store outside Oxford in 1992 as part of this campaign. EF! (UK) shifted its issue focus towards anti-roads campaigning in the same year (Wall 1998).

During the 1990s anti-road protest has been the most visible form of environmental direct action, with the years between 1992 and 1996 seeing sustained mobilisation. This wave of action started in February 1992 with 'protesters from the radical green group Earth First ... arrested during a weekend of protests against plans to extend the M3 motorway ... . Environmentalists and local people had occupied two Victorian bridges over the Waterloo to Weymouth line which had been due for demolition' (*Independent* 19 February 1992: 1). FoE subsequently established an anti-roads camp, the first in Britain, at Twyford. When they left, identity-oriented neo-tribalists the Dongas stayed on and when they were violently evicted a third camp was established by EF! (Bryant 1996; Lamb 1996; Lowe and Shaw 1993). Anti-roads camps were created at over a dozen sites including the M11 in East London, Pollok in Glasgow, the Lizard, Norfolk, East Devon, Preston and Newbury with thousands living full-time lives of protest. EF! were the catalyst for action but protests against construction were usually launched by local conservation groups such as the Twyford Down Association, supported by pressure groups like FoE and groups such as the Dongas (see Cathles, this volume). Action against road construction was also sustained by networks such as ALARM UK and Road Alert who were to maintain communication between such diverse networks (Wall 1999). Identities were blurred with many activists crossing boundaries and holding multiple affiliations.

Anti-road action has not merely sought to halt the construction of new routes, protesters have also occupied existing roads. On the last Saturday before Christmas 1991, South Downs EF! 'carried out the first road blockade in the Carmageddon campaign' in Brighton, suffering one arrest (*Action Update* (AU) 1991, 2: 1). A London blockade on 15 May 1992 occurred with around eighty people obstructing Waterloo Bridge (Collins interview).[1] EF! (UK)'s Reclaim the Streets (RTS) campaign aimed to 'do imaginative and non-violent direct actions, and to reclaim the streets of London from cars and traffic and give it back to people' (Anon. 1992: 4). The concept of a street party, where pedestrians occupy and enjoy road space, gradually evolved from these early carmageddon actions. In 1996, 7,000 protesters occupied a motorway and in 1998 simultaneous street parties held in Brixton, south London and Tottenham, north London, drew around 3,000 each.

RTS has grown and moved towards becoming an overtly anti-capitalist campaign, influenced by anarchism and, through the journal *Aufheben*, Marxism (see Anon. 1994). In 1999, at least 6,000 individuals, including RTS supporters, took part in the 'Carnival against capitalism' in the financial centre of London, doing at least £2 million worth of damage (Hartley-Brewer 1999: 11).

The mid-1990s also saw protest camps established to try and prevent the expansion of Manchester Airport. Action against quarrying and open-cast mining continued throughout the 1990s often with the support of former miners. Large-scale development such as the creation of leisure centres at sites such as London's Crystal Palace have also been fought. By 1999 the focus of action had shifted to genetically modified crops.

The contrast between this frenetic activity and green direct action during the 1960s, 1970s and 1980s is striking (Doherty and Rawcliffe 1995; Rootes 1992). Direct action against car culture, for example, was extremely limited in the thirty years prior to 1990. Between 1970 and 1972, young environmental activists blocked major roads and held street parties in a small number of cities including Cambridge and Edinburgh (Shipley 1976). Young Liberals formed a NVDA environmental group, Commitment, which protested against pollution by blocking Oxford Street and Piccadilly Circus in actions heralding the EF!'s RTS campaign twenty years later (Anderson interview). In the mid-1970s John Tyme of the Conservation Society disrupted public inquiries held prior to the construction of motorway routes (Twinn 1978; Tyme 1978).

Greens were active in both the movement against nuclear power in the mid- and late 1970s and in the resurgent peace movement of the 1980s (Parkin 1989: 222; Taylor and Young 1987: 294). A third area of activity was within the animal liberation movement (Maycock 1987). Direct action against roads in the 1980s appeared to be absent along with campaigns dealing with rainforest conservation, quarrying and other 1990 mobilisation targets (Robinson 1992). Yet specific repertoires utilised in the 1990s have evolved from those in the 1970s, 1980s and perhaps earlier.

Snowballs

During 1998 and 1999 numerous GenetiX Snowball actions have taken place in Britain with participants visiting a site where genetically modified crops have been planted. They dig or pull up a number of plants, wrap them neatly in biohazard bags and then turn themselves over to the police. Genetic concern has been the environmental issue of the late 1990s. The Green Party crusaded for a ban on such research during its successful 1999 European election campaign and concern has gone far beyond the green movement, drawing in William Hague's Conservative Party, tabloid newspapers and Labour MPs. Thus GenetiX Snowball is far from distinct in their sentiments, but virtually unique in their legalistic approach to the destruction of property. One GenetiX Snowball participant states 'We are very fluffy … . We don't go for balaclavas. We believe in being open. We are the acceptable face of direct action' (Arlidge and Paton-Walsh 1999: 7).

Their newsletter further outlined their philosophy and aims:

> GenetiX snowball is a campaign of nonviolent civil responsibility. It encourages and supports open and accountable nonviolent direct action to safely remove genetically modified (GM) plants from release sites, and other parts of the food chain, in Britain. The campaign is calling for
>
> 1 a five year moratorium on the deliberate release of GM plants in Britain, except for government sponsored ecological health and safety tests (in enclosed systems), and
> 2 the removal by government agencies, farmers or the biotechnology companies of all GM plants already existing.
>
> (July '99 Update GenetiX Snowball)

The term 'Snowball' was coined by activists in the 1980s campaigning against nuclear weapons:

> Snowball … the enforce the law campaign came out of my direct action experience of Greenham and wanting to carry Greenham home and also from trying to make direct action more accessible to ordinary people. So it was devised really to make it very easy to confront the military, sort of all you had to do was cut one bit of chain link fence with a hack saw blade. That was technically criminal damage and we would argue that nuclear weapons were in breach of the genocide act. It was a way of finding something for people to do for expressing politically through the court system their opposition to nuclear weapons.
>
> (Zelter interview)

Angie Zelter, originally a peace activist, became involved in EF! when she met its co-founders Jason Torrance and Jake Burbridge on an action against a shipment of nuclear waste:

> [How did you get involved in Earth First!?]
> Just by chance through meeting Jason and Jake, at a ship action to do with a nuclear flask coming to Sizewell in East Anglia near where I lived and we met on the action and chained ourselves to each other on the ship and, uh, they told me about this SOS Sarawak and so I got involved really because of the Sarawak forest issue rather than because I'd heard about Earth First! and wanted to get involved with Earth First!

Zelter travelled to Sarawak in Malaysia with other activists including US and UK EF!ers, where she was imprisoned for trying to prevent logging. Increasingly active in forest campaigns, on return to Britain she helped develop the concept of 'ethical shoplifting'. In the mid-1990s she became active in the Ploughshares movement utilising a similar repertoire to oppose arms sales to Indonesia (Pilger 1996: 5). The activists would attack the planes with hammers, a reference to the biblical notion of beating swords into ploughshares, before presenting themselves to the authorities. In all these campaigns direct action is legitimated and utilised with reference to existing legal forms. In the early 1990s Zelter propagated so-called ethical shoplifting. Here, timber which had been taken, allegedly illegally, from areas of rainforest is seized by 'Ethical Shoplifting' EF!ers and other rain-forest campaigners. Such actions were seen as humorous and ironic and in contrast to EF! (US)'s early acts, non-threatening. One participant observed, 'We took it to Tottenham police station and they were just completely amazed at people taking wood in from the local Jewsons and saying we want to report a crime ... they filled out a proper crime report like when somebody is attacked' (Interview with Durham).[2]

Because of their tokenistic or iconic approach to direct action, their humour and compliance, however tenuous with legal structures, Zelter's tactical adapta-tions were seen as providing an easy entry into direct action for new participants (Tilly interview). Rowen Tilly, a key supporter of such Snowball actions and like Zelter, a former Greenham Common peace camper has been highly active in GenetiX Snowball (Arlidge and Paton-Walsh 1999: 7).

The original peace movement Snowball campaign was a product of Greenham, but perhaps most particularly of Gandhian rather than feminist assumptions. Snowball activists such as Tilly and Zelter remarked on their debt to Gandhi and there is a lineage of UK peace movement activity built on his philosophy stretching back to the 1950s. Gandhian non-violence, of course, uses ritualistic acts to persuade and legitimise through 'truth force' or 'satyagraha'. It is about winning support from opponents rather than seeking their defeat.

> 'Passive resistance' conveyed the idea of the Suffragette Movement in England. Burning of houses by these women was called 'passive resistance' ... such acts might very well be 'passive resistance' but they were no 'satya-graha'. ... Satyagraha is not physical force. A satyagrahi does not inflict pain on the adversary; he does not seek his destruction ... . If someone gives us pain through ignorance, we shall win him through love.
>
> (Gandhi in Mukherjee 1993: 125)

Quaker forms of bearing witness also fed into peace movement campaigns in the UK, possibly indirectly influencing snowball repertoires.

Rather more playful attempts to win support by parodying symbols and rituals of authority can commonly be found within the environmental direct action of the 1990s. Alex Begg, an anti-road protester, EF!er and Green Party activist, discussing an anti-road protest near Preston, commented:

> I helped paint the outside of the Eco-police station that later got flat-
> tened.
> [What was the Eco-police station?]
> That was a farm house on the route and they painted it completely green
> with a checked stripe right around the middle and a great big badge
> saying Eco-police and it was really good, we were chuffed to bits with it.
>
> (Begg interview)

Doherty talks of commonly constructed situations of 'manufactured vulnerability', a Gandhian variant which, rather than using criminal damage however
tokenistic, dares the authorities to sacrifice activists to bulldozers and chainsaws
(Doherty 1999, also this volume).

Elves

Some activists enter fields of genetically modified plants armed with a different
set of assumptions to those of the Gandhian and Greenham-inspired GenetiX
Snowball. In July 1999 the media reported how 150 genetically modified trees
had been destroyed by anonymous saboteurs at the Zeneca Agricultural
Research Centre near Bracknell, Berkshire.

A communiqué received from the Zeneca saboteurs noted:

> We have been forced to take this action ourselves because the biotechnology
> companies have used their wealth and power to subvert not only the process
> of scientific innovation but also the democratic process. Genetic manipula-
> tion of trees is a major threat to the world's environment. Forests maintain
> our atmosphere and climate, and sustain thousands of independent species
> of animals and plants. Those who are manipulating the DNA of trees, using
> very powerful but new and dimly understood technology, show contempt for
> our planet and the life it supports, including human life. They respect only
> profit for themselves and their shareholders.
>
> (Brookes and Brown 1999: 3)

Various other anonymous acts of 'ecotage' have occurred throughout the 1990s.
Acts of arson transpired during the campaign to prevent the building of the M3
across Twyford Down. At Pressmennen Woods in southern Scotland, trees were
spiked with ceramic nails to reduce the value of timber around 1997. Shortly
before their first national gathering in April 1992 a communiqué sent to the
media claimed EF! (UK) responsibility for sabotaging a Fison's peat digging
operation in South Yorkshire (see also Maples, this volume). Some EF! activists,
at the time, believed that it would be legally difficult for them if the network
publicly endorsed such 'ecotage'. It was agreed at the gathering to divide the
network in two with the ELF indulging in secretive criminal damage and EF!
using public non-violent direct action (Wall 1998).

The noun 'elf' and the verb 'elving', sometimes mutating into 'pixieing', evolved from the acronym ELF. Elves aim to do rather more than manipulate symbols; rather than seeking to embarrass or win over authority, they believe in directly and physically dealing with the ills around them. Anonymity is vital, so that activists can avoid arrest and maximise their ability to destroy more perceived sources of ecological ills. The acronym ELF was playfully taken from the ALF initials of the Animal Liberation Front.[3] Repertoires of covert sabotage practised by the ALF were an obvious source of inspiration for such activists, who used animal liberation networks to recruit others sympathetic to their approach into EF! (UK). One early EF! (UK) supporter formerly active in the animal liberation movement noted:

> a good way in was to approach the hunt saboteurs because they are already into [a] sort of direct action and it is quite easy to show them the links ... if you are going to save the fox from the hunt why let it be killed by a contractor ... from that Plymouth EF! was set up ... the thing that really appealed to me initially was the deep ecology that I saw as an extension of the animal liberation idea.

> (Molland interview)

Within sections of the animal liberation movement there is a tradition of using covert and disruptive direct action. The Hunt Saboteurs Association (HSA) was created in the 1960s to attempt to use direct action physically to prevent the pursuit of fox, deer and other fauna (Ryder 1989). In turn, HSA activists established the Band of Mercy in 1973, 'to use non-violent methods to liberate animals from all forms of cruelty'. The group destroyed hunting vehicles, lit fires at Hoechst Pharmaceuticals in opposition to vivisection and burnt seal culling boats in the Norfolk Wash (Roberts 1986: 9).

Band of Mercy co-founder Ronnie Lee has situated strategies of direct action in the context of frustration with traditional methods of lobbying, '100 years of campaigning hasn't got anywhere – through the legal methods, peaceful protest and petitions, etc.'. He was not enamoured with a Gandhian approach and he rejected actions where individuals admitted to sabotage, 'If we did a lot of damage openly ... it would end up with lots of people in prison being arrested and those people couldn't go out the next week and save animals again' (Lee 1983: 11).

The ALF, as the Band became known in 1976, has emphasised direct action as an economic strategy rather than a means of gaining public support through 'truthforce':

> If you go and damage a laboratory they have to pay to put it right and to install extra security measures (because often they won't get insurance unless they put in extra security). This money often comes out of their research budget and would be spent on experimentation. A lot of people criticize the

fact that damage is done, saying that property is sacred. I think it is important to point out that damage to property does save animals.

(Lee 1983: 10)

One link between an ALF approach and the ELF has been via several tiny green
anarchist networks. *Green Anarchist* (GA), a newspaper produced by radical greens,
has long championed the ALF and sought to diffuse EF! to UK. Chris Laughton
who wrote for GA, attempted to use it to launch EF in the UK in 1987 but
failed. The growth of the EF! (UK) in the early 1990s was also aided by GA
(Noble and Torrance interviews). Another joint EF/GA activist noted, 'a key
model throughout the 80s was the Animal Liberation Front, ... they were
directly resolving things in a clandestine manner' (interview with 'Mix'). A
second network, Greenpeace London, also had early links with EF! and was
sympathetic to the ALF.

While green anarchist and animal liberation linkages were important,
attempts were also made to import repertoires of 'ecotage' from North America.
EF! in the US was notorious for its advocacy of ecologically motivated acts of
criminal damage. Such sabotage was propagated in the group's journal and in a
handbook *Ecodefense* outlining techniques for disabling vehicles, felling or burning
billboards, wrecking animal traps and otherwise using robust repertoires to
protect wildlife (Foreman and Haywood 1993). A genealogy of such ecologically
motivated sabotage clearly existed in the US via actions in the 1960s and 1970s
along with the writing of earlier deep ecologists such as Leopold and Muir.

In *Ecodefense*, Foreman and Hayward suggested that:

It is time for women and men, individually and in small groups, to act hero-
ically in defense of the wild, to put a monkeywrench into the gears of the
machine that is destroying natural diversity. Though illegal, this strategic
monkeywrenching can be ... effective in stopping timber cutting, road
building, overgrazing, oil and gas exploration, mining, dam building, power
line construction, off-road-vehicle use, trapping, ski area development, and
other forms of destruction.

(Foreman and Haywood 1993: 8–9)

Those in the UK sympathetic to 'ecotage' seem to have been influenced more by
the ALF than EF! in the US. 'Ecodefense' was technically suited to the Deep
South of the USA and advocated tactics that were not also applicable in the UK.
Equally, US advocates of ecotage such as Edward Abbey and 'Ecodefense' editor
Foreman were criticised by UK activists as misanthropes:

the stuff I read I didn't feel entirely happy with it and I felt it was anti-
human, and I wasn't into that Deep Ecology stuff and I wasn't aware of it
at the start ... and finding out about it put me off. ... we were missing a
whole political critique.

(Durham interview)

Skimmingtons?

In July 1999 I took part in a genetics action that, while involving yet more criminal damage, worked in a rather different way from the Gandhian snowball or
the secretive assault on Zeneca. Around five hundred individuals attended a rally
near Watlington in Oxford against genetic crop testing. We listened to rousing
speeches from, among others, the Labour MP Alan Simpson and George
Monbiot, who had been active in a range of environmental direct action
campaigns during the 1990s. My children were given models of bumble bees
made from recycled material, representing the insects that might transmit genetically modified pollen into local holly. It was very much a family event and
reminded me rather of childhood trips to rural steam engine fairs in the 1970s.
The sun shone and music played. We had been offered white paper whole-body
suits and masks. The majority put them on and were entirely anonymous. After
the speeches we marched on the field of genetically modified oil seed rape on the
neighbouring Model Farm. The majority ran into the crop, trampling it, pulling
it up and even rolling bodily, so as to wreck the test before the rape could flower.

A few weeks earlier in June 1999 a 'stop the city' action, where green activists
and others had mobilised around 6,000 individuals as part of a 'carnival against
capitalism' resulted in over £2m of damage (Hartley-Brewer 1999: 11). Fast-
food outlets, expensive cars and commodity exchange centres were targeted.

Criminal damage undertaken as part of events like the Carnival against
Capitalism differs from much of the criminal damage undertaken by the ALF,
the ELF or EF! (US) in one respect at least. Such 'ecotage', far from being the
product of small secretive cells indulging in night work, originated out of mass
actions involving hundreds and sometimes thousands of individuals. Such mass
actions have a festive and celebratory aspect.

Mass actions involving criminal damage have been linked by its sympathisers
and exponents to historical tradition of riot, revel and resistance. Searle sees
modern green protest as a product of centuries of grassroots rebellion by the
British mob (1997). An article in *Do or Die!* links 1990s environment action,
including sabotage, to the Luddite machine breakers of the early nineteenth
century (*Do or Die!*, 1997, 6: 70). Freedland celebrated such a tradition in a
Guardian article shortly after the 'Carnival':

> The parallels are certainly striking. The June 18 or J18 demo was billed as a
> Carnival against Capitalism, a street party replacing 'the roar of profit and
> plunder with the sounds and rhythms of carnival and pleasure!' Until things
> got out of hand, that's how it was: live music, jugglers, stilt-walkers and
> magicians filling the streets usually occupied by pinstripes and mobile
> phones. Protesters were urged to come in disguise, in order to blend in … .
> How sensitive to tradition these radicals were. Exactly 160 years earlier, the
> Rebecca Rioters of rural Wales also donned costume – to protest against the
> capitalist evil of their day … . Their target was … the series of tollgates
> erected along the country of Wales … . Every time they led their sheep to

market they had to pay up. So dressed as Rebecca (associated with gates in the book of Genesis), these Welsh farmers staged an elaborate piece of street theatre by each of the offending gates – before promptly smashing and burning them … . Just like then, the Rebeccas knew how to stage the perfect blend of costume, drama and force.

(Freedland 1999)

Actions such as the 'Carnival against Capitalism' and the anti-road street parties closely resemble that mainstay of the mob the skimmington. Skimmingtons are ritual processions, marked by cross-dressing, partying and the ridiculing of authority (Underdown 1985). In the seventeenth century:

> The customary world had been turned upside-down by enclosers; the protesters symbolically turn it upside-down again (dressing as women, parodying the titles and offices of their social superiors) in order to turn it right-side-up. The prominence of women in enclosure and grain riots is well known and is one more sign of rejection of the submissive ideal. Female rioters were often joined by men disguised in women's clothes.

(Underdown 1985: 111)

There is a longing in many accounts to see contemporary environmental militancy as part of a whole history of grassroots action. Yet, unlike the more historically immediate snowballs and elves, such a lineage is far more difficult to sustain. Street parties have gradually moved from small acts of road occupation in Brighton in 1991 to large-scale events such as the 1996 occupation of the M41 motorway in London. The festive element seems to be linked to politicised forms of music, ranging from Reggae to Punk and on to more hedonistic rave (Anon. 1993). The expression 'street party' may be a call for an ironic replay of the parties held by communities to mark the end of the Second World War and events such as royal weddings!

The political heritage of, perhaps all, historical repertoires is richly ambiguous. They may, for example, diffuse to counter movements; in the 1990s the pro-hunting Countryside Movement has borrowed tactics from the environmentalists (Doherty 1999). In the 1930s the British Union of Fascists used direct action to protect farmers from being shut down (Carter 1973: 22).[4] The practice of cross-dressing in skimmingtons during the seventeenth century was often part of the ritual punishment of 'scolds' rather than a celebration of female militancy. The London mob pursued conservative as well as radical causes; Jacobites, after all, proclaimed different kings when advocating regicide. Jacobins, such as the Gordon rioters, burnt Irish homes as well as rough handling their lordships. The seventeenth-century skimmingtons were more often practised by supporters of the Court rather than revolutionary Puritans who sought to throw away church ales, maypoles and all the other Conservative, Catholic and ultimately pagan traces. Openly pagan opponents of the Crown such as the Ranters were sadly marginal. Movements, let alone repertoires, are impure.

Conclusion

I am sympathetic to attempts to construct lengthy genealogies and have even had a go myself (Wall 1994), thus I might be accused by readers of this brief cartography of hypocritical and pedantic empiricism. In my defence I would like to suggest that we have now moved beyond a situation where it is necessary to disprove that green movements are new and much has been published on this topic (Veldman 1994). Green historical analysis has other tasks to undertake. As an eco-Marxist I am interested in the hermeneutics and mechanics of direct action undertaken by greens because I believe we must constantly refine tactics and wider strategies for contesting a productivist, exterminist capitalism. Counting red-green flags is only a start; to challenge capitalism more effectively, I feel that deeper reflection is necessary. We need to understand where our repertoires have originated so as to fight the war against sleep and adapt tactics to evolving needs. The more modest task of mapping diffusion is a first step towards such reflexivity.

Repertoires diffuse between movements over time, yet diffusion cannot simply be asserted via correlation. It is all very well to claim that because group A in the 1970s were using a tactic similar to one employed by group C in the 1990s diffusion must have taken place. While historical progression via a group B in the 1980s may have occurred, equally independent reinvention is a possibility. Illegal street parties that blocked roads as an anti-car tactic took place in both the early 1970s and 1990s in London. Yet there seems to be no direct or indirect link between the individuals involved in Commitment in 1972, mainly Young Liberals concerned with pollution, and the Reclaim the Streets activists using a similar repertoire twenty years later (Wall 1999). Supposed continuities over centuries are even more difficult to trace, although perhaps not impossible. Genealogies that snake backwards and forwards between hybrids are likely. Diffusion may be indirect with Group C borrowing Group B's repertoires via the media. When a wave of student protest spread across continents during the late 1960s, repertoires were carried by individuals moving from one country to another and via impersonal imitation with young activists borrowing from each other via the television, newspapers and other media sources (McAdam and Rucht 1993). Sources of diffusion, direct and indirect, as we have seen, may be multiple. My essential point is that before examining how and why repertoires diffuse, the researcher must show that diffusion has actually occurred. In perhaps all forms of cultural cartography one should not:

> collapse the lengthy and complex process of stylistic development into too narrow a moment of analysis, and thus neglect how certain aspects are taken up or become imbued with an especial significance at particular moments and in relation to particular events.
>
> (Clarke 1976: 182)

Repertoires can be traced back to previous decades of the twentieth century, but lineages that moved through centuries of continuity and growth are more difficult to map. Skimmingtons demand the continued use of a question mark, for the time being at least.

Notes

1   All interviews were undertaken as part of doctoral research between 1994 and 1997.
2   Jewsons escaped prosecution!
3   Tolkien got a look in, too, according to one ELF I interviewed during doctoral research.
4   I have, of course, long criticised those who discover or even invent far right links to direct action as a convenient means of discrediting radicals. From the Hackney squatters to Stop the City to Hunt saboteurs, convenient neo-Nazi links have been constructed to aid the bulldozing of oppositional movements (see O'Hara 1993).

Bibliography

Anon. (1992) 'Road fury', *Wild*, 1: 4.
—— (1993) 'Dancing on the edge', *Green Revolution*, 4: 5–9.
—— (1994) 'Auto-struggles: the developing war against the road monster', *Aufheben*, 3: 3–23.
Arlidge, J. and Paton-Walsh, N. (1999) 'Do I look like an anarchist weirdo?', *Observer*, 16 June, 7.
Brooks, L. and Brown, P. (1999) 'Felled in the name of natural justice', *Guardian*, 13 July, 3.
Bryant, B. (1996) *Twyford Down*, London: Chapman and Hall.
Carter, A. (1973) *Direct Action and Liberal Democracy*, London: Routledge and Kegan Paul.
Clarke, J. (1976) 'Style', in S. Hall, J. Clarke, T. Jefferson and B. Roberts (eds) *Resistance Through Rituals*, London: Hutchinson.
Diani, M. (1994) *Green Networks*, Edinburgh: Edinburgh University Press.
Doherty, B. (1999) 'Manufactured vulnerability: eco-activist tactics in Britain', *Mobilization*, 4, 1: 75–89.
Doherty, B. and Rawcliffe, P. (1995) 'British exceptionalism? Comparing the environmental movement in Britain and Germany', in I. Bluhdorn, F. Krause and T. Scharf (eds) *The Green Agenda: Environmental Politics and Policy in Germany*, Keele: Keele University Press.
Foreman, D. and Haywood, B. (1993) *Ecodefense*, Chico, Ca: Abzug Press.
Freedland, J. (1999) 'The theatre of riot', *Guardian*, 23 June, 15.
Friends of the Earth (FoE) (1998) *Checkout Chuckout! A Directory for Campaigners Against Superstore Developments*, London: FoE.
Hartley-Brewer, J. (1999) 'Riot police inexperience blamed', *Guardian*, 29 July, 11.
Kriesi, H., Koopmans, R., Duyvendak, J. and Giugni, M. (1995) *New Social Movements in Western Europe*, London: UCL Press.
Lamb, R. (1996) *Promising the Earth*, London: Routledge.
Lee, R. (1983) 'Free the 4,344,843', *Peace News*, 2201: 5–6.
Lowe, R. and Shaw, W. (1993) *Travellers – Voices of the New Age Nomads*, London: Fourth Estate.
McAdam, D. and Rucht, D. (1993) 'The cross-national diffusion of movement ideas', *Annals of American Academy of Political and Social Science*, 528: 56–74.
Maycock, B. (1987) 'Animal liberationists are peace campaigners too!', *Peace News*, 2289: 7.

Melucci, A. (1996) *Challenging Codes*, Cambridge: Cambridge University Press.

Mukherjee, R. (1993) *The Penguin Gandhi Reader*, Harmondsworth: Penguin.

O'Hara, L. (1993) *A Lie Too Far: Searchlight, Hepple and the Left*, London: Mina.

Parkin, S. (1989) *Green Parties*, London: Heretic.

Pilger, J. (1996b) 'An inspiration to us all', *Red Pepper*, 28: 5.

Roberts, J. (1986) *Against All Odds*, London: Arc Print.

Robinson, M. (1992) *The Greening of British Party Politics*, Manchester: Manchester University Press.

Rootes, C. (1992) 'The new politics and the new social movements: accounting for British exceptionalism', *European Journal of Political Research*, 22: 171–191.

Roseneil, S. (1995) *Disarming Patriarchy: Feminism and Political Action at Greenham*, Milton Keynes: Open University Press.

Ryder, R. (1989) *Animal Revolution*, Oxford: Basil Blackwell.

Searle, D. (ed.) (1997) *Gathering Force*, London: The Big Issue.

Shipley, P. (1976) *Revolutionaries in Modern Britain*, London: Bodley Head.

Swidler, A. (1986) 'Culture in action: symbols and strategies', *American Sociological Review* 51, 2: 273–286.

Tarrow, S. (1994) *Power in Movement*, London: Cambridge University Press.

Taylor, R. and Young, N. (1987) 'Britain and the international peace movement in the 1980s', in R. Taylor and N. Young (eds) *Campaigns For Peace*, Manchester: Manchester University Press.

Tilly, C. (1986) *The Contentious French*, Cambridge, MA: Harvard University Press.

Twinn, I. (1978) *Public Involvement or Public Protest: A Case Study of the M3 at Winchester 1971–1974*, London: Polytechnic of the South Bank.

Tyme, J. (1978) *Motorways versus Democracy*, London: Macmillan.

Underdown, D. (1985) *Revel, Riot and Rebellion*, Oxford: Oxford University Press.

Veldman, M. (1994) *Fantasy, the Bomb and the Greening of Britain*, London: Cambridge University Press.

Wall, D. (1994) *Green History*, London: Routledge.

—— (1998) 'The politics of Earth First! in the UK', unpublished PhD thesis, University of the West of England.

—— (1999) *Earth First! and the Anti-Roads Movement*, London: Routledge.

5   Modern millenarians?

Anticonsumerism, anarchism and the
new urban environmentalism[1]

Jonathan Purkis

A short story

It is one of the last Saturdays before Christmas. Shoppers scurry around the
gleaming city arcades, dodging each other and the tinsel displays which bedeck
every entrance. There is a feeling of claustrophobia and grim commitment to
getting what is needed and leaving as fast as is possible. In the midst of a crush at
the entrance of the Arndale Centre a small child grabs hold of her hassled
mother's arm and points along the crowded pedestrian precinct to where something quite unfamiliar is taking place. More people follow the shout of 'Look
Mummy' and stop to watch. Five figures wearing large 'alien' heads and clad in
bright orange robes move slowly – even eerily – along the street, pointing thin
green hands at shop windows and appearing fascinated with their surroundings.
Shepherding them along is a silver-suited man carrying a megaphone and a sign
inscribed 'Galactic Tours'.

'Come along now, aliens, follow the sign,' he booms into the megaphone.
'Don't miss this next bit of the tour. The people you can see here are called
Christmas Shoppers. At this time of the year they all buy lots of things to make each
other happy. The shop here sells different types of shoes. Why don't we go and
have a look at them?'

The gathered crowd crams into the shop and watch the aliens inspect a
variety of different items of sports footwear.

The tour guide explains: 'Those are very expensive shoes because they have a
special squiggle on the side. People on Earth are very happy to be given these
shoes for Christmas because it makes them feel that they are better than people
who have shoes without a squiggle on. The people who make the shoes with a
squiggle on are not very happy because they have to work very hard.'

By now several security staff have surrounded the tour guide, although they
have failed to notice non-costumed men and women handing out leaflets which
are inscribed with the words 'Why we are here'.

The tour guide keeps talking into the megaphone.

'Pay attention, aliens. This is a security guard. His job is to make sure that
everybody in the shop is happy. He is telling me that we are making people in the
shop *unhappy* because we are preventing them from buying the special shoes

which make them feel happy. He is telling me that if we don't go out of the shop, which will make him very happy, he will telephone some of his special friends with hats and they will come and make us all very unhappy. Shall we go and look at other shops?'

Introduction

In recent years, the number of political actions concentrating on the negative impacts that the consumer classes of the rich countries are having on the world's eco-systems, its poorest populations, and the psyches of those who have more than enough already, has mushroomed. Based largely on a critique of the intrusion of the commodity into all aspects of daily life and the endless pursuit of material accumulation for its own sake, most of these actions have been carried out by small, well-networked, usually leaderless groups who engage in direct actions of a highly theatrical, inventive and iconoclastic nature. This has involved anything from embarrassing large multinational corporations in the courts, unsettling liberal opinion on the best way to save the world, to providing alternative entertainment in huge shopping centres for small children. What has become clear is that this emerging web of anticonsumer groups not only have a complex and largely unpalatable message to deliver to governments, business and the general public, but that they have also had an impact on the more mainstream non-governmental organisations (NGOs) dealing with matters of the environment, poverty and justice. As a result, whole new areas of public debate have opened up and discussion on the limits of consumerism appeared viable, where once it was the kiss of death to a campaigning group.

Despite this, the anticonsumer groups appear to have very different agendas as well as organisational structures from the mainstream NGOs. It is the aim of this chapter to outline what these differences are and how we can understand them in a historical context. My claims are that millenarianism is a useful touchstone for exploring and theorising the radical, anti-authoritarian aspects of contemporary protest around consumption. This can be seen in two ways. *First*, there is an emphasis on 'non-material' values, which runs through the history of such movements, whether achieving a 'state of grace' in earlier pre-modern manifestations through to processes of 'self-actualisation' in the late twentieth century. *Second*, we should see such grassroots activity as also part of the history of anarchism, both in terms of their theory and practice. Whilst it is frequently acknowledged that there is a strong historical relationship between millenarianism and anarchism (Cohn 1970; Bookchin 1982; Perlman 1983; Walter 1971), there is considerably less agreement about their relationship in the twentieth century. In this respect I will use the concept of social ecology as a means of understanding the importance of making the link between anti-authoritarian, non-materialist practices and the ecological crisis which has, to all intents and purposes, motivated the current attitudes to consumerism.

This is by way of contrast with the eco-philosophy of 'deep ecology' – which enjoys favoured status among some 1990s UK radical environmentalists, but lacks both philosophical consistency or historical coherence. So, rather than blaming the ecological crisis and the excesses of human society on humans per se, a social ecological perspective concentrates on the interconnected nature of social and ecological problems, suggesting that it is the manner in which human societies have organised themselves which can be seen to underpin the ecological crisis. It is for this reason that the location of so many anticonsumer protests become significant. The contestation – indeed the '(re)-colonisation' – of urban spaces brings into focus a plethora of social, political and ecological problems that were absent when groups opposed to materialism simply attempted to withdraw to more rural or 'natural' surroundings and adopt an isolationist method of protest. Moreover, it is debatable whether, given the concentration of corporate power, a non-urban radical environmental praxis is even valid at all, at least in the West.

The argument is organised in this fashion. The first section discusses the definitional problems which have existed around the terms 'millenarianism' and 'anarchism' and suggests that social ecology offers us a framework for the early twenty-first century. The second section outlines the general history of anticonsumerism, moving the argument from a critique of excess wealth and the belief in voluntary simplicity to a critique of ecological impact and a belief in a limits to growth. The third section moves this critique into a contemporary geographical context with a consideration of recent anticonsumerist praxis. In the final section I consider the extent to which we can really regard the 1990s protests against consumerism as fulfilling the theoretical criteria which I now outline below.

Millenarianism, anarchism and social ecology

Regardless of the extent to which readers are familiar with either of these three concepts, it should be said that what follows is something of a departure from both popular and specialist wisdom in any of these areas.

Millenarianism

In the popular imagination millenarianism is the belief in the end of the world or the arrival of a major cataclysmic epoch-making event. It has become associated with the radical utopian visions and practices of a series of small iconoclastic non-conformist religious communitarians from fifteenth-century Europe who believed in the imminent Second Coming of Christ and the establishment of a heaven on Earth. Most famously documented by Norman Cohn in his book *The Pursuit of the Millennium: Revolutionary Millenarians and Mystical Anarchists of the Middle Ages* (1970), such groups as the Brethren of the Free Spirit, the Hutterites and the Anabaptists believed in the diffusion of all religious boundaries between the deity and the devotee – thus by-passing the hierarchical religious establishment. These beliefs were profoundly heretical against prevailing religious dogma which millenarians regarded as responsible for creating evil in the world.

The religious heresies took the most individual of forms, often focused on the body as an agent of societal transformation. This occurred through the belief in 'this-worldly salvation', whereby one could achieve an individual 'state of grace' (moral and spiritual perfection) in everyday life. These were linked to the creation of a utopian society – the 'heaven on Earth' – in the sense that such actions embodied the desired society. Sometimes these practices could vary from the very austere and ascetic to wild promiscuous hedonism. Unsurprisingly, millenarian groups were seen as dangerous fanatics and were hounded throughout Europe. Four hundred were expelled in 1421 from the city of Tabor for believing that they were already in the kingdom of the elect and that laws had already been abolished (Rexroth 1974: 89). The communities which were established by millenarian groups, such as the Anabaptist's New Jerusalem at Münster in 1535, were usually short-lived and such peoples were frequently mobile. They were also demographically marginal peoples, attracting the dispossessed, dissident priests or scholars, vagrants, journeymen: Cohn calls these people the 'voluntary poor'.

> [They] formed a mobile, restless intelligentsia, members of which were constantly travelling along the tradesroutes from town to town, operating mostly underground and finding an audience and a following amongst all the disoriented and anxious elements in urban society.
>
> (Cohn 1970: 157)

For some commentators, there are clearly traceable millenarian currents from the fifteenth century which keep resurfacing in all manner of books, pamphlets and speeches (Barkun 1986: 180). The next famous period of millenarianism is that of the English Revolution in the seventeenth century, as documented in Christopher Hill's excellent *The World Turned Upside Down* (1982). Many of the groups of this period such as the Fifth Monarchy Men, the Ranters, the now much-celebrated Diggers, as well as many Quakers, took on similar characteristics to their fifteenth-century counterparts in terms of emphasis on self-expression, freedom from religious hierarchies, the development of alternative communities and societies. The pursuit of sensuous and ascetic activities was as equally polarised as their predecessors (sometimes providing new liberating practices for women – see Grant 1993: 23–27).

From here on there is some disagreement as to the manifestations of millenarianism. According to Cohn, the idea of creating a 'heaven on earth' becomes secularised around the time of the French Revolution and the utopianism of Enlightenment politics. So, the major 'utopian' ideals of the twentieth century – Bolshevism and the Nazi 1,000-year Reich – are seen to embody this millenarian tendency, in terms of their sense of common and exclusive destiny, their demonisation of other cultural or political groups and their charismatic leadership. Thus, what Cohn appears to be doing is trying to locate the roots of totalitarianism in the hopes and fears of the most marginal and excluded of groups. This is where, I think, Cohn is wrong.

An important departure from this view is the critique offered by Fredy Perlman in his strange but beautiful *Against His-story Against Leviathan* (1983: 183). Perlman maintains that Cohn ignores the political visions behind the religious rhetoric and completely misses the fact that the key characteristic of millenarianism is its deep anti-authoritarianism and self-organisation. If we recognise this, millenarianism appears a much transformed concept and, for our purposes, provides the theoretical overlap between anarchism and social ecology.

However, to understand social ecology we need to understand anarchism, and it is to the difficulties presented by defining anarchism that I now turn.

Anarchism

Apart from the common misconceptions which exist around the term, anarchism also suffers a problem of periodisation. It is often the case in political theory that anarchism is seen to be exclusive to the emergence of Modernity, a political movement emblematic of the political turbulence throughout nineteenth-century Europe (and, to a lesser extent, America). The collected works of Pierre-Joseph Proudhon, Michael Bakunin and Peter Kropotkin are seen to exemplify the political philosophy of the 'anarchist moment' which is often regarded, argues Moore (1997: 157), as ending in the 'failure' of the Spanish Revolution of 1939. This view is flawed in two significant ways: first, it concentrates on the history of groups who call themselves anarchist, as opposed to those that behave anarchistically but do not ascribe a label to themselves; and second, it fails to see that behind the ideology of 'anarchism' is a form of organisation common to many historical situations which stands outside the assumptions of bourgeois historians (Chomsky 1969). What Colin Ward (1982: 14) calls the 'theory of spontaneous order' is, I want to suggest, both as relevant to political formations in the pre-Enlightenment period as they are to contemporary radical environmentalism and anticonsumerism.

The 'classical anarchist' era, however, has provided a number of influential principles: that political actions must be based on voluntary association allowing maximum participation; that the means of an action should be equated with its ends; that all forms of authority and power are regarded as morally unacceptable; and that the future is seen as being determined by activists in the unfolding of a revolutionary situation rather than in accordance with specific blueprints. These were based on an essentially *psychological* critique of power that recognised how human activities could be equally egoist or sociable, hence a belief that organising in a co-operative and non-hierarchical fashion was paramount to prevent political corruption (see Morland 1998).

The re-emergence of anarchist ideas in the post-war era is well documented – in the New Left and the American counterculture (Apter and Joll 1971; Ehrlich *et al.* 1979) – as well as being influential in the events of May and June 1968 in France (Cohn-Bendit 1968). However, theorists of the so-called New Social Movements (NSMs) that emerged in the 1960s with new and apparently radical agendas – on race, gender, sexual preference, nuclear technologies and the environment – have been less effective at identifying the anarchist lineage. Such writers as Touraine (1981), Offe (1985) and Habermas (1981) ascribed non-hierarchical, anti-bureaucratic and participatory decision-making characteristics to the new movements, yet, when many of them developed into large bureaucracies and even multinational companies, there seemed to be very little work on *why* these movements had 'failed'. The tendency to 'talk up' the anti-hierarchical characteristics of many of these movements in the literature has been noted (Bagguley 1992), although for some (Stammers 1995) this was actually to miss the point: it was *only* the 'radical currents' of the NSMs which were exciting theorists in the first place.

However, recent advances in NSM theory (Joppke 1993; Duyvendak 1995; Koopmans 1995) which have recognised the importance of looking at protest movement *culture* rather than 'political opportunities'[2] to engage with electoral politics, government or the Civil Service, has resulted in more comprehensive understanding of the vast differences which can exist within a movement culture. Such welcome developments have also resulted in attempting to decipher the 'radical currents' within contemporary environmental politics and the extent to which they can be considered to be part of anarchism (Welsh and McLeish 1996; Hart 1997). Contemporary challenges to consumerism occupy this position but, as with the problem of assessing the 'old' NSMs, we should not be lulled into any false sense of security as to exactly *how* radical these groups are.

It is for this reason that we need to understand the issues which have not only driven people to fuse anarchism with eco-politics, but to determine how this is manifested.

Social ecology

Arguably the principal achievement of anarchist thinking in the twentieth century has been its attempt to incorporate new circumstances such as the ecological crisis and the intrusion of technology into daily life into an essentially nineteenth-century critique. Foremost in this respect is the sometimes controversial work of American eco-anarchist Murray Bookchin and the development of the philosophy of social ecology.[3]

Described by fellow-thinker John Clark as a 'holistic conception of the self, society, and nature' (1992) social ecology attempts to incorporate ecological notions of interconnectedness with a dialectical philosophy that does not totally abandon concepts of either rationality or teleology. Social ecology argues that the roots of the ecological crisis lie in the evolution of social hierarchies and that it is the oppression of people by people (and mostly men) which underpins the domination of the natural world. Bookchin suggests that it is possible to chart the evolution of these hierarchies in the long transition from the organic societies of the preliterate Neolithic Period to the ancient civilisations of Mesopotamia and the Mediterranean basin,[4] disrupting the interdependent equilibrium of existing human and non-human ecosystems. These hierarchies manifested themselves at both a *material* level (the creation of agricultural technologies and surplus, the rise of patriarchal domestic roles and the growth of cities) and at *subjective/psychological* levels (the steady internalisation of command structures; the acceptance that authoritarian behaviour is natural). Bookchin calls these command structures 'epistemologies of rule', and what he tries to do in *The Ecology of Freedom* (1982) is to document the significance of when these structures break down, covering much of the same ground that Cohn does. Central to his method is identifying when the dualistic concepts which form these epistemologies such as Man/Nature or God/Man are challenged.

This model, I argue, helps us to understand contemporary consumerism as an epistemology of rule and any attacks upon it as part of a history of small-scale resistance based on non-material values, which in both theoretical and practical ways dissolve prevailing dualisms.

The challenge to consumerism

The identification of clear and coherent movements that can be seen to constitute an anticonsumerist tradition is, I argue, not always easy and appears to be based around a series of 'moments', social experiments and interventions in everyday life. Since some of these 'moments' span several decades, or even centuries, and vary in context from the religious to the secular, a number of important methodological issues require definition.

Defining premises

The first of these is the fact that when we are talking about the emphasis on non-material values in such 'moments' the resistance to wealth and excess is not necessarily the same as the resistance to consumerism. Thus, we should see the *denial* of material possessions as manifesting itself differently in each era. For instance, whilst Durning points out (1992: 137ff) that the cultural roots of consumerism are shallow, on the grounds that all of the main world religions have involved the preaching of moderation rather than excess as a virtue, we should remember that such views were born of historical eras plagued by issues of scarcity and less control over food supplies. Indeed, as Cohn points out, some of the very early millenarian movements of the twelfth century were in part reacting against the growth of wealth in Europe and felt the need to adopt a life of 'voluntary poverty', where they could concentrate on more spiritual matters (Cohn 1970: 156). Thus the *point* about attempting to trace such a history is that non-material values will manifest themselves in opposition to dominant ideas and practices of the time, be they social, political, economic or cosmological in nature.

Second, with respect to understanding consumerism as an 'epistemology of rule' we need to tread on sociological eggshells. Studies of consumption have sometimes been only too quick to regard people as 'cultural dopes' in much the same way as the Frankfurt School of Critical Theory did consumers of popular culture in the 1930s and 1940s – passively buying daydreams to cushion the blow of everyday life. This is a position which still holds considerable sway among political activists of all shades of black, red, pink and green. It is one which ignores both the complexities of consumerism as a cultural practice and how power is constituted around it. With respect to the former, consumerism is not 'just capitalism', but 'the outcome of a complex interplay of forces – political ideology, production, class relations, international trade, economic, cultural and moral values' (Gabriel and Lang 1995: 26). Consumerism is capitalism's alter ego, weaving together local and global cultures and spaces, raising new questions about power and oppression. In many ways, the configuration of power in consumer society evokes the work of Michel Foucault (1980) in terms of how, rather than it being applied by a central authority, power is produced and repro- duced by everyone, 'percolating' through the social body to become a significant way of organising and ordering social life, from breakfast cereal to car culture. Contemporary consumerism may be vastly complex, but protesters understand it from precisely this analytical perspective: that there is a need to transgress – albeit temporarily – the ways in which it organises our social world.

I have already outlined a starting point for tracing anticonsumerist practices in the context of early millenarian movements and then the various religious groups of the seventeenth century: now I want to look at the period of moder- nity and Enlightenment.

Romantics and industrialists

The religious context for non-material values being a resistance to domineering and dualistic ideas can be seen to adopt a particular stance during the Industrial Revolution. In the late eighteenth and early nineteenth centuries all manners of writers and movements were critical of the impact industrialisation and urbani- sation were having on the human psyche. This included the American Transcendentalists and English Romantic poets such as Henry Thoreau, Waldo Emerson, Walt Whitman and Mark Twain on the one hand and William Wordsworth and Samuel Taylor Coleridge on the other. Although not neces- sarily all as anti-authoritarian or utopian as the likes of William Blake or William Godwin, these people did – to use Arne Naess's words – 'ask deeper questions' about the relationships between humans and nature (Devall and Sessions 1985: 74), including adopting a non-anthropocentric view of the world. The blurring of dualisms such as Man–Nature are therefore to be considered relevant here given the fact that industrial capitalism required 'Man' to be above Nature and most of these thinkers thought somewhat differently.

Concerns about the impact and injustices of industrialisation fed into many small-scale religious and political experiments in Europe and North America that arguably bear the millenarian inheritance, although this is not something which the aforementioned books by Cohn or Barkun really pick up on. These projects varied considerably in terms of their founder's motivations. They were frequently in rural locations, and sometimes embracing what we might today call eminently sustainable lives, but were previously seen merely in terms of thriftiness[5] and utilitarianism.[6] Moreover, often they were committed to radical democratic ideals, a daily diet of self-discovery and re-learning of meaning (see D'Aneri *et al.* 1990; Taylor 1987) and unorthodox sexual relationships (Grant 1993). Murray Bookchin sees two figures from this period as offering social ecological sensibilities: the utopian socialists Robert Owen and Charles Fourier. The former not only revolutionised the factory system by developing a working textile mill community at New Lanark committed to shorter working hours, available education for all, freedom from disease or accidents, but also formed an (ultimately unsuccessful) utopian community in America (New Harmony). Owen's vision of an 'industrial village' is, for Bookchin, a forerunner of Kropotkin's ideals of communal living in balance with the natural world (1982: 332). Fourier's vision of a small self-governing community (a phalanx) based on rotating work patterns, non-bourgeois family structures and pursuit of individual freedoms are also considered by Bookchin to be similarly part of a social ecological history.

Thus, as well as expressing a critique of industrialisation and materialism in these experiments and visions, there was still a sense of the need to integrate a healthy sense of self into a functioning alternative community; the kind of issues which we might understand today as consistent with self-actualisation or, as Erich Fromm (1993) put it, 'being' rather than 'having'.

What I would suggest is that there is in the nineteenth century – just as in the fifteenth and seventeenth centuries – a millenarianism which expresses according to different religious, political and economic situations. Moreover, that it defines itself as being separate from the ever-pervasive 'evils in the world' and practises anti-authoritarian methods of organisation (to varying degrees) with an emphasis on transcending the dominant ideas and ideologies of the time. As I have suggested earlier in the article, it is the translation of such millenarian notions into the twentieth century which is the difficult part of this intellectual journey. In order to do this, an excursion into some of the twentieth-century critiques of consumerism is necessary, mainly because of their subsequent impact upon the contemporary environmental movement.

Intellectuals and surrealists

As suggested above, some of the intellectual critiques of consumerism require sociological caution owing to often determinist interpretations of everyday practices. It is strange then, that some of the most elitist avant-garde theorising of the twentieth century is actually essential for understanding contemporary praxis. Here I am thinking of the avant-garde art movements of Dadaism, Surrealism, Lettrisme and, perhaps most importantly, Situationism (see Home 1988). In different ways, these movements from the 1920s onwards have each attempted to explode the ideological division between art and life, through the juxtaposition of images and materials, to draw attention to commodification and social alienation. It is the translation of some of these ideas into popular culture which is of importance to the argument, especially the Situationist's radical synthesis of

Marxism and anarchism. Since the heady days of May 1968, when Situationist ideas and 'art' found their expression on the streets of France in the form of graffiti, political pamphlets and 'manifestos', the works of Guy Debord (1987), Raoul Vaneigem (1967) and more recently Larry Law's pocketbook 'primers' have done much to inspire protest against consumer culture. Throughout the late 1970s and the 1980s much of the alternative and underground British punk and post-punk cultures utilised Situationist imagery (Goaman 1997), finding its way into alternative university prospectuses, *Vague* magazine, numerous fanzines and even spoof supermarket flyposters advertising free food.

The concept of 'subvertising' for instance – widely used in environmental politics – comes directly from the Situationist notion of *détournment* whereby the meaning of an advertisement or cultural text is transformed by the substitution of a radical message. Moreover, the creation of 'situations' (sometimes referred to as 'happenings') as a way of shocking people out of their experience of everyday 'oppression' is something which has subsequently become part of contemporary protest inheritance.

Some consumer protest does not fit into this chronology of anticonsumerism. For instance, in cultural studies and sociology there have been lively debates about the extent to which consumers can 'rebel' within the framework of post-war capitalist society. Largely prompted by the optimistic work of John Fiske (1989), for whom ripped jeans and shop-lifting can be equated with the activities of Third World freedom fighters, the debates have weighed up the extent to which (particularly youth) cultures actively produce and reproduce their own forms of resistance. Although there is not space to explore these debates fully, what appears pertinent is, as Gabriel and Lang note (1995: 150), that there is a world of difference between consumers whose rebellion can quickly degenerate into style and those who are actively saying 'no' to consumerism. It is this strand of protest to which I now turn.

From Grosvener Square to Go-Tan

The reaction of the 1960s counterculture to their parent's generation came out of a need for liberalisation, but it was also a reaction against materialism and Western exploitation in an increasingly globalised world (largely focused on American involvement in Vietnam). Appropriately perhaps, there was an explosion of interest in non-material values and 'self-actualisation' during this period, from the revering of Eastern religions to the glamorisation of 'simpler' lifestyles of indigenous people around the globe. Books such as Herbert Marcuse's *Eros and Civilisation* (1966) – which inspired hopes for a socially and sexually liberated society without high-tech consumer enslavement and looked to the developing world for exemplification – seemed to epitomise this.

In terms of activism, the 1960s counterculture in the US and UK did not just oppose imperialism and conformist materialism, it attempted to transform the cultural as well as political underpinnings of the society. This involved the kind of spaces and practices that these days would be called temporary autonomous zones (Bey 1996)[7] – such as the Roundhouse in London or the work of the Living Theatre. Surrealist influences seemed evident in actions against 'the system' such as the stunt by the Youth International Party (or 'Yippies') of throwing real money into the Wall Street Stock Exchange and the much-eulogised 1968 Christmas action whereby Santa and his little helpers handed out free presents in London's Selfridges (Neville 1973: 17).

Although there was a strong Left/Marxist critique associated with these activities, what was significant about this time was the emergence of environmental critiques of the impact which the mass consumer societies were having on the natural world. There had been precursors – in particular Rachel Carson's *Silent Spring* (1962) – but the early 1970s demonstrated the fact that specifically environmentally-focused strategies were needed. As Joe Weston points out (1986: 12), the symbolism of Friends of the Earth's first demonstration – dumping non-returnable glass bottles outside Schweppes, the manufacturers – cannot be underestimated: it was as though they were 'questioning the "right" of capitalism to accumulate wealth at the expense of society and the environment'.

The kind of questions which emerged from this critique of Western material accumulation and expansionism underscored the rise of radical new environmental movements and led to the kind of arguments about resource depletion and rising pollution levels which appeared in the *Limits to Growth* report (Meadows *et al.* 1974). The new eco-political awareness translated into many social experiments throughout the Western world attempting to create more fulfilling lifestyles, based on 'appropriate technologies' and a philosophy of 'small is beautiful' (coined from F.S. Schumacher's book of the same name – 1976). In Britain, these varied from the free festival music scene to the Findhorn Community near Inverness, the Centre for Alternative Technology and Tipi Valley (both in Wales but very different), as well as hundreds of small semi-rural communes springing up, following the self-sufficiency ethic of writers such as John Seymour. In America during this period there was the coining of the phrase 'voluntary simplicity' and a philosophy of 'living lightly on the earth' (so that others may simply live), again sometimes taking the form of alternative communities, but also entering more mainstream contexts. As Durning (1992: 139) notes, 'the goal is not ascetic self-denial, but a sort of unadorned grace ... [where] ... clotheslines, window shades, and bicycles have a functional elegance that clothes dryers, air conditioners, and automobiles lack'.

In order to understand the emergence of the 'second' wave of environmental politics to sweep Britain in the late 1980s, we need to contextualise it in terms of the socio-economic climate which young people were growing up under during that decade and the steady institutionalisation of the movements which had led the way two decades before. Although awareness of the ecological crisis intensified in the post-Chernobyl period (1986), the conditions and opportunities for many of those concerned about it actually decreased, largely thanks to the Thatcherite philosophy of sink or swim in a sea of reduced employment opportunities, welfare benefit cuts, housing shortages and increasingly repressive state legislation. The upshot was to produce a generation of new young voters who saw politicians as increasingly irrelevant at making very real differences to global or individual lives and who preferred to do it themselves (Mulgan 1994). Added to this decline in deference has been a feeling that the critical edge of the 'first generation' of environmental campaigners has been lost, with many of their demands watered down: 'zero growth' becoming 'sustainable development', 'small-scale/appropriate technology' becoming 'cleaner production' and the 'anti-elitism' of protest culture becoming 'professionalisation'. As a consequence, the dominant political formations in environmental politics during the 1990s have been much more anarchistic and direct in nature, emphasising civil disobedience, co-operative decision-making and self-determination at individual and group levels. Earth First!, the Donga Tribe, Reclaim the Streets and campaigns against the Criminal Justice and Public Order Act of 1995 have been in the vanguard of these political cultures. The protest camp, especially those associated with anti-road protests, has become indicative of a generation's desire to live in different ways.

Like their 1960s and '70s counterparts, the 1990s activist's critique has been international and extremely partial in terms of pointing the finger at governments, multinational corporations and international financiers. The difference, I would suggest, is that the level of research done – identifying the connections between social injustice, ecological devastation and everyday consumer practices – is much more sophisticated. Moreover, the rise of ethical and green consumerism, has served to develop the concept of the 'personal is political' to new levels, placing even the most moderate activist in a complex and interrelated series of lifestyle decisions. Yet, for an anticonsumerist, the task is to subvert the very assumptions of consumerism as a means to try to create a better society. It is to the locations and characteristics of some of these subversive practices that we now turn.

Doing it in the shopping malls

One of the most significant aspects of environmentally-related protest during the 1990s is the way in which city centre locations have become a focus for a variety of occupations and theatrical stunts. I am not suggesting that this is new or distinctive, more that as protest strategies have become more sophisticated and befitting of a highly globalised information-driven society, environmental protesters have recognised the multiple possibilities of urban action as opposed to limiting their actions to defending the 'wild' areas under threat. As I have argued elsewhere (Purkis 1996), these strategies are significant for a number of different reasons. First, there is the 'colonisation' of 'private' or capitalist 'space' such as banks, superstores, company HQs and annual general meetings (turning them into alternative 'spaces' or 'temporary autonomous zones'). Second, many of the processes of globalisation can be used against the companies, through on-site demands for information on company activity. As a consequence, the attendant public, workers, shareholders, and so forth, are accessible to protesters in ways that they would not be through public demonstrations in market squares, parks or roads.

The varieties of anticonsumer activities in the last two decades are, as I have suggested, quite considerable and I think this is the point where we have to separate out the kinds of actions that might be considered part of a social ecological outlook and those which are somewhat more nihilistic and/or typical of stereotypical notions of anarchism. This is not to suggest that the latter might be somehow irrelevant, more that they should be seen as two ends of an activist spectrum which emphasises the inevitable creative destruction of change in different ways.[8] For instance, in the mid-1980s, the anarchist group Class War targeted the consumer excesses of 'yuppies', who gentrified parts of London, through highly symbolic 'Bash the Rich' events, but showed little interest (as indeed was typical of much of the 'official' UK anarchist scene at that time)[9] in consumerism as worthy of further analysis as an issue in itself. Perhaps more appropriate in terms of location as anticonsumerist actions were the two anarchist 'puke-ins' against consumerism in Canberra (1989) and Seattle (1990), which took place in large shopping malls. The Antipodean side of anticonsumerism has been quite strong, in particular the BugaUp group (Billboard Utilizing Graffitists Against Unhealthy Promotions), with its history of Situationist billboard subversion. Associated activists also organised an innovative 'Celebration of the Life Under Capitalism Day' in Melbourne during 1992 deliberately timed to coincide with an Australian 'right to work' march (Scott and David 1996), and the Brisbane Culture Jammers Collective has been one of a number of groups to take part in International Buy Nothing/No Shop Days (see below).

From a UK perspective, the reclaiming of the phrase 'anticonsumerist' belongs to a campaigning group from Manchester called 'Enough: the anticonsumerism campaign', who have been pivotal in accelerating the debate about the impact and extent of consumerism amongst UK environmentalists. In April 1993 two activists with considerable experience in development politics – Paul Fitzgerald and Anna Thomas – called a public meeting proposing a campaign specifically on the issue of consumerism. They cited their influences as a 1980s group called Whose World? (then based in Manchester), the slick Canadian outfit The Media Foundation (from Vancouver) who organised a Buy Nothing Day as well as producing *Adbusters* magazine, and an earlier attempt of a Buy Nothing Day in the UK by Liverpool and Leeds activists. In their position booklet *Never Enough: a critical look at consumerism, poverty and the planet* (1995) the group make it clear where they stand: 'Any proposed solutions to the problems of world poverty, environmental destruction and social alienation will fail, unless they also address the role that the consumerist lifestyle plays in creating these problems.'[10]

Enough's literature places particular emphasis on the importance of anticonsumerism consisting of living differently rather than through denial, in terms not dissimilar to what Durning (1992) says about voluntary simplicity movements. Whilst much of the group's concerns appear to concentrate around international issues, it has tried to tap into the annual debate about whether Christmas is socially beneficial as a way into wider issues such as the social and ecological impact of accelerating global consumerism.

The group – which also runs workshops and conferences – has become known for co-ordinating No Shop Day in the UK, which may take place in anything between a dozen and twenty towns and cities. Popular protest themes have been: 'rat races' (where costumed activists chased each other around super-markets and shopping centres urging each other on with 'work harder' and 'buy more things' signs); spoof product launches ('Happiness – now in a can', or 'Bags of Happiness' for sale); 'shopping-free zones' (essentially a living room trans-ported into pedestrian precincts with free hot drinks plus a leaflet); the 'Prophets of Consumption' (where purple-clad 'acolytes' carried an 'altar to consumerism' around shopping centres, chanting the slogans shouted out by a sharp-suited sales director) and the Christmas Liberation Front (green Santas non-violently removing decorations from shops which advertised Christmas prior to December). Anticonsumerist Christmas carols have been sung in malls from Manchester to Montreal, 'No Shops' have appeared in several cities throughout the Western world and anticonsumerist videos/productions have appeared in as high profile contexts as CNN. Anticonsumerism has been particularly strong in the Netherlands, and in recent years actions have taken place in Sweden, Eire, South Africa, New Zealand and the United States.

Although the media have been quick to acknowledge Buy Nothing/No Shop Day, the established environmental and development organisations have been somewhat slower – at least publicly. In the UK the only supporters of Enough for the first few years of No Shop Day were *New Internationalist* magazine, the Women's Environmental Network and the New Economics Foundation, before Friends of the Earth officially joined in for some of the 1998 actions. However, the highly anti-capitalist nature of the anticonsumerist message has been partic-ularly successful at a grassroots level and Enough managed to tap into the activist culture based around the anti-roads movement, much of which practised low impact lifestyles anyway, either in their everyday lives or on protest camps, thus swelling the ranks of those interested in anticonsumerism around Christmas time. The overlap with Earth First! and the then-named Third World First (now People and Planet) also ensured that the international dimension to consumerism was covered in the campaigns. In addition, the high-profile 'McLibel' case (Vidal 1997) moved the debate about McDonalds – which in the 1980s had been mostly targeted from an animal rights angle – to a more general one concerning the interconnectedness of Western lifestyles with human rights, ecological and civil liberties issues, and this overlapped considerably with anticonsumerist messages. At the time of writing, direct action on issues of consumerism has become very regular on the genetically modified food issue, with many of the offending supermarkets and company premises receiving activist attention that displays the imaginative kind of tactics and protest aesthetics discussed above.

Modern millenarians: some concluding remarks

What has been apparent about many of the aforementioned activities is that they are taking place in spite of what politicians or more established organisations are doing. The new radical environmental networks are not only advocating anticonsumerist lifestyles – tapping into the alternative economic tradition of Local Exchange Trading Systems (LETS) and credit unions – but also taking their messages into the court rooms and confronting huge multinationals such as McDonalds and Monsanto. It is entirely appropriate that the new networks – or countercultures – consist of either people who have been marginalised in some way by changes in the social and economic landscape or by those who have seen what is available and decided not to be part of it.

Western consumer societies have become the focus for much contemporary radical environmental protest simply because they embody or evoke the worst aspects of capitalism and an alienation – economic, political or psychological – from individual and collective fulfilment. In the sense that consumerism can be seen to organise much of everyday life – whether wittingly or unwittingly – it can be considered an 'epistemology of rule' in the sense that Murray Bookchin maintains.

Although we are a long way from Münster in 1535, and it is far from clear what the current notion of New Jerusalem actually is in terms of contemporary anticonsumerism, there are still some connecting themes which, despite their different 'moments', are worthy of consideration. The first is that of language. Modern millenarians may well use the rhetoric of disaster and world collapse on occasions, but what exists behind this are notions of creating a profoundly ethical–moral–just society (a 'Heaven on Earth' if you like) through individual lifestyle practices united with self-organised radical political campaigning around consumerism. Then there is a critique of materialism which is based around the need to achieve a more fulfilling state of being – whether defined in religious or secular terms. In addition, we also need to consider how – from an anticonsumerist perspective – dominant dualistic processes come to be broken down in the same way as some of the earlier millenarian theological divisions were undermined.

First, there is evidence of a collapsing of the 'common-sense' separation of the First and Third worlds. This is something that serves to maintain the legitimacy of current trade practices and obscure the kind of injustices that lie behind many aspects of consumerism. So, by using an urban context as a protest site, anticonsumers attempt to collapse both of these 'spaces' into the same one. Following on from this is the *second* dualism, that of public and private actions. Here we see issues of responsibility being written into the very purchases (or non-purchases) that delineate everyday life but also can be seen to determine processes of self and self-actualisation. *Third*, in terms of the very political practices being used, there is a deliberate attempt to break the expert/lay leader-led authoritarian structures which many contemporary activists feel has taken over the first wave of environmental organisations. Thus the language of DIY protest – anarchism in all but name – serves as an indication of the fact that people want to develop their own protest cultures and communities. *Fourth* (and this is by default), the rejection of consumerism is often associated with the rejection of work since, many activists assert, the whole argument about keeping consumerism going hinges on jobs, and if society is to be changed to reject current patterns of consumption then notions of work must be redrawn. In this respect the identification of fulfilling and 'self-actualising' work processes deconstruct the work–leisure dualism. *Last*, consumerism is frequently associated with progress, and technological progress at that, something which is rooted in notions of Gross National Product (a concept which even includes production geared to helping environmental problems, thus pollution boosts the economy (Nicholson-Lord 1995)). The suggestion that quality of life indicators should be foremost in the assessment of the health of a society, and that this need not mean some kind of feudalism but more an appropriate use of technology, undermines the dualistic notion – progress/stagnation or even civilisation/nature.

On 18 June 1999 thousands of environmentalists, opponents of the arms trade, anarchists, anticonsumers, development and human rights activists occupied the centre of London in a diverse, spectacular, anti-authoritarian gesture against contemporary political and economic systems. Dubbed the 'Carnival against Capitalism' it echoed the mid-1980s 'Stop the City' actions, but embodied a much broader set of issues. After hours of peaceful protest, when trouble 'broke out' the buildings which were burnt out or trashed – the London International Financial Futures Exchange and a branch of McDonalds – epitomised the kind of problems of the late twentieth century. Despite the many different accounts of the day – who was to blame, and so forth – a couple of incidents seemed to me to sum up much of contemporary protest. One, a photograph in the next day's papers showed two slightly punky activists dancing on top of a police van holding cans of beer in their hands and appearing to be having the time of their lives. The second was an interview with a slightly older, self-confessed anarchist, who said that he hadn't had a job for over ten years but in this time he had never worked so hard in his life trying to create alternative communities, campaigning on globally important issues or just by growing organic vegetables in his allotment.

If the history of millenarianism can tell us anything, it is that at times of enormous existential crisis – when the incumbent social order appears unable to fulfil non-material desires, and what it represents comes under attack from a range of divergent, largely marginalised interest groups – the potential for huge political and cosmological shifts becomes apparent. If there can ever be an event which epitomises the undermining of dominant discourses and the optimism of unified collective struggle against – in Fredy Perlman's terms – the Leviathan of late twentieth-century life, then it surely must be the Carnival against Capitalism.

Notes

1   Many thanks to the editors for their enthusiastic and supportive comments throughout. Also to Nicole Matthews for an Australian perspective on these issues and Chayley Collis for keeping my feet on the ground. In recent years campaigners on these issues seem to favour the term 'anticonsumerism' without the hyphen, seemingly on the grounds that it becomes something other than a negative definition.

2 The theory of Political Opportunity Structure is mostly associated with the work of Tarrow (1994).
3 This is not to be confused with the social or human ecology models of the Chicago School of Social Theory in the 1920s and 1930s.
4 Bookchin is not using the word 'organic' to mean having the properties of an organism, but rather as a society which is 'spontaneously formed, noncoercive, and egalitarian' (1982: 5). Social ecologists are keen to avoid fetishising more 'primitive' societies and are interested in what we can learn from their attitudes to nature and to each other, particularly their tolerance of difference, their preferring 'wise' rather than 'authority' figures, and the concept of usufruct.
5 Judging from a number of nineteenth-century literary works – Charles Dickens' *Christmas Carol*, Oscar Wilde's *The Happy Prince*, Jerome K. Jerome's *Three Men in a Boat* – it is clear that not tying one's hopes to the accumulation of material goods as an end in itself was something of a concern even if it was sometimes expressed in the language of thrift.
6 As Bookchin notes (1982: 332), not all of these were particularly egalitarian.
7 I use Bey's concept of the temporary autonomous zone cautiously as it is in itself sociologically vague, but is also used to discuss anything from aspects of club culture to road-protest camps.
8 Here, I acknowledge the somewhat different 'take' on some of the same ground that I am covering by Greil Marcus in his book *Lipstick Traces: A Secret History of the Twentieth Century* (1990). I would suggest that these can be, and often are, part of the same 'moments' and depend largely on what one chooses to emphasise. In modernity, no matter how creative one is, there is always an element of destruction in any process which aims to make a change to the existing order.
9 The publication *Green Anarchist* would be an exception to this, I would suggest.
10 1995: 4, available from Enough, c/o One World Centre, 6 Mount Street, Manchester M2 5NS.

Bibliography

Apter, D. and Joll, J. (eds) (1971) *Anarchism Today*, London: Macmillan.
Bagguley, P. (1992) 'Social change, the middle class and the emergence of "new social movements": a critical analysis', *The Sociological Review* 40, 1: 26–48.
Barkun, M. (1986) *Disaster and the Millennium*, New York: Syracuse University Press.
Bey, H. (1996) *The Temporary Autonomous Zone*, Camberley: Green Anarchist Books.
Bookchin, M. (1982) *The Ecology of Freedom*, Palo Alto: Cheshire Books.
Carson, R. (1962) *Silent Spring*, London: Hamish Hamilton.
Chomsky, N. (1969) *American Power and the New Mandarins*, Harmondsworth: Penguin.
Clark, J. (1992) 'What is social ecology?', *Society and Nature* 1, 1: 85–92.
Cohn, N. (1970) *The Pursuit of the Millennium: Revolutionary Millenarians and Mystical Anarchists of the Middle Ages*, New York: Oxford University Press.
Cohn-Bendit, D. (1968) *Obsolete Communism: The Left Wing Alternative*, London: André Deutsch.
D'Anieri, P., Ernst, C. and Kier, E. (1990) 'New social movements in historical perspective', *Comparative Politics* 22: 445–458.
Debord, G. (1987) *The Society of the Spectacle*, London: Rebel Press.
Devall, B. and Sessions, G. (1985) *Deep Ecology: Living as if Nature Mattered*, Salt Lake City: Peregrine Smith.
Durning, A. (1992) *How Much is Enough?*, London: Earthscan.

Duyvendak, J. (1995) *The Power of Politics: New Social Movements in France*, Oxford: Westview Press.

Ehrlich, H., Erlich, C., De Leon, D. and Morris, B. (eds) (1979) *Reinventing Anarchy*, London: Routledge and Kegan Paul.

Enough (1995) *Never Enough: a critical look at consumerism, poverty and the planet*, Manchester: MARC (available from Enough, c/o One World Centre, 6 Mount Street, Manchester M2 5NS).

Fiske, J. (1989) *Understanding Popular Culture*, Boston, MA: Unwin Hyman.

Foucault, M. (1980) *Michel Foucault: Power/Knowledge*, C. Gordon (ed.), Hemel Hempstead: Harvester Wheatsheaf.

Fromm, E. (1993) *To Have or To Be?*, London: Abacus.

Gabriel, Y. and Lang, T. (1995) *The Unmanageable Consumer: Contemporary Consumption and its Fragmentation*, London: Sage.

Goaman, K. (1997) 'Youth culture, Situationism and anarchy' (Review Article), *Anarchist Studies* 5, 1: 77–82.

Grant, L. (1993) *Sexing the Millennium*, London: HarperCollins.

Habermas, J. (1981) 'New social movements', *Telos* 49: 33–37.

Hart, L. (1997) 'In defence of radical direct action: reflections on civil disobedience, sabotage and violence', in Purkis, J. and Bowen, J. (eds) *Twenty-First Century Anarchism*, London: Cassell.

Hill, C. (1982) *The World Turned Upside Down*, London: Penguin.

Home, S. (1988) *The Assault on Culture: Utopian Currents from Lettrisme to Class War*, Stirling: AK Press.

Joppke, C. (1993) *Mobilizing Against Nuclear Energy: A Comparison of Germany and the United States*, Berkeley: University of California Press.

Koopmans, R. (1995) *Democracy From Below: New Social Movements and the Political System in West Germany*, Oxford: Westview Press.

Marcus, G. (1990) *Lipstick Traces: A Secret History of the Twentieth Century*, Harvard: Harvard University Press.

Marcuse, H. (1966) *Eros and Civilisation*, Boston MA: Beacon Press.

Meadows, D., Meadows, D., Randers, J. and Behrens, W. (1974) *The Limits to Growth*, London: Pan.

Moore, J. (1997) 'Anarchism and post-Structuralism', *Anarchist Studies* 5, 2: 157–161.

Morland, D. (1998) *Demanding the Impossible?* London: Cassell.

Mulgan, G. (1994) *Politics in an Anti-political Age*, Cambridge: Polity Press.

Neville, R. (1973) *Playpower*, Frogmore St Albans: Paladin.

Nicholson-Lord, D. (1995) 'The end of consumerism?', *Earth Matters*, Winter.

Offe, C. (1985) 'New social movements: challenging the boundaries of institutional politics', *Social Research* 52, 4: 817–868.

Perlman, F. (1983) *Against His-Story, Against Leviathan*, Detroit: Black and Red.

Purkis, J. (1996) 'The city as a site of ethical consumption and resistance', in J. O'Connor and D. Wynne (eds) *From the Margins to the Centre*, Aldershot: Avebury.

Purkis, J. and Bowen, J. (eds) (1997) *Twenty-First Century Anarchism*, London: Cassell.

Rexroth, K. (1974) *Communalism: From Its Origins to the Twentieth Century*, New York: Seabury Press.

Schumacher, F.S. (1976) *Small is Beautiful*, London: Sphere.

Scott, B. and David, G. (1996) *How to Make Trouble and Influence People*, Sydney: Political Hooligan Publications.

Stammers, N. (1995) 'New social movements and civil society: learning the lessons from Eastern Europe', in C. Barker, P. Kennedy and M. Tyldesley (eds) *Alternative Futures and Popular Protest Conference Papers – 4–6 April*, Manchester Metropolitan University.

Tarrow, S. (1994) *Power in Movement*, Cambridge: Cambridge University Press.

Taylor, A. (1987) *Visions of Harmony: A Study in Nineteenth Century Millenarianism*, Oxford: Clarendon Press.

Touraine, A. (1981) *The Voice and the Eye*, Cambridge: Cambridge University Press.

Vaneigem, R. (1967) *The Revolution of Everyday Life*, London: Left Bank/Rebel Press.

Vidal, J. (1997) *McLibel: Burger Culture on Trial*, London: Macmillan.

Walter, N. (1971) 'Anarchism in print: yesterday and today', in D. E. Apter and J. Joll (eds) *Anarchism Today*, London: Macmillan.

Ward, C. (1982) *Anarchy in Action*, London: Freedom Press.

Welsh, I. and McLeish, P. (1996) 'The European road to nowhere: anarchism and direct action against the UK roads programme', *Anarchist Studies* 4, 1: 27–44.

Weston, J. (1986) 'The Greens, nature and the social environment', in J. Weston (ed.) *Red and Green*, London: Pluto Press.

6 Coming live and direct
Strategies of Earth First!

Benjamin Seel and Alex Plows

> The name Earth First! [EF!] is an exclamation, hence the exclamation mark. It is not the name of an organisation, it is a philosophy ... EF! has no central office, no paid workers, no decision-making bodies, and is not even an organisation in the normal sense of the word. EF! is a network of autonomous local groups ... who decide for themselves what campaigns they run and how they run them.
>
> (EF! UK web site)

> [EF! is] not a cohesive group or campaign, but a convenient banner for people who share similar philosophies to work under. The general principles behind the name are non-hierarchical organisation and the use of direct action to confront, stop and eventually reverse the forces that are responsible for the destruction of the earth and its inhabitants.
>
> (EF! *Action Update* May 1999, No. 58)

EF! is based upon small, local, often urban-based groups. At any one time it consists of the people taking part in its ongoing direct action issue campaigns or in local EF! groups. The EF!er becomes a road, airport, arms sales, opencast mine, deforestation or genetically modified organism (GMO) protester simply through their presence on particular actions. Activists do not just affiliate with different campaigns; they become them. EF! also exists as a latent movement in potential – as a cultural and informational network which only becomes more publicly visible during protest mobilisations.

Most activists avoid definitions of who or what they 'are' like the plague. But the 'similar philosophies' referred to in the *Action Update* newsletter quoted above involve a particular kind of worldview and cognitive praxis. Most important to EF! activists is the idea that direct actions speak louder than words; in particular they are thought to speak louder than the words of the traditional lobbying techniques of more institutionalised environmental organisations. Identification with EF! is primarily based on a collective valuation of direct action, rather than a wish to perpetuate EF! as an organisation. Nevertheless, small core groups of individuals involved in EF! have also focused on the day-to-day administration of information and networking organisations like Road Alert! (which linked direct activists from different road protests, but is now defunct), or the ongoing

Genetics Engineering Network (GEN) or Corporate Watch (a group that researches companies' malpractice). EF! also has two main publications: a monthly *Action Update* newsletter (available in paper and electronic mail forms) and a roughly annual journal called *Do or Die.*[1] The editorial board of the *Action Update* is rotated between different local groups on an annual basis. Similarly, *Do or Die* is taken on, one issue at a time, by a small group of activists.

The direct action movement is a series of overlapping and biodegradable networks that continuously change and adapt. We will suggest that this form of organisation, or as activists like to say 'disorganisation', has strategies implicit within it. In some ways it is impossible to separate EF! from the wider direct action networks and groups like Reclaim the Streets (RTS) who have a similar kind of philosophy, because belonging to each network tends to be a nebulous and transitory affair. Nevertheless, EF! is just one banner and network within this series of networks which comprises the direct action movement.

EF! is also perhaps the network with the most strongly articulated sense of strategy and its own collective identity, having been instrumental in initiating and propelling the 1990s wave of direct action. It is at EF! summer and winter gatherings, and in the pages of *Do or Die*, that one finds the most evidence of strategic discussion and thought in the direct action movement. The influence of EF!'s ideas in terms of articulating reasons for mobilising, particularly in the pre-Twyford (1992) era, when a new cycle of protest activity was beginning, fits with Snow and Benson's concept of an 'elaborated master frame'. 'Movements that surface early in a cycle of protest are likely to function as progenitors of master frames that provide the ideational and interpretive anchoring for subsequent movements in the cycle' (Snow and Benford 1992: 144). For these reasons, we have chosen EF!'s strategy, rather than that of the direct action movement more generally, as the focus of this chapter.

A shared worldview?

Autonomy and philosophical diversity are central tenets of EF! ideology. It is essential to stress that there is much variety in beliefs and values amongst EF!ers; some may even disagree quite fundamentally. Rather than this being a problem, Melucci (1996: 78) suggests the typical new social movement (NSM) collective identity is, 'always plural, ambivalent, [and] often contradictory'.

> Collective identity as a process involves cognitive definitions concerning the ends, means and the field of action ... this cognitive level does not necessarily imply unified and coherent frameworks ... rather, it is constructed through interaction and comprises different and sometimes contradictory definitions.
>
> (Melucci 1996: 71)

The idea of a shared worldview should be understood in this context. Both worldview and strategy are constructed around the value and exigencies of direct *action*. Identification with shared values and worldviews happens around site campfires, in tree houses, squatted buildings or tunnels, on top of bulldozers and in police cells. It is in these kinds of situations, as well as in local EF! group meetings and at EF! national gatherings, where activists refine and redefine the reasons they take action.

The Transformation of Environmental Activism (TEA) research team's protest event study of the *Guardian* newspaper between 1988 and 1997 found that, in a glut of newspaper coverage of environmental protest between 1995 and 1997, journalists quite often referred to the rise of 'single-issue' protest politics.[2] However, detailed interview-based and ethnographic research carried out by both the authors suggests that EF!ers have always been consciously 'multi-issue' since their inception in Britain in 1991. They combine a concern with global and systemic issues of political economy with a focus on particular targets. Protests against the import of tropical timber, peat extraction on SSSIs (sites of special scientific interests), the arms trade, opencast mining, road building and GMOs have been followed up with the recent (1999) J18 protests which targeted finance capital in the City of London and 'global capitalism' itself. Each 'single issue' or protest event is located in an analysis where environmental, socio-economic, cultural, and sometimes spiritual, factors are seen as intrinsically interconnected. As we shall see later, there has also been a shift in strategic focus over time – from the particular to the systemic.

The shared worldview that mobilises activists is partly based on a pragmatic assessment of the unsustainable nature of present political and economic practices and at the same time is based on something more conceptual, a challenge to the value system which permeates the structural targets activists identify. Activists are explicitly seeking a 'paradigm shift' away from capitalist systems, structures and values, referring disparagingly to 'progress culture', 'straight society', and very often 'global capitalism' to describe what it is they are mobilising against. They see exploitation of the Third World, the global poor, women, animals and the environment as a product of hierarchy, patriarchy, anthropocentrism, racism and, most prominently, capitalist economic relations. There is a strong sense of moral outrage in the EF! activist worldview where an ethical stance is taken revaluing what they believe is not being sufficiently valued. For example, activists protesting about British arms sales to Indonesia highlight the fact that British jobs and the economy are considered of more value than the lives of the East Timorese, and road campaigners challenge the values and corporate interests which assert that cutting a few minutes off the journey time between Southampton and London was worth the loss of Twyford Down.

There is a mass of literature on ecophilosophy, 'biocentrism' and environmental ethics. It is rare for activists to espouse specific academic ideas on these topics, but it does seem that these kinds of ideas have influenced some sections of the EF! milieu. In so doing they have dovetailed with a social analysis drawing upon the American anarchist, Murray Bookchin's (e.g. 1995) 'social ecology' and an 'eco-socialist' analysis of political economy (see, for example, Pepper 1993) of the forces driving environmental degradation and social exploitation.

Ecofeminism, deep ecology and spirituality also play a part in defining the ethical meanings that some individual activists construct (Plows 1997). In general terms, activists identify a sense of alienation from nature – nature seen as 'other' and as worth less than humanity – as being part cause, part effect of a hierarchical, capitalist, 'progress culture'. In this way ethics, values and politics are interwoven and symbiotic in EF!ers' worldview; theirs is both a systemic analysis and an argument for a shift in values.

Does EF! have a strategy?

Rucht defines *strategy* as, '[A] conscious, long-range, planned, and integrated general conception of an actor's conflict behavior based on the overall context (including third parties and potential allies), and with special emphasis on the inherent strengths and weaknesses of the major opponent' (Rucht 1990: 161). *Strategy* then, is the 'how' of political actors and social movements. Collective actors have certain goals, and strategy is the principles or concepts that guide the methods which such actors use in the attempt to affect their social environment. Strategy can be differentiated from *tactics* in that tactics are the techniques chosen for particular situations, whereas strategies are the more generalised conceptions of how changes can be effected. As such, tactics may change from one situation to another (Rucht 1990: 174); in contrast strategic concepts are more stable and sustained even though they may be applied in different ways in different situations.

The April 1992 EF! national gathering defined three aims which would be pursued under the EF! banner. These aims are still referred to in contemporary EF! publications. They are:

- To defend the environment.
- To confront and expose those destroying the environment.
- To realise a human lifestyle that exists in balance and harmony with the natural world and that has respect for all life.

The same gathering also came up with a set of (less quoted) 'methods':

- Empowering individuals and groups to take direct and focused action against those destroying the environment.
- Networking information and contacts between action groups to facilitate the growth of a movement and encourage group autonomy.
- Raising funds for direct action campaigns and networking costs.

Putting these aims and methods together, it is clear that EF!'s main strategy is to use direct action protests physically to defend environmental sites threatened by economic 'development' and to confront and expose those economic and political groups whom they see as perpetrating environmental degradation.

While this is a general 'strategy', it is clear that in terms of the fairly traditional definition given above, EF! has a relatively unformulated strategy. In an interview at the 1999 EF! summer gathering, for example, an anonymous EF! activist said: 'Maybe I've just been missing something, but "strategy" doesn't seem to happen.' Strategy is not formulated or planned by a policy unit as it might be in more professional environmental movement organisations (EMOs). But of course EF! is not an EMO, it is an anarchist NSM and to have a centralised policy structure would run against the nature of the movement and its core principles. In this sense EF! strategy is not 'planned and integrated' as in Rucht's definition of strategy. However, local group autonomy prefigures the kind of non-hierarchical political organisation that EF!ers want to see and, following a theme found in parts of the anarchist tradition, they believe the kind of organisation and methods that a movement uses, influences the political, social and cultural outcomes of their actions. That is, they see means and ends as closely related. Local group autonomy is also consciously regarded as having the strategic advantage of making EF! groups less predictable and more innovative, fluid and flexible, thus able to respond more effectively to change on the ground and to throw multiple spanners in 'the system's' works. The lack of certain elements of traditional 'strategy' is thus itself actually part of EF!'s strategy.

However, EF! remains in general an action-based movement. When asked why they engage in the actions that they do, activists might sometimes speak of 'intuition', 'instinct' or 'gut feelings', or otherwise just tell you that it is because a particular corporation is 'shafting people and the planet', rather than explain a complex social analysis. Too much intellectual discussion of either 'the system' they are opposing or the principles of how direct action might achieve change is often seen as a distraction from action. EF!ers tend to think that it bogs people down in endless unnecessary discussions.[3] Thus, their action-oriented ethos is a conscious and deliberate response to the factionalism and schism documented amongst left-wing groups where excessive strategic discussion and debate has contributed to organisational splits. In contrast, direct actions or protests create a feeling of solidarity in a group that makes it more unified (see Hetherington 1998). It is enough for an EF! group to agree that protest should be made on a particular issue, rather than how that issue fits into a wider societal formation or the specific mechanisms by which their action might cause change. EF! has a dearth of resources such as people, time and money, so focusing upon performing direct actions on particular issues is partly a pragmatic use of their scarce resources. Nevertheless, it is a taken for granted set of political and strategic analyses and worldview based on past experience, which triggers activists to devise tactics for particular actions 'instinctively'. That is, actions draw upon shared values and social analyses that are further worked out and argued over during the course of the action. In what follows we hope to explain some of the lines of strategic thought underpinning EF!'s emphasis on direct actions. Not surprisingly, there are several competing themes.

The radical flank effect

The radical flank effect can be understood as working in two main ways. In the first, direct actions can be understood as functioning to prevent EMOs becoming too de-radicalised or 'sucked in' to a policy-oriented politics of reform through exposing them to radical critique. The introduction to this book described how 1990s direct action emerged partly as a response to the institutionalisation and professionalisation of EMOs like FoE and Greenpeace. Radicals saw these processes as having led the environmental movement too far down a path of 'reformist tinkering'. At the same time such EMOs were seen as lacking a partic-ipatory ethos. On this issue Wall (1999: 123) believes frustration with FoE influenced early EF! activists most of all.[4] In contrast, EF!ers are keen on main-taining a systemic critique rather than working on a single-issue basis:

> Conventional 'green' campaigning is not enough to stop the destruction that is happening. Politicians and companies ignore letters, petitions and public enquiries; they reject overwhelming evidence because it goes against their interests. Conventional campaigns are all too often narrow, and are seen as single issues; the scale of change needed is forgotten. While the world burns, environmentalists debate recycling beer cans.

> (EF! UK website)

Discussing the limits of lobbying for policy changes, an EF! activist asks:

> What in fact could you offer us? The end of the industrial system – can you offer us that? An end to the assault against the life systems of the earth … can you offer us that? Of course not! … The modern ecology movement is over 30 years old; in the bowels of your [government's] office there is a whole forest of reports on the ecological stupidity of what you are doing. You know the situation.

> (*Do or Die* 1995: 5)

Hence, EF! questions the efficacy of the policy directed and reform oriented strategies of EMOs, arguing that the state is actually deeply implicated in perpetuating the process of ecological degradation through encouraging economic growth, rather than being a neutral body open to plural influences. Writing reports for government or researching policy options is seen as helping government maintain the illusion that environmental action is being taken while the 'business as usual' that is reckoned to drive ecological degradation continues. Direct action and radical rhetoric can be understood as functioning to make EMOs reconsider the extent to which they compromise their ideals for the sake of insider status and nominal influence upon government policy.

Unlike formal EMOs, EF! actions are not compromised by either a fear that they will lose their insider status, nor by the threat of sequestration of assets through legal action, because EF! has no formal organisation or assets.

EF! campaigns are always consistent with our slogan: 'No compromise in defence of the earth'. For example, when other groups have backed down to court injunctions or police threats, we refuse to be intimidated into inaction. EF!ers quite often have to break the law (especially thanks to the CJA) to achieve their ends, but this is not a drawback – it's fun!

(EF! UK website)

Unlike formal EMOs, the EF! information network can communicate plans for quick and flexible direct action responses to state or business initiatives because they have no committees to go through. They simply post details of a proposed action on the web or on an emailing list (usually the *Allsorts* list) so that those who wish to participate can get in touch, turn up or plan supportive actions. In this way, EF!'s lack of formal organisation is a conscious strategy allowing for rapid and radical responses.

Since the early 1990s, EF! activists have become much more concerned with the development of their own movement rather than being primarily concerned with how their activities influence EMOs. Nevertheless, their direct action strategy does seem to have been initially formed partly as a response to the short-comings of EMOs and in this sense this first version of the radical flank effect has been strategically significant. Moreover, EF! actions can be understood as having this radicalising affect on more mainstream groups, regardless of contemporary activists' intentions. FoE refused to co-operate with early EF! actions, seeing them as lacking public support and risking their funding. FoE even publicly disowned EF!ers' actions at the M3 protest at Twyford Down in 1992. The result of this was that between 1992 and 1995 there was overt hostility towards EMOs like FoE and Greenpeace amongst some direct activists. In response to EF!ers' criticisms, FoE has since tried to develop a more friendly approach to direct action. While they do not perpetrate it in the radical forms that EF!ers do, by 1995 they were training local groups in NVDA (Wall 1999: 156). They have also tried to support EF! actions in the media and have provided support to some protest camps. For example, during the battle over the Newbury bypass the FoE Newbury office dealt with the media side of direct actions as well as providing physical support to activists living in trees. At the Keele University 1997 Direct Action Conference, the FoE representative, Simon Festing, said FoE now sees the new wave of direct action as complementing their own activities.

While the vehement criticism of EMOs that followed FoE's actions at Twyford are no longer so prominent, when asked, many EF! activists are still quite dismissive of EMOs, especially interest groups like the National Trust which are seen as part of 'the establishment'.[5] Their participatory direct action ethos means they have not tended to be interested in groups or organisations with policy-oriented or conservation management type concerns. Nevertheless, some prominent EF! members maintained their Green Party membership after becoming involved in EF!, even after the moderate Green 2000 group had taken control of the party at national level (Wall 1999: 123) and groups like FoE and Alarm UK (who had links with direct activists from Road Alert!) participated in the Transport Activists' Roundtable forum linking EMOs focused upon transport issues (Rawcliffe 1998: 137). EF! activists themselves have also combined with Greenpeace and FoE activists on quite a few actions. This has been evident most recently in anti-GMO demonstrations at test sites. Greenpeace also sometimes give 'under the counter' financial assistance to local EF! groups or particular issue campaigns (anonymous interview at EF! summer gathering, 1999).

All this suggests that while EF!ers are often critical of EMOs, direct action and the more professional activities of EMOs may also complement one another strategically. In the second kind of radical flank effect, direct actions can be understood as making the reforming activities of EMOs more effective. The US EF! activists, Foreman and Haywood, used this kind of strategic thought in their seminal *Ecodefense*:

> The actions of monkeywrenchers invariably enhance the status of more 'reasonable' opponents. Industry considers the mainline environmentalists to be radical until they get a taste of real radical activism. Suddenly the soft-sell of the Sierra Club and other white-shirt-and-tie eco-bureaucrats becomes much more worthy of serious negotiation.
>
> (Foreman and Haywood 1987: 22)

The idea is that corporations and government become more willing to compromise with moderate environmentalists out of a wish to avoid bad publicity and to prevent their operational costs spiralling from delays, security costs and sabotage of machinery and equipment. We will look at the logic behind cost escalation more closely later. For now we can note that the shifting of the middle ground that is sought by the radical flank effect is achieved through public pressure on government and corporations. The perception of such public pressure comes, in large part, through media coverage of direct action. Thus, some activists have seen one of the goals of direct action to be to make symbolic challenges to hegemonic ideas, assumptions, social groups and practices in order to achieve media coverage and the perception of public pressure on government or corporations to make reforms.

Symbolic challenges

The most prominent form of direct action used by UK EF! has been the protest camp obstructing construction (most often of new roads). Simply by being there, protest camps escalate the political conflict over the particular project and bring it into the public eye. Activists normally realise that the particular sites that they occupy in this fashion are unlikely to be saved, but the physical process of eviction required to remove them is often photogenic and newsworthy. The process of eviction can also reveal issues of power to onlookers and for this reason EF!ers always try to prolong it by using whatever tactical innovations or delays they can come up with (see Doherty, this volume). Other environmental groups like the FoE might make a British or European high court challenge to the legality of a scheme; activists in trees or tunnels gratefully accept such opportunities to prolong their battles. The combination of state police and private security implicates the state as siding with big corporations and promoting economic growth, infrastructure extension and the destruction of countryside as being equal to 'development' or 'progress'. In this way, direct action can be understood as making symbolic challenges to dominant assumptions about the role of the state and about what 'development' or 'progress' are. Even when individual site 'battles' are lost, they are fought vehemently for their part in a longer environmental struggle; an activist at the Pollok Free State, for example, referred to the struggle against the M77 extension as like 'a battle in a war'.

Groups like The Land Is Ours (TLIO) and Reclaim The Streets (RTS) are integral parts of the direct action milieu that are both closely inter-linked and overlapping with the EF! network. Their main strategy is to take temporary control of private or public spaces to create what Bey (1996) has called temporary autonomous zones, (supposedly) free from state or corporate influence. RTS, as its name suggests, reclaims sections of streets. The busier the street, or even – as in July 1996 when 7,000 or more occupied the M41 in London – the motorway, the better, since these actions aim to disrupt the domination of city life by cars. In the case of TLIO, it is private land that is occupied in order to protest at its private ownership and the uses to which it is being put – there was a TLIO occupation of a GM crop site in 1999 for example. In both kinds of events there are attempts to prefigure the kind of future that activists want to see. TLIO occupations usually establish demonstrative permaculture plots, self-composting toilets and environmentally friendly temporary shelters. At the RTS occupation of the M41, part of the motorway was dug up and trees were planted and at another RTS event a section of the street was covered with turf and children were then encouraged to play on it. Rave music and carnival atmosphere dominates RTS parties; drumming and acoustic instruments are found at TLIO occupations. Furthest to the lifestyle and tribal end of the direct action spectrum have been the setting up of permaculture 'eco-village' projects like those of the recently established Natty Trust in Sussex. Such settlements can provide havens for some direct activists among like-minded people, where they replenish their energies in a rural location and enjoy alternative kinds of cultural practices like yoga or sweat-lodges. While for some, such activities might help them avoid the burn-out that plagues radical political movements, others seem to move on to lifestyle activism after a period of direct action protest.

Roseneil suggests that the word *strategy* has 'connotations of instrumental rationality, cost-benefit analysis and military-like planning' (Roseneil 1995: 98). In traditional conceptions of strategy, means are sharply separated from ends, which are specific and explicit. The classical strategist calculates the most effective means to achieve discrete and definable goals. EF! groups do work for specific objectives such as to prevent a particular road being built or to try to get an opencast mine or production plant shut down. But another part of EF! strategy is to make symbolic challenges to non-quantifiable, but widely held, assumptions or 'dominant codes' which underlie the particular projects undertaken in the name of 'progress'. Such symbolic challenges sometimes work in a prophetic manner (Melucci 1994: 125) where dominant ideas are revealed by the alternative embodied in activists' lifestyles or organisation. The idea of a prophetic symbolic challenge sheds light on some of the activities of RTS and TLIO described above. It is clear that EF! strategy involves cultural and identity-oriented, as well as instrumental, activity.

The Pollok Free State road protest camp in Glasgow provides an example of this. Tolkien imagery of Lothlorien harmony with nature and Mordor-like desolation was difficult to resist in seeing the camp alongside the M77 construction site. Photographers got shots of dreadlocked Free State participants, perhaps sporting Celtic symbols. Behind them would be carvings of indigenous Scottish birds and animals, a totem pole, or perhaps the 'in-nature' architecture of a tree house or the impressive camp tree-lodge. The aesthetics of the camp can be understood through Melucci's concept of 'prophecy'. 'The message is that the possible is already real in the direct experience of those proclaiming it. The struggle for change is already incarnate in the life ... of the group' (Melucci 1994: 125). The Pollok Free State's iconography was strategically designed to communicate to both visitors to the camp, and to a wider public through the media:

> So this is a message, everything that comes out of here is a message to the community that surrounds it because we are being watched ... I came down here two years ago with leaflets and a lot of talk; and most people won't read a leaflet. The majority of people will glance through it just because you have given it, but it won't penetrate ... so what we've done is make it inter-esting ... we have tried to make it a bit different ... . Crazy carvings and that attract people and they can make their own judgement about the situa-tion. But if we can get their attention for a small moment as they are passing through then it becomes apparent to them in view of their own instincts and intelligence that the forest is a beautiful place.
>
> (Free State and EF! activist Colin McCleod, interview, 1995)

The camp drew attention to what would be lost in the construction of the M77 project: mature woodland, a place where people could play or walk, and wildlife, indicated by carvings around the camp of extinct Scottish animals and birds. A carving of a chainsaw cutting into a tree trunk, inside which is a human, seemed to signal humans' dependency upon nature, the idea that damaging nature harms humans too, and the unity of social and environmental struggle that many direct activists ascribe to. By showing what 'could have been' and what was being lost in the construction of the M77, the Free State raised the wider issue of whether the extension of infrastructure and multiplication of construc-tion projects 'to create jobs' (or profit) really improves people's well-being. In this way, the camp, while ostensibly a single-issue campaign against a particular road, also played a prophetic role revealing and questioning the dominant encoding of development and progress. (For more on the Pollok Free State, see Seel 1997.)

Building a movement?

EF!ers are keen to try to 'empower' more people to take direct action in order to build a radical environmental movement with a participatory ethic. What gets called 'grass roots liaison' with local community groups is generally seen as the most prominent strand of this empowerment. Rawcliffe (1998: 133) describes how, 'strengthening grass-roots protest ... has begun to shift the emphasis of ... local campaigns from NIMBY on to a more environmental footing'. Protest sites seem to have gone some way towards breaking down barriers between 'crusty' eco-activists and 'respectable' middle-class professionals and other locals, since their common opposition to particular development schemes have created the basis for dialogue as part of the practical processes of fighting campaigns. Media stereotypes can be overcome by face-to-face contact with direct activists. Time and again, initially suspicious and worried residents cross boundaries by visiting a protest site, accepting the grimy cup of wood-smoke flavoured tea and discovering that grubby, dreadlocked or nose-pierced raggle-taggle youth can (gasp) hold a friendly, perhaps even perceptive, conversation.

At many sites, activists have used on-site rallies, 'open days' and guided tours of threatened land as techniques to enable locals to meet activists in a familiar, 'people-friendly' format. Throughout 1992, the Donga Tribe held many small events, such as a Teddy Bear's Picnic for children, to encourage locals to visit. That October, the Bishop of Winchester even held a service at the Donga camp on Twyford Down, which was attended by over 100 local people. The tribe, faces painted for the occasion, sang 'Jerusalem' with the flower-arranging, tweed-wearing backbone of the parish. The A30 Fairmile camp in Devon 'dug in' for two years before the eviction process and many activists who arrived at the beginning, expecting to be there for only a few months, found that they had time on their hands. Wanting to be more accepted by the local community and to communicate their values and social and political analyses to locals, they set up a group called the 'Green Dreamers'. They used their costume-making, music and storytelling skills to produce plays with environmental messages which children participated in at schools. In response to these kind of initiatives, locals have sometimes returned with children at the weekend to paint banners or, as at the Brewery Fields campaign pursued by North Wales EF!, to participate in a 'find the species' day. Through such processes, activists explain face-to-face why they are taking direct action and constructive dialogue can ensue.

At the end of a campaign, locals often witness evictions first-hand; this may involve violence by security guards or the breaking of safety laws by bailiffs, things that are rarely portrayed in the media. It is easy for activists and academics, who may already have some degree of scepticism about so-called 'development' or the social role of the state and the police, to forget that mass evictions can challenge an onlooker's acceptance of the benevolence of state agencies. At the M11 protest, a local lollipop lady was sacked for participating in a demonstration while wearing her uniform; she reported that, after thirty years of teaching respect for law and order, she no longer trusted the justice of the state.

The most important point strategically for EF!ers is that NIMBYs can be radicalised through contact with activists, or just discover that they do have some shared opinions. The importance of strong communities and the decentralisation of political power are standard anarchist themes shared by EF!ers. In the case of the Brewery Fields campaign against new housing on a green field site in Bangor, North Wales, direct action acted as a trigger for shared political agendas to be fully understood and articulated. The residents, almost without exception, rapidly began to understand the main issue for them as being one of reclaiming the local democratic process. They were politically empowered and forced the council to respect their wishes. Johan, a Pollok Free State activist, commented in an interview in 1995 that 'escalating the costs of Wimpey is … more of a side issue, … in a more lasting kind of way we want to affect the consciousness of the local people'. Residents first protested on NIMBY grounds, arguing, 'that Corkerhill would suffer whilst others would benefit' (Robinson 1998: 4). Contact with EF!ers at the Pollok Free State allowed local people to make connections between their situation and other types of environmental degradation in other parts of the world by talking about how their practical local concerns were tied into wider social, political and economic structures. Robinson (1998) presents interview and survey evidence to show that many locals who came into contact with direct activists perceived themselves as having been radicalised by the process. Direct action tactics, such as building tree-houses, were also taken on by some local campaigners, who even set up their own protest camp to fight alongside the Pollok Free State.[6]

Direct action protests like tree-sitting may be too radical and too legally and physically risky for many people, but EF!ers have tried to emphasise that such direct actions require all sorts of support roles and also positive lifestyle initiatives, alliance building and campaign work, which are not so risky, to complement them strategically. Tentative affiliations with other radical groups such as the Liverpool dockers have been initiated, but the EF! network is still only a small movement with 1,000 or, at the most, 2,000 frequently active members. Protest sites have made it easy for interested people to make contact with direct activists; those that liked what they found on sites sometimes later got involved in a local EF! group. But with the fall of the 'Roads for Prosperity' road-building programme, there are now fewer protest sites with activists living at them. Local EF! groups are not as easily approachable as protest sites, especially since many activists are concerned about infiltration by police, private investigators and journalists. This became a problem for EF! in the late 1990s; one response seems to have been to set up squat cafés which provide an alternative entry point into the movement.

While some local people who come into contact with protest sites may come to question the role of the state and the benefits of capitalist 'development', and a small number even become politically active in radical networks, for others the effect of contact with EF!ers may not be so radical. There are often vast divergences between direct activists and locals when it comes to overall philosophies, ideologies and ways of life. At many protest sites the relationship between direct activists and local campaigners may have been little more than a temporary coalition where locals motivated by NIMBY concerns co-ordinated with direct activists only because it helped them gain publicity for their campaign. One North Wales EF!er, for example, after canvassing door-to-door opinion about the proposed housing development on the Brewery Fields, was distressed to learn that several residents opposed the development because they had heard that the houses were for single mothers. At Mobbeley, in the affluent belt of North Cheshire, some of the locals who have supported protest camps against the proposed second runway for Manchester airport were motivated more by a concern about their house prices than with the global warming caused by air travel (Wain 1997: 1). (For more on local campaigners' relationships to direct action, see Cathles, this volume.)

Many activists are also aware of a common strategic shortfall in following their grassroots liaison through properly – after a site has been physically lost to developers, direct activists have tended to move on to new protest sites. A desire to improve and build upon grassroots liaison comes up repeatedly during discussions at EF! gatherings and other meetings like the 1999 'Gathering Visions Gathering Strength' conference.[7] But the movement's small numbers of committed activists limits the number of initiatives they can make with respect to both local campaigning and other types of outreach, such as that to other radical political groups. Organic vegetable box schemes, LETS and similar kinds of positive alternative local initiatives which EF!ers support in spirit as part of their aim to help the development of environmentally friendly lifestyles, tend to require large investments of time. If they got too involved in this sort of activity, EF! groups would risk neglecting high profile direct action protest and becoming part of mainstream environmentalism. Since such grassroots activity does not get media attention, it is more difficult to assess to what extent it is going on, but high profile direct action protests certainly seem to remain the mainstay of EF! activity. Direct action is more glamorous and exciting than grassroots campaigning, and it seems to fit better with activists' sense of their own identities. They perceive direct and immediate threats such as the planting of GM crops as being a more important priority, leading them to focus on the more specialised, confrontational and radical actions for which they are best known.

Live and direct

We suggested earlier that some EF! activists have seen direct action as a way of making symbolic challenges to dominant ideas and practices through the media attention they can attract. This was undoubtedly the case in the earlier years of EF!. However, throughout its short history in Britain, other sections of the EF! network have criticised the notion that direct actions should be deliberately aimed at achieving newspaper and television coverage. Since the mid-1990s, EF! activists have become considerably more hostile to both the media itself, and strategic perspectives that understand EF!'s influence as medium-oriented. In interview (anonymous, 1999), an EF! activist described this as the result of a learning process where experience had shown that newspaper and television coverage tends to exaggerate and sensationalise violent and lifestyle aspects, while trivialising the issues motivating protests (see Paterson, this volume). The majority of the EF! network now reject the idea that direct actions are performed as media spectacles to raise issues and create a climate conducive to reforms for EMOs. They are often unhappy about the way they are portrayed in the media:

> I feel a lot more comfortable being denounced accurately as a dirty, dole scrounging, anarchist than being lauded as someone trying to get publicity for their single issue concern in the hope that the government will do something to stop it. In the end I came to the conclusion that my whole outlook was so radically different from that of the mainstream media that it was a straight choice between being hated for what I am or loved for what I'm not.
>
> (*Do or Die* 1998: 36)

Neither do they see the mass media as in any way neutral, or equally open to different interests:

> The people who control the mass media have broadly the same outlook and some of the same interests as the people who own opencast sites and build roads. To get good coverage we risk pandering to their outlook in the mistaken belief that it represents the thoughts of the general public.
>
> (*Do or Die* 1998: 37)

One advantage of media coverage is seen as its potential to 'get people out of their armchairs' and down to protest sites (*Do or Die* 1998: 36; Seel 1997: 121, 125). But, in general, media attention is increasingly tolerated rather than sought after: 'Mainstream publicity is a bit like getting arrested. It is a fact of life and it is sometimes necessary, but it isn't the point and you don't make it happen for its own sake' (*Do or Die* 1998: 37).

Rather than being media-oriented, increasing numbers of EF!ers have preferred to understand their strategy as aiming for a more direct influence upon both environmentally unfriendly opponents and potential allies. A reviewer of the *Big Issue* book, *Gathering Force* (Brass and Koziell 1997), complains that it presents direct action as an effort to un-block 'silted up' democratic channels; 'a sort of pep-me-up tonic to rejuvenate British democracy' (*Do or Die* 1999: 139). This is seen as playing up liberal aspects of the direct action movement, suggesting that all direct activists want is better representation, while downplaying anarchist and anti-capitalist tendencies. 'This utterly naïve expectation that the state has any interest in listening to us ... demonstrates that the authors have no understanding of the state as having radically different interests to ourselves' (*Do or Die* 1999: 140). In one EF *Action Update* (July 1999, No. 60) an article suggests of the J18 City of London protest:

It was not a campaign or a message. It was an attempt to physically prevent the destructive machine processes of capital from going on. It was an act of self defence in a life or death struggle with those who kill to cling on to power and privilege.

RTS flyers and posters often state that, 'Direct action is not a last resort, it is a preferred way of doing things', and the same ethos is prevalent under EF! banners. Proudly adorning the cover of the 1999 *Do or Die*, for example, is a quotation from William Brigham, ex-chairman of Norfolk National Farmers' Union and the owner of a trashed GM site: 'This is not just about GMOs – it's about whether we want democratic government or anarchy.' Irony aside, EF!ers certainly do not believe that British government is democratic. Many seem to believe that political participation in direct actions organised on anarchist principles is a kind of direct democracy. We have seen in the previous section how EF!ers hope to influence and empower local campaigners through direct contact with them. Below we explore some of the other ways in which they hope to achieve change through live and direct influence.

Cost escalation

The goal of escalating the costs of those engaged in environmentally unsound projects has often been expressed as a strategy by EF!ers in Britain. In the campaign against the M77 extension through Pollok Park in Glasgow, for example, it was satirically proposed that 'Giving free play to the imagination, all manner of direct actions will be effected to act as a "market force"' (*Do or Die* 1995). The basis of the cost escalation strategy is that while corporations often do not want to understand the arguments or values of radical environmentalists, the one thing they do understand very well is a balance sheet. Thus, activists enfranchise their views directly, in terms of sterling costs. The 'Roads to Prosperity' road-building programme has experienced the brunt of direct action in Britain. Costs were escalated by as much as 20–25% at the Newbury bypass. Even some relatively small evictions have turned out to be very costly. In general, cost escalation is likely to have a more decisive effect when the scheme in question is not being funded by central government.

Pixieing

Abbey (1975) and Foreman and Haywood (1987) called covert sabotage of machinery, equipment, vehicles and buildings for the purposes of environmental protection 'ecotage'.[8] In Britain, it has become known as 'pixieing', and, when asked about such sabotage, EF!ers will often publicly attribute it to pixies. This draws playfully upon pagan influences and portrays the earth, or earth-beings, as consciously against 'development', giving protesters the moral high ground. Drawing upon the example of 1980s US EF!, some British activists see covert sabotage as a legitimate part of the EF! repertoire of actions. Wall (1999: 60) notes, for example, that the South Downs and South East London groups supported covert sabotage having also been influenced by the British animal liberation movement. In contrast, activists drawn from peace networks were uneasy about the use of covert repertoires. They preferred open and publicly accountable forms of sabotage, which they saw as more useful in making symbolic challenges. At the 1992 summer gathering, it was agreed that a new group called the Earth Liberation Front (ELF) would carry out covert sabotage. Civil disobedience would go under the EF! banner, but it was agreed that, publicly, EF!ers would 'neither condemn nor condone' covert sabotage, and that EF! and ELF would be mutually supportive rather than competitive.

Disruption

'The earth is not dying, it is being murdered and the people doing it have names and addresses' (EF! slogan). Believing strongly that they hold the moral high ground, EF!ers sometimes confront the companies that they see as representing an example or worst instance of wider practices exploiting people and the environment on those companies' own territory. In the 1995 picketing of Shell stations, for example, they sought to emphasise the connection between pollution and car use in Britain and environmental degradation and human rights abuses in Oginiland, Nigeria. In 1997, an Undercurrents spokesperson on Radio 4's Afternoon Shift said: 'You don't just sit on the fringes ... you go into the castle.' This happens when company offices and equipment are occupied and sometimes damaged. The intention, it seems, is to bring home to individuals working for particular organisations that their individual actions are promoting a development that others find morally reprehensible and anti-social. In some cases this may be done in a good-willed spirit of moral appeal; in others it may be done more aggressively (but very rarely violently) to make individuals face close proximity, real life (not paper) opposition. But even if such actions do not actually influence the individuals involved in particular developments, they are still valued by activists for their disruptive and cost-escalating qualities.

Radicalisation

Systemic critique

It is interesting to note that British EF! has articulated an increasingly systemic critique as the 1990s have progressed. A letter in *Do or Die* in 1995 (72–73) argued, 'If we don't fight against the totality of the system by understanding a campaign in the context of the wider struggle, capitalism will just rear its ugly head elsewhere.' The last couple of years of the decade in particular saw British EF! articulate a critique of capitalism itself where, in the early 1990s, they were more likely to communicate about particular issues. In EF! literature it has become more commonplace to read statements like: 'Capitalism is at the heart of our ecological and social problems ... London Animal Action state that "animal abuse is as transnational as capital" and that goes for genetics and the arms trade and everything else too' (J18 flyer in EF! *Action Update* Issue 58). At the 1999 summer gathering, an (anonymous) activist said in interview that this systemic critique had existed earlier but had been implicit rather than articulated.[9]

McKay (1998: 12) has accurately documented some anti-intellectualism and anti-academic attitudes within the 1990s wave of environmental direct action. At the outset of this chapter we stressed that EF! has an action-based strategy; this remains the case. But at recent EF! national gatherings there has been an increasing willingness to discuss theoretical questions about the nature of 'the system' EF!ers oppose. From 1998, an annual Winter Moot has been set up to make space for such theoretical and long-term strategic discussion. In 1999, the Summer Gathering, which has tended in the past to eschew theoretical debates, also had a workshop on 'Targeting Capitalism'. The questions the workshop aimed to ask were: '(1) What do we mean by capitalism?; (2) Is capitalism "the heart of the beast" or is this a simplified analysis?; (3) Is this analysis alienating? [to the general public]; (4) How do we target capitalism?'. Some defined 'capitalism' as private ownership of the means of production and others saw it more vaguely as encompassing all forms of hierarchy and patriarchy. While being influenced by Marxian ideas about the profit accumulation imperative inherent in capitalist organisation, the superstructural role of the state as an adjunct to capital accumulation and mass culture as heavily influenced by commodity fetishism, those EF!ers who have started to espouse a revolutionary perspective do so in anarchist terms. It is not just capitalism, but all forms of hierarchy that they oppose; in the long term they would not seek to take over the state but to destroy it. The workshop ended in typical EF! fashion with a pressing sense of the need to get back to the practicalities of fighting big business rather than talking about it:

> So we're against capitalism 'and that' then?! [amused agreement]
> We're in agreement that we are against a totality ['of oppressions', 'of the system'], so shall we discuss that at the Winter Moot?
> Can it be a practical discussion of the totality and how to hit it?

Moves towards militancy

EF! has recently become more militant in its rhetoric. We use the term 'militant' here to mean accepting violence as a necessary part of struggle. Much NVDA has a radical agenda and radical tactics. Office occupations, climbing bulldozers and spending weeks down tunnels are all radical and predominantly non-violent. Economic sabotage is also often undertaken by activists – like the Ploughshares women who damaged Hawk jets in 1997 – who explicitly define themselves as non-violent. But crucially, the term 'NVDA' is used less in contemporary EF! literature. What was known as a 'spiky–fluffy' (violence–non-violence) debate was common in the mid-1990s, but is now rarely heard at EF! gatherings. However, mailing lists such as *n30@listbot.com* do include some debate about violence, and many participants still seem to favour a predominantly non-violent position while supporting damage to property and the individual's right to defend oneself against attack. On its own this is not that significant a shift, since many EF! activists in the early 1990s would instinctively defend themselves when facing assault by security guards, as evidenced by fighting and scuffles at Twyford Down in 1992. The dropping of the claim to a strict non-violence is thus partly just an acceptance of what was happening anyway. However, more significant is that non-violent perspectives have increasingly been dismissed as 'counterrevolutionary' or 'liberal' in debates at EF! national gatherings by a number of prime movers within EF!. Some non-violent activists have become tired of such refrains and this rhetoric of violence may have been a factor contributing to a recent shift of activists into other, more explicitly, non-violent networks such as the GEN, and into positive lifestyle initiatives like the setting up of eco-villages or co-operatives. At the risk of propounding stereotypes, it is nevertheless interesting to note that there have been rather less of the dreadlocked 'tribes' and more 'urban anarchists' with short hair and black clothing at recent EF! gatherings. Gone are the days of holding hands to 'attune' before a meeting, and at the 1999 summer gathering the 'healing area' was deserted in comparison with previous years.

Militant rhetoric has also fed through into actions in 1999. The 1999 EF! *Action Update* described the J18 protests as 'an attempt to physically prevent the destructive machine processes of capital from going on'. There was a physical attempt by a small number of activists to storm the LIFFE (London International Financial Futures Exchange) building, which was repelled by security guards and traders at the top of the escalator leading to the first floor. The first group of (non-riot) police that tried to get into the LIFFE building while this was taking place retreated after bottles and cans were thrown at them. Some activists later expressed respect for those who, on 18 June, had thrown stones and bottles or fought with advancing riot police lines because they saw this as 'defensive violence' vital to be able to 'hold the space' territorially.

EF!ers' anarchism has an individualist quality in that there is little attempt to make members abide by common codes on what are and are not acceptable tactics and conduct. The small affinity groups in which EF!ers often conduct direct actions decide by consensus on their boundaries before they carry out an action, but in bigger protests such collective agreements on what is acceptable do not exist. While this may be empowering for individual activists, it can be off-putting for other participants. Some found J18 exhilarating, others may avoid such demonstrations in the future because they do not agree with violence. While the anarchist ethos can empower some people to make up their own kinds of direct actions, it can also put others off getting involved because they see some actions performed under the EF! banner as being too militant or because they perceive EF! activists as protest 'specialists' involved in legally and physically risky tactics unsuited to those with children or concerned about their occupational security or personal safety.

There has, however, been negligible violent environmental direct action in Britain in the past decade (see Rootes, this volume), and the J18 and N30 violence of 1999 may not be sustained. It is also important to note that not all EF!ers subscribe to the need for defensive violence; for example, the North Wales group remains committed to non-violence. The violence–non-violence issue is tied in with the wider issue of the future of EF!. Some activists obviously envisage the EF! network as a small and covert network of anarchist 'cells' perpetrating attacks on corporate property. However, these voices are also countered by others who are keen to avoid 'the dangers of being forced underground' (anonymous, EF! workshop, 1999) by the state through having a violent agenda.[10] Instead, these activists want to build on grassroots connections and they emphasise the strategic need for mass participation.

Conclusion

'EF!' is the banner of a network in which strategy is not unified, homogeneous, fixed or clear. Respect for difference and a fierce belief in the independence of local groups underlie a refusal to lay out a unified national strategy. This lack of unification means EF! does not have a traditionally defined strategy. The activists in the EF! network turn over, and, as they do so, EF!'s collective identity and strategic praxis is renegotiated and changes emphasis. But we have suggested that, despite the heterogeneity of strategic thought in the EF! network, it would be wrong to suggest that EF! does not have a strategy. Local groups' autonomy is itself actually a sustained strategic principle that makes EF! both organisationally prophetic of the decentralised, directly democratic future its activists want to see, and more innovative, flexible and unpredictable, and therefore harder to police.

Refusal to define a single primary motivation for direct action has helped to make the EF! network inclusive of different kinds of direct activists. But, whilst an affective solidarity is achieved through collective protest action, the different kinds of strategic reasoning that we have explored do not always simply fall together in easy synthesis. There are contradictions, for example, between desires to propound an increasingly radical systemic critique and militant methods, and others' wish to build an inclusive formation in which local opinion can be courted, participation can be increased and alliances built with other groups. The lowest common denominator of what EF! activists are unified by is their belief in, and actual taking of, direct action. An emphasis on action and scepticism about the efficacy of prolonged strategic debates has allowed diverse motivations and reasoning to co-exist thus far without the serious internal divisions or constant splintering that have plagued some radical movements.

The predilection for action rather than words remains in EF!, but an increasingly articulated form of anarchism has emerged alongside an anarchism of the deed. At the turn of the century, British EF! is building upon its links with overseas activists in Europe and the US and is ambitiously focused upon 'the downfall of global capitalism', even while its active numbers have dwindled a little. Whether a systemic focus will be sustained and developed to contribute to the formation of a counter-hegemonic twenty-first-century environmental movement remains to be seen.

Notes

1 As of the 1999 edition, *Do or Die* became independent of EF!.
2 This stage of the TEA research was carried out by Ben Seel, Sandy Miller and Debbie Adams, and supervised by Chris Rootes and Dieter Rucht. The TEA research is based in the Centre for the Study of Social and Political Movements at the University of Kent and funded by the EC, contract number: ENV4-CT97–0514. On this research, see also Rootes, this volume.
3 Email lists are set up for discussion of issues such as strategy and personal motivation. Even here, however, some activists seem to be suffering from information overload and have little time for reading these.
4 FoE has local groups of environmental activists, but Andrew Lees, FoE Campaigns Manager from 1989, was hostile to radical FoE grassroots activism, seeing it as endangering FoE's professional reputation (Wall 1999: 122). Even though Greenpeace had never claimed to encourage grassroots activity, many EF! activists are also hostile to both its hierarchical organisation and its co-operation with some government and corporate activities.
5 The National Trust, in particular, has come under fire because of sale of its land at sites like Pollok Park in Glasgow (to make way for the M77 extension) and North Cheshire (to make way for Manchester airport's second runway).
6 Direct activists have been vociferously supported by several other local communities, apart from the examples mentioned here – for example, South Wales ex-mining communities in campaigns against opencast mining.
7 Gathering Visions Gathering Strength was, in its own words, 'A gathering to bring together people from different movements and communities to explore self organising for radical social change'.
8 Abbey pioneered the idea of covert sabotage as a strategy for radical environmentalists through his novel *The Monkey Wrench Gang* (1975).
9 She added that personally she finds the new systemic focus on 'global capitalism' disempowering because she feels her group's direct actions will have so little effect on such a megalith. Similar examples of dissenting voices could be found on most issues in EF!.
10 The 1999 Prevention of Terrorism Bill aims to redefine terrorism to include, 'the use of serious violence against persons *or property*, or the threat to use such violence to intimidate or coerce the government, the public or any section of the public for political, religious or ideological ends'. The Bill also proposes a new criminal offence of being 'connected with' such terrorism. It is clearly plausible that the implementation of such measures could force EF! groups further underground, especially if they wish to pursue a militant agenda.

Bibliography

Abbey, E. (1975, republished 1991) *The Monkey Wrench Gang*, London: Robin Clark.
Bey, H. (1996) *TAZ: The Temporary Autonomous Zone, Ontological Anarchy, Poetic Terrorism*, Camberley: Green Anarchist Books.
Bookchin, M. (1995) *Re-Enchanting Humanity*, New York: Cassell.
Brass, E. and Koziell, P. (1997) *Gathering Force: DIY Culture – Radical Action for those Tired of Waiting*, London: The Big Issue.
Do or Die (1995) *Do or Die: Voices of Earth First!*, Vol. 5.
—— (1998) *Do or Die: Voices from Earth First!*, Vol. 7.
—— (1999) *Do or Die*, Vol. 8.
EF! UK web site: http://www.snet.co.uk/ef/

Foreman, D. and Haywood, B. (eds) (1987) *Ecodefense: A Field Guide to Monkeywrenching*, Tucson, Arizona: Ned Ludd.

Hetherington, K. (1998) *Expressions of Identity: Space, Performance and the Politics of Identity*, London: Sage.

McKay, G. (ed.) (1998) *DIY Culture: Party and Protest in Nineties Britain*, London: Verso.

Melucci, A. (1994) 'A strange kind of newness: what's "new" in NSMs?', in E. Larana, H. Johnston and J.R. Gusfield (eds) *New Social Movements: From Ideology to Identity*, Philadelphia: Temple University Press.

—— (1996) *Challenging Codes: Collective Action in the Information Age*, Cambridge: Cambridge University Press.

Pepper, D. (1993) *Eco-Socialism: From Deep Ecology to Social Justice*, London: Routledge.

Plows, A. (1997) 'Roads protest/Earth First and "multi issue" new social movements: beyond the dualisms of the "red/green" debate', in C. Barker and M. Tyldesley (eds) *Alternative Futures and Popular Protest 3: Conference Papers*, Vol. 2, Manchester: Manchester Metropolitan University.

Rawcliffe, P. (1998) *Environmental Pressure Groups in Transition*, Manchester: Manchester University Press.

Robinson, A. (1998) 'From NIMBY to NOPE: residues of reform on Glasgow's Southside', in C. Barker and M. Tyldesley (eds) *Alternative Futures and Popular Protest IV*, Vol. 2, Manchester: Manchester Metropolitan University.

Roseneil, S. (1995) *Disarming Patriarchy*, Milton Keynes: Open University Press.

Rucht, D. (1990) 'The strategies and action repertoires of new movements', in R.J. Dalton and M. Kuechler (eds) *Challenging the Political Order: New Social and Political Movements in Western Democracies*, Cambridge: Polity Press, 156–175.

Seel, B. (1997) 'Strategies of resistance at the Pollok Free State road protest camp', *Environmental Politics* 6, 4: 108–139.

Snow, D. and Benford, R. (1992) 'Master frames and cycles of protest' in A.D. Morris and C. Mueller (eds) *Frontiers in Social Movement Theory*, New Haven/London: Yale University Press.

Wain, G. (1997) 'Keys to the feel-good factor', *ECOS* 18, 1: 1.

Wall, D. (1999) *Earth First! and the Anti-roads Movement*, London: Routledge.

7 'It's just not natural'?

Queer insights on eco-action

Wendy Maples

Radical eco-protests such as those engaged in by Earth First! (EF!) or Reclaim the Streets are significant political movements in the period of advanced capitalism. Eco-activism, as a diffuse, decentralised and non-hierarchical, mutable and diverse set of practices challenges the status quo and disrupts conventional conceptions of political engagement and thereby constitutes an important aspect of contemporary politics. In this chapter, I accept the premise that the current historical period (described as the period of 'postmodernity' or, less contentiously, 'advanced capitalism') constitutes a distinctive epoch that is evident in cultural, political and economic divergences – as well as continuities – with previous periods. I take as given that something called 'politics' is still relevant in this period,[1] though I contend, with others in this volume, that some of the widely held conceptualisations of politics must be reconsidered. Connected to this is the need to reconsider 'eco-identity' as a social marker and lived experience of contingency, belonging and difference and, as such, an important cultural and political formation.

Other theorists have sought to explore the identity of the eco-activist asking: In what ways is eco-activism developed through the experiences of activists 'on-site'? What are the possibilities for expressing an identity organised around ecological concerns? These are important questions. Authors such as Maffesoli and Hetherington have developed intriguing insights regarding the identity formation of 'protest performances'. They see the identity formation of eco-activists as contiguous with that of, for instance, green consumers or vegetarians. However, as Szerszynski contends, these analyses are not adept at 'discriminating between the public performance of protest and the more general performance of cultural memberships ... [nor have they] the capacity to acknowledge the full social and political significance of contemporary protests' (Szerszynski 1999: 220). Though there may be only a fine line between the performance of cultural memberships and that of public protest, Szerszynski is right to suspect the limitations of these understandings of 'identity formation' with regard to eco-protest.

There is something compelling about eco-protest that speaks of an ecological identification – or, as Dave Foreman would have it, the decision to 'stand ... on the side of the bears' (Foreman 1991: 107) – as well as producing 'new meanings for ourselves as persons and as citizens' (Szerszynski 1998: 2) which, as

Szerszynski argues, 'should be seen as "signs" to society as a whole' (Szerszynski 1998: 2).[2] This connection between identity formation and a publicly articulated politics suggests the need to consider the eco-activist as a 'cultural figure' (*vide* Seidman)[3] and identity and politics as formed discursively through everyday life, juridical codes, popular culture, etc. This brings us to a different sort of question: What is the significance of eco-activism as a politics in the period of advanced capitalism?

This can be analysed in a number of ways, but I will contend that a very useful way of understanding the politics of radical eco-action is by reconsidering the concept of identity and the wider political context of the present historical moment – as explored by what has come to be known as 'queer theory'. The critical rearticulation of politics and identity by theorists such as Judith Butler, Nancy Fraser, Shane Phelan, Steven Seidman, Stanley Aronowitz, and others writing within the field of queer theory, suggests the possibility of analyses not only of political formations organised around sexuality, sex and gender, but other 'new' political formations as well.

This chapter does not seek to reconcile the ideas of queer theory with those of ecologism: instead the aim is to consider how queer theorists' analysis of political identity formation, explication of collectivity and perspectives on 'political legitimacy' might inform an understanding of the political significance of direct eco-action. I suggest that eco-activism has potential to challenge critically dominant conceptions of political activism and to rearticulate the political in the 'postmodern' period. I consider the significance of eco-activism as a forum of collective identity formation. The prime considerations of the chapter, then, are identity, collectivity and the implications of their reconceptualisation for contemporary politics. I begin by exploring some of the problematics of an 'ecological identity'.

When I was ten ...

When I was ten and living in the USA, I wrote to the President of the United States, Richard Nixon, asking what, exactly, he was doing about pollution. In reply I received a letter thanking me for my concerns, pamphlets explaining the roles of the various government departments with environmental responsibilities, and booklets, aimed at a youth audience, with suggestions about how 'we kids' could do our bit to save the planet.

I noticed that Nixon had not signed that letter himself. The pamphlets were full of platitudes and statistics but didn't really say what was being done. The suggestions for how we kids could save the planet were patronising and limited to encouraging us to recycle glass and getting our parents to warm up the car engine so that, when driving, fuel use was more efficient. Although I was pleased to have received a parcel from the President, I therewith developed a sense of why my parents were not fans of 'the most powerful man on the planet'.

Around this time the first 'Earth Day' was celebrated and, on some level, my anxiety about the environment and despair with the government was corroborated. But at the same time, I had doubts about the 'real' importance of environmental concern.

As a white Anglo-American[4] and (regardless of my liberal-socialist parents' financial struggles) a member of the aspirant middle classes, my early concern with the environment was part of a matrix of social conscience concerns, mostly organised under the liberal discourse of 'rights', such as animal rights, education rights, nuclear weapons (right to be free from) and equal rights for women and blacks. I came to understand that each of these issues was separate: concerns with 'nature' or the environment on one side, and 'social' concerns on the other; each requiring a different set of solutions and each needing to be approached with segregate goals in mind. I was aware that black people were disproportionately poor and that poor people were disproportionately subject to polluted environments: but I understood poverty, pollution and racism as coincidental, not institutionally contingent.

I gathered that my subject position (white, middle class, etc.) would 'naturally' lead me away from some concerns and towards others. My gender allowed me to speak with feeling and some authority about women's rights: but this marked the full extent of my 'authentic subjectivity' with regard to those issues falling under the category of 'social'. It was apparent that this authenticity was conferred by dint of the essential nature and oppression of my sex. Other aspects of my identity, situating me firmly within the ranks of the dominant majority, were to all intents and purposes non-issues as there was evidently little need to concern myself with the 'rights' of the middle class or whites.

'Authenticity', like 'ethnicity', was somehow the preserve of 'minority' or politically recognised groups. The dominant liberal discourse of the day meant that the prime goal prescribed for such groups was 'equality' or (individual) 'rights'. The anthropocentrism of this liberal discourse relegated a concern with the environment to secondary status: it was inappropriate to speak of environmental 'rights' and, moreover, for the category of 'nature' or 'the environment', there was no authentic subjectivity of which, or from which, to speak. Even with the continuance of environmental campaigns through the 1970s and 1980s, and a number of important victories for environmentalists during this period, environmental issues lacked the authenticity, and therefore credibility or legitimacy, of other 'new social movement' concerns.

In retrospect, this was in some way compounded by the rise of identity politics in the 1980s. Here again, authenticity was a paramount attribute of engagement with issues of identity. And though the scope of concern had widened with, for example, many middle-class authors exploring, as I have just done, their anxiety regarding their identity, their desire to affiliate with the underdog, or grasping at some long-forgotten history of oppression, much of the early identity work still relied on a claim to authenticity. The increasingly conservative discourses of the late 1970s and early 1980s encouraged me to believe that my concerns about the environment persisted in part because, as a white, middle-class, liberal 'do-gooder', I had nothing else to complain about.

But in the early 1970s, I was a girl who felt entitled to write to the President and who, as a prospective voter and young citizen, expected a reply. I was annoyed at being fobbed off with slickly designed pamphlets. I went on anti-Nuke vigils, protested against vivisection, signed petitions against toxic waste dumping and, despite an impressive lack of artistic skill, drew flowers and trees and wrote poems about nature on the walls of our garage.

The distance of years has not eliminated the inclination to cringe at these memories. But there is something more to it than embarrassment at youthful naïveté. There is also the defensiveness of feeling that protest from a position of apparent social or cultural privilege is somehow secondary and the residual sense that these concerns lacked the credibility conferred by culturally recognised 'authenticity'.

Identity: queer theory and the constitutedness of eco-protest

Other authors in this collection have discussed what it means to be an eco-activist (Seel and Plows) and have suggested that identity formations occur in relation to the constituency of the protest. In other words, people may come to identify themselves *in situ* as 'protesters' or 'activists' and, like the Dongas at Twyford Down, may make deeper identifications with particular actions. This identification is easily recognised as not one born of an ostensibly 'authentic' or 'essential' subjectivity: unlike 'race' or gender, it is evidently not 'fixed' at birth, nor is legitimacy conferred by dint either of centrality/domination or marginality/oppression. Nevertheless, as argued elsewhere in this volume, the identity formation of the eco-activist is a significant one. The 'elective identity', as Kevin Hetherington terms it, establishes important allegiances. Hetherington rightly emphasises that:

> the logic of a non-essentialist view of identity, and the politics associated with it, is that we are all making choices about identity, even within the oppressive conditions of marginality, just as there are always constraints when we make those choices ... . Acts of resistance are choices, whether they be choices about fighting racist violence born out of one's own experiences or about trying to live a life in which one is responsible towards the environment ... . Alongside ... expressions of identity politics associated with issues such as race, class and gender, we also see ... an identity politics around issues of the environment, animal rights, vegetarianism ... . It is not a question of making a judgment whether one is more real or authentic than the other but about recognising that the politics of identity is broader than issues of class, gender and ethnicity ...
>
> (Hetherington 1998: 27–28)

Hetherington usefully argues against an essentialist view of identity: and yet, he differentiates 'elective' identities (Hetherington 1998: 6, 49, 101). Furthermore, this implicit abrogation of 'authenticity' is apparent both in mainstream and 'identity politics'. Certainly, the politics of identity are 'broader than issues of class, gender and ethnicity', but it is necessary to acknowledge that the narrow conception of identity is the prevailing one. The 'givens' of birth, and the non-congenital development of other affinities are commonly seen as at odds: one an entitlement, the other implicitly less significant, 'elective', 'made up'.

The idea that any identity, 'elective' or otherwise, might be essentially fixed, or 'naturally' determined, is most persuasively challenged by queer theorists.[5] 'Queer theory' has been concerned to express the complexity of identity formation and contingent politics of sex, gender and sexuality. Of course, central to this questioning of identity for queer theorists is the construction of sexual identities. But, for my purposes here, it is the broader implications of 'queer' thought that are significant.[6] According to Phelan, '[u]ltimately, queer theory's target is identity itself – the assumption of unity or harmony or transparency within persons or groups' (Phelan 1997: 2). For what is proposed is a deeply politicised conception of identity, one which challenges essentialisms and points to the levels at which even the most intimate aspects of identity are (at least in part) constructed through cultural and social expectations, institutions, discourses. More broadly speaking, queer theory throws into question assumed certainties regarding identities and posits the possibility of empowering rearticulations in social, cultural and political life.

Certainly, there are crucial differences in the politics and implications of 'identities' organised around environmentalism or ecologism, on the one hand, and gay, lesbian or 'queer' identities on the other. However, there are also similarities between the 'constitutedness' (*vide* Butler)[7] of these two subject positions that may shed light on the ways in which, more broadly, we are able to understand the changing meanings of radical political activism, and perhaps politics more widely, in Britain in the 1990s and into the new millennium.

First, though, a brief historical note is necessary. Without dispute, histories of environmental and gay activism in Western democratic societies long precede the 1960s, but a political sea change is often considered to have occurred in the 1960s, with a flowing towards the creation and recognition of a range of 'new social movements', including lesbian and gay politics and environmentalism. NSMs marked a move away from singular class-based politics, seeking recognition for other fields of struggle that cut across simple, bipolar distinctions of, say, 'left' and 'right'.

For theorists of the new social movements, the significance of (social and political) 'rights' was seen as inherently attached to 'identity' (in an early formulative phase, literally the identification of marginalised social and 'politically legitimate' groups), and in the 1970s and 1980s 'identity politics' came to influence 'progressive' political agendas. Unified identities, constructed in opposition,[8] suggested another form of political expression. No longer could 'rights' be understood as merely about juridical equality, they became understood in terms of what Judith Butler has identified as 'contingent foundations'; the underlying cultural and social assumptions which enable the very establishment of inequalities (Butler 1992: 7, 16). Identity politics sought to challenge these often punitive assumptions regarding the 'essential' nature of different social groups, discrediting normative social and political approaches.

A rejection of essentialism was an important part of the identity politics project of the late 1980s. And yet, in terms of both mainstream and self-representation, normative constructions and essentialisations still dog many social groups, environmentalists and ecologists, lesbians and gays among them. Unsurprisingly, mainstream representations of environmentalists have tended to polarised stereotypes (fastidious NIMBYs or fanatical eco-warriors),[9] but even within the 'movement', subtle arguments or nuanced issues have been glossed, often in the name of clarity or a united front.

But this is a false unity, an obfuscating 'clarity'. For instance, the home truth that green politics are neither left nor right – that is, they cut across conventional political divides – is not very satisfying, while the assertion, initially made by die Grünen in their claim for seats in the Bundestag, that Greens are 'in front' merely begs the question: 'In front of what?'. 'The opposition' is not always evident. Even if it were, this should not be taken to predicate a need for a unified collectivity of protest. Different parts of the movement have accordingly approached environmentalism in different ways.

On the other hand, the lack of 'eco-unity' may be read as the success of liberal individualistic thought and the hegemonic machinations of capitalism. Throughout the 1980s, in fact, many environmentalists were concerned by the subsumation of 'green' politics into 'green consumerism'. They feared that eco-politics might be reduced to mere 'lifestyle' options, and that a sincere concern with the environment or ecologism could be supplanted by an individualised set of 'shallow' practices – for which new corporations (or old companies with new labels) were keen to provide products and services. The public assertion of environmental concern in the form of purchases from the Body Shop, or trips (in the car) to the recycling centre, the ingestion of the odd organic vegetable, can be seen as mere placation of 'real' environmentalist demands and a *reductio ad absurdum* of ecologism.

Interestingly, in the literature on queer politics a similar scenario is described. Chris Woods, for instance, suggests that for gays and lesbians the apparent empowerment of the 'new consumerism' is more accurately seen as exploitation rather than as a recognition of the power of the 'pink pound'. More stridently, Woods argues that '[t]he commodification of homosexuality has less to do with the politics of liberation or community than with the cynical creation and maintenance of a gullible niche market' (Woods 1995: 41).

> By implication, gays and lesbians who opt for a commodified lifestyle merely trade one closet for another: As wider society begins to question the values which bind it, perversely many homosexuals seek comfort in a poor replica of a discredited past, whether in the glorification of consumerism or a misguided belief that Britain's non-democracy can deliver us from evil.
>
> (Woods 1995: 60)

There are undoubtedly problems with Woods's invective – not least his distress at what he identifies as the depoliticisation of queer politics – which cannot be tackled here. Yet his concerns echo and illuminate some of the issues raised by environmentalists, ecologists and greens about the political role and viability of 'eco-protests'.

One starting point is the use of the term 'queer'. While Woods suggests that the 'queering' of politics is a 'nebulous' move, 'not [organised] around ideological goals ... but upon a politics of transgression for its own sake' (Woods 1995: 29), other theorists and activists have embraced the term, arguing that it offers a collective yet mutable identification. This reclamation of a term of abuse is analogous to the reclamation inscribed in phrases like 'Black is Beautiful' or, perhaps more ambiguously, 'Girl Power'. But significantly, 'queer' provides not only a rallying cry ('We're Here, We're Queer, Get Used To It') but also a political – and cultural – perspective. More to the point, 'queer theory', 'queer politics' and 'queer activism' do not describe a singular, fixed perspective, but instead what Judith Butler, writing in another context, analyses as 'constitutedness' (Butler 1992). This concept is not an essentialising or determining one: mutability is inscribed in the continuous recontextualisation of the lived experience. The 'unity' of 'queer' is, ideally, a 'provisional' one. In proposing a coalitional feminist politics, Butler argues that this 'antifoundational approach' (Butler 1990: 15) can be radically transformative and disruptive of the 'insistence in advance on coalitional "unity" ... which assumes that solidarity, whatever its price, is a prerequisite for political action'. Butler asks, rightly: '[W]hat sort of politics demands that kind of advance purchase on unity?' (ibid.: 14).

Alexander Doty evokes this sense when explaining his use of the term 'queer':

> I ... wanted to find a term with some ambiguity, a term that would describe a wide range of impulses and cultural expressions, including space for describing and expressing bisexual, transsexual, and straight queerness ... . My uses of the terms queer readings, queer discourses, and queer positions ... are attempts to account for the existence and expression of a wide range of positions within culture that are queer or non-, anti-, or contrastraight. I am using the term queer to mark a flexible space for the expression of all aspects of non- (anti-, contra-) straight cultural production and reception. As such, this cultural 'queer space' recognizes the possibility that various and fluctuating queer positions might be occupied whenever anyone produces or responds to culture.
>
> (Doty 1995: 72–73)

This way of understanding collectivity – as a set of practices, taken up in a variety of 'spaces', as well as a sense of self, contingent upon other practices, contexts, senses of self – may be useful in understanding the collectivities of eco-activism.

Earth First!: a 'unity in flight'

The eco-protests of Reclaim the Streets, EF!, and various direct action campaigns, provide ideal examples of 'unities in flight' (see Young 1995: 201) and, as such, are expressions of postmodern identity politics. These radical environmental protests establish collectivities over a limited period of time; they are dispersed and reconstituted in different locations and for different purposes, but maintain a sense of contingent 'unity'.

Not so long ago, EF! was the shining light of the radical environmental movement with a plethora of actions, and adherent activists, the rapid evolution of new groups and an impressive sense of achievement. EF! protest styles such as 'digger diving', 'tree-sitting', and the amassing of eco-bodies, remain popular on-site tactics. But EF! had shaky beginnings in the UK. The first ever gathering was marred by anxiety: this anxiety stemmed from a perceived need to present a 'united front' in the mainstream public sphere.

Fisons and the first Earth First! gathering

The phone rings: it's a journalist from a national newspaper. He has heard that machinery at Fisons' peat works has been badly damaged by eco-activists protesting against the decimation of the last remaining English peat bogs. No, he's not interested in any comments about peat or the environment. No, he doesn't want to wait to talk with anyone who might know more about the 'issues'. What he wants is a quote from EF! about the 'criminal damage' to Fisons' property. No philosophising, just the answer to the question: Is EF! 'for it' or 'against it'?

On the day the Fisons' works were attacked EF! was a barely nascent group. The following day, EF! had its first 'national gathering'. Between twenty and thirty people camped in a clearing under a chalk cliff near Brighton to talk about building an EF! movement in the UK. Before the logistics of this endeavour could be addressed, however, there was the matter of Fisons – or rather, the matter of the media interest in EF!'s reaction to the 'attack' on Fisons. A lengthy debate resulted in the adoption of the phrase 'EF! neither condemns nor condones' the destruction of property used to destroy the environment. In making this statement, EF! established a unity of sorts: a near universal agreement about the importance of presenting a single voice to the media. This small evidence of unity was hard won and was regularly contested by individuals who argued that direct action would sometimes necessitate 'criminal damage': of course, therefore, we did sometimes condone this destruction if it averted the more heinous destruction of the countryside.

A second, and more important unity was, however, forged over the weekend: the unity of commitment. 'We' – and talk of 'we' increased as day turned to night – were committed to the ideal of 'Earth First!' and wanted to do actions in the name of 'Earth First!' and to find others committed to the aims of 'Earth First!' and let the wider public know that 'Earth First!' styles of direct action were to be an important part of the environmentalists' political repertoire in the UK.

'We' sought to challenge the conventions of mainstream politics in two distinct ways: first, we wished to prioritise environmental concerns and to work towards ecological principles in all areas of politics. Second, we sought to utilise direct action as a means of halting the destruction of the environment and, where the simultaneous opportunity arose, as a tactic for forcing ecological issues onto the media's agenda. At the time, though the political role of the media was taken seriously, the newsworthiness of actions was considered subordinate to the main objective of interfering with environmental destruction.

But within EF! there were factions: people keen to associate EF! with the IWW,[10] others willing to work with Friends of the Earth, still others interested in exploiting the possibility of media exposure, and others opposed, sometimes vehemently, to all of these *modus operandi*. 'Unity' in no way reflected conformity nor did it suggest an 'essential' identification. Importantly, too, this temporary unity dispersed – and reformed and dispersed again – over protracted periods of time. New ways of working emerged, new alliances were forged, but forged in context – or, to rearticulate Butler, in contingency.

As noted above, Butler proposes that it may be fruitful to expect not long-term or presupposed unity, but instead 'provisional unities [which] might emerge in the context of concrete actions' (Butler 1990: 15). But instead of provisionality being a weakness, a tentativeness that never takes on a solid formal shape, this mutability is presented as strength.[11] In this sense, the 'flight' of unity; the shifts and changes of coalitions, the flocking and dispersing of groups is echoed, or exemplified, in the actions which groups like EF! engage. The physical convergence and flight, necessitated by the desire, for instance, to evade capture by the police is an important aspect of group formation (however temporary and tenuous). The continual reinvention of the group, in service of 'Earth First!' or 'Reclaim the Streets' – both simultaneously mottoes, ways of working, and 'disorganisations' of committed individuals and networks – is a powerful expression in the face of structured political forces. But it is also powerful in the face of the 'new networks' of power of advanced capitalism. 'It is', according to Manuel Castells:

> this decentred, subtle character of networks of social change that makes it so difficult to perceive, and identify, new identity projects coming into being. Because our historical vision has become so used to orderly battalions, colorful banners, and scripted proclamations of social change, we are at a loss when confronted with the subtle pervasiveness of incremental changes of symbols processed through multiform networks, away from the halls of power.

> (Castells 1997: 362)

This is a 'guerrilla semiotics' (Eco 1986: 145) that, albeit tentatively, marks a serious challenge to contemporary conceptions of protest and thereby of the exercise of power and the formation of politics. A struggle against the 'foundationalism' of democratic politics is apparent in the physical manifestation of 'provisional unities' of eco-protest.

When I became an adult ...

When I became an adult, though I held on to the possibility of electoral politics providing a forum of democratic representation, I was inclined to see our elected representatives as having similar core attributes to (former) President Nixon. I still believed that governments exercised some power, however deeply constrained by corporate interests, but felt my individual vote was limited in effect. I chose to engage in NVDA political protest. EF! actions provided an important forum of protest: unlike voting, 'cause and effect' were evident in our actions and, while the effects were limited and frequently unintentional, there was a sense of 'real' engagement. Later, I took part in 'Reclaim the Streets' protest parties which I saw as innovative expressions of a 'postmodern' politics: a politics of 'dis-organisation', de-centralisation, and reclamation of desecrated space. Like EF!, RTS marked a move away from the ballot box to a politics of immediacy, rich with multifaceted symbolism and disregard for (and an implicit attack upon) normative expectations of 'political action'. For the sake of clarity and because I am arguing that specific contexts are essential in understanding radical 'eco-protest', I will look at one protest, a 'Reclaim the Streets Party' held in Bristol in 1997.

Reclaim the Streets, Bristol, Summer solstice, 1997

> To 'street party' is to begin reconstructing the geography of everyday life; to re-appropriate the public sphere; to rediscover the streets and attempt to liberate them. To 'street party' is to rescue communality from the dissection table of capitalism; to oppose the free market with a vision of the free society. This vision which the street party embodies, is collective imagining in practice. It radically dissolves in a utopian expression: a utopia defined, not as 'no-place', but as this-place, here and now.
>
> (Anon./RTS 1997: 6)

On 21 June 1997, Bristol city centre inadvertently played host to a 'Reclaim the Streets' street party, initiated by a recently reconstituted Bristol EF! group, to 'celebrate the solstice' and protest against Bristol's car culture.[12] Bristol, which is home to a large population of students and ex-students, is known in some circles as a haven for 'alternative lifestyles'. Bristol's central shopping precinct is largely pedestrianised, but is also ringed by a series of busy roads and multi-storey car parks which lure the automotive to drive in to the city-centre shops.[13] The site for the protest, the inner ring road, is a location without community, of transit and waiting. It is the space between going and arriving and, as such, serves the car almost exclusively, to the detriment of cyclists and pedestrians.[14]

RTS was, and is, a London-based eco-protest group which (re-)formed during the period of mass protest against the Criminal Justice Bill and was, in this incarnation, comprised predominantly of people involved in the 'No M11' campaign.[15] 'Reclaim the Streets' sought to challenge the dominance of car culture. Explicitly anti-car, much of the impetus of RTS was to reclaim the public space of the street: to (re)create a geographically located or 'community-based' public sphere.[16] But the phrase 'reclaim the streets' took on a wider meaning within the roads protest and environmental movement of the 1990s. Interestingly, 'Reclaim the Streets' saw itself as a group which could serve as an information organisation for other groups wishing to arrange street parties and city-centre roads protests, but the name 'Reclaim the Streets' took on a life of its own, becoming the phrase used to describe and advertise certain types of anti-roads actions.[17]

The Bristol 'Reclaim the Streets' action began on Saturday morning as a gathering on a grassy verge at the edge of the inner ring road. As numbers of people grew, drummers drummed and whistlers whistled and the people formed a slow procession through the main shopping area, disrupting the flow of cars, only minimally hampered by the directions of police. As the procession, with banners waving and dancers parading, emerged through the pedestrianised section of the shopping precinct there was a temporary interruption to the proceedings: protesters slowed to shout abuse at the McDonald's restaurant and were hustled away from this section of the planned route by the police. The desire of the police to protect McDonald's created enough of a diversion for a group of protesters to manoeuvre out of the pedestrianised section of the shopping precinct and onto a major section of the inner ring road, stopping traffic. A van, carrying a mobile sound system stopped in its tracks near the area of the planned action. Other protesters pushed through the thin lines of police and gained access to the road. The drums arrived, the food stall and children's play area were set up, the police asked drivers to reverse out of the instant street party: we won.

The day largely consisted of dancing, talking, eating and wandering in and out of the action. At the end of the day, a further procession was to lead people to a free party. Although this was instigated, the exit procession was ultimately disrupted. Despite attempts to move the protest away from the city centre, a hard-core group – mostly of locals – were determined to hold the site and an even more hard-core group of police on horseback were determined to clear it. Running battles ensued with horses charging into groups of protesters, police swinging batons at individuals and occasional, though ineffectual, retaliations from the protesters. The day ended with a tremendous downpour. The protesters mainly dispersed of their own accord though the police carted off a couple of van loads of assorted aggressives and innocents.[18]

The paucity of conventional political engagement

In Western liberal democracies the notion of individual inalienable rights is deemed sacrosanct. But the individual has limited means of political engagement, usually restricted to elections. Elections themselves are regulated to ensure small numbers of individuals are eligible candidates, particularly at the higher levels of government and this tends to decrease voter involvement. The evident surprise demonstrated by pollsters and elected representatives at the poor voter turn-out for most elections belies the public disengagement which underscores much of intra-electoral politics. This apparent desire on the part of elected representatives to decrease the involvement of the public is further compounded by the legal restrictions on political activism outside of party politics/voting which in recent years – particularly with the introduction of the 1994 Criminal Justice and Public Order Act (CJA) – has actually limited even further individual rights to political engagement. But this focus on the individual in fact misses the point – or at least capitulates to the dominant ideology of political engagement – and in so doing limits the possibilities for thinking about what might constitute the political.

Challenging the legitimacy of the state

The period of advanced capitalism has seen the emergence of a range of radical extra-parliamentary forms of political engagement in Britain, RTS amongst them. Although sharing some of the concerns of the new social movements of the 1960s and 1970s, an important feature of these more recent political formations is a 'disdain' for 'legislative and electoral niceties' (Aronowitz 1995: 366), which, though emulating some of the protest culture of the 1960s and '70s, takes as given the extreme paucity of franchise and the material and political wealth not of elected government but of big business. A further feature is the desire to elude simple categorisation (especially by the media) and to create a range of cultural formations and associations which challenge the presumptions of legitimacy of the state. Groups with concerns about issues ranging from the representation of women in municipal art collections (Guerrilla Girls) to AIDS and HIV awareness and health provision (ACT-UP) to ecological degradation (Earth First!) have increasingly questioned the authority and legitimacy of governments and have utilised direct action tactics in a bid to alter existing policy and/or behaviour.

Stanley Aronowitz (1995) argues that the direct action tactics of ACT-UP are a response to a political system which has lost its claim to legitimacy: the liberal claim to 'representation' no longer holds in light of the concessions given by the state to big business and the prioritisation of private capital over public interests. But while complicity with the interests of big business is cynically accepted by most politicians, it is still not the done thing to admit this to the electorate. For this reason, high visibility protest groups which utilise the media as a tactical resource can achieve results where low-key campaign groups may not. This analysis of ACT-UP suggests resonances with the aims and actions of Reclaim the Streets. One key difference, however, lies in the 'address' of the protest.

For Aronowitz, an indication of ACT-UP's success rests on the achievement of change to political-economic policy.[19] But the critique of electoral politics implicit in the organisation and execution of direct action protest may not be an end point that results in state policy response. In fact, as a number of theorists have suggested, much radical protest is aimed increasingly at 'global financial and retailing concerns' while 'the nation state and its political institutions are [deemed] irrelevant' (Scott and Street 1999: 22).

In the RTS action, the 'demonstration' is simultaneously a 'party'. Food, banners, dancing, brings the living room, the rave, the children's play area into the street. The attention paid to the global retailer, McDonald's, is both a protest and a mock protest, a diversion. The procession, the disruption of the everyday of shopping and automotive mobility, rewrites space and movement. The individual consumer is displaced (however temporarily) by the 'unity in flight' of the protesters, the isolation of the car supplanted with public movement, music and pedestrian locomotion. The authority of the state (embodied in the police) concede (temporarily) to the protesters: the balance of power is redrawn.

Significantly, the challenge is not created by a 'centralised' or 'hierarchical' group formation: the planning for the event, certainly, requires organisation, but the event itself mutates at different stages, taking advantage of weaknesses in the 'thin blue line' of power to 'reclaim the street', articulating itself as a 'party' (which is also a protest, which is also a gathering, which is also a reconstituted space) and later, a 'battle' (with the epic formulae: the heavy lines of horses coming up over a grassy hill, the passions of the protesters, the dissolution and re-establishment of police control, the torrential downpour). The object of protest is also not singular or 'central', it is instead 'contingent'; reclaiming the street is a 'moment' of protest against, among other things: car-culture, consumerism, capitalism, the physical coercive power of the state, the degradation of the environment and everyday life. But the day is also 'celebratory': at odds with conventional concepts of politically-marginal protest as sombre, trudging events, enlivened only by the occasional banner or placard. The success of the event cannot be measured in changed policies, newspaper column inches or the 'winning' of a parliamentary post; it is deeper than this. The success of the event is its playfulness and provocation and the fact that it 'happened' at all.

For Butler, the challenge of the protest event lies not in its formal end-results. In discussing the semiotic subversion of queer protest, she argues that:

> it is right to say that any attempt at subversion is potentially recuperable. There is no way to safeguard against that. You can't plan or calculate subversion. In fact, I would say that subversion is precisely an incalculable effect. That's what makes it subversive ... I ... think that subversive practices have to overwhelm the capacity to read, challenge conventions of reading and demand new possibilities of reading.
>
> (Butler 1996: 121)

Butler goes on to suggest that the 'die-ins' ACT-UP have performed were a 'shocking symbolization':

> It was a new adumbration of a certain kind of civil disobedience ... . It made people have to read what was happening ... . The [actions] ... that challenge our practices of reading, that make us uncertain about how to read or make us think that we have to renegotiate the way in which we read public signs, these seem really important.
>
> (Butler 1996: 122)

Likewise, the multiplicity of meaning of 'Reclaim the Streets' – a 'dis-organisation', a 'moment' of protest, a political 'movement' – requires a renegotiation of the politics of protest and of the structures and location of political power itself. As such, actions, like those of EF! and RTS, articulate new political forums: they are themselves alterior public spheres. And, as Nancy Fraser points out, 'public spheres are not only arenas for the formation of discursive opinion; in addition they are arenas for the formation and enactment of social identities' (Fraser 1993: 16). We might wish to add that the inverse of this formulation is also evident in the politically challenging formations of radical direct action such as Reclaim the Streets or ACT-UP.

Conclusion

The important question for activists and theorists of eco-activism is what is the significance of eco-protest as politics? Of course, in terms of maintaining the currency of ecological concerns, a healthy activist culture is essential: we need people to draw attention to issues such as the destruction of the countryside; the capitulation of urban areas to car culture; the complicity of government at both the local, national and transnational levels with processes of ecological destruction; the role of multinationals in hastening those processes. How these issues might be addressed is not, however, predictable: activists can work in a variety of political fora and through different media, such as letter-writing campaigns which target local government, or actions where ecological destruction is physically challenged. These two activities alone suggest widely differing skills and approaches to the political process. The roles that activists assume over the course of a particular campaign vary and the activist 'identity' may fluctuate accordingly. The culture of activism itself is variable and not easily subjected to a totalising or homogenising analysis. It is for these reasons, however, that I argue that eco-activism is a deeply significant political category in the period of advanced capitalism.

The argument has been posed in relation to three interlinked elements: identity, unity or collectivity, and challenges to democratic electoral politics. Eco-activism has been proposed as providing evidence of a rearticulation of the contemporary political context. The concept of 'legitimate' identities has been challenged and, instead, the question of legitimacy has been turned on the 'contingent foundations' of such identity formations. Challenges to the claims of legitimacy of formal state politics have been identified in the temporary and tactical formations of collectivities and unities, and in the semiotic potential of public actions. This is seen as running parallel to the economic challenges posed by multinational corporations and other big business concerns which also undermine the independence and political authority of government at local, national and transnational levels. Government, in this analysis – and implicitly in the actions of eco-activists – is increasingly a cipher for corporate power. Though not addressed in this chapter, a more recent shift in eco-protests has seen activists addressing corporate power directly (e.g. the 1999 'Carnival Against Capital').

In *The Power of Identity* Manuel Castells considers the role environmentalism might play in reconstituting politics. He suggests that perhaps the only politics in the late twentieth century to overcome the obstacles posed by the political shifts inherent in what he has identified as the 'network society' is environmentalism. The 'disorganisations' of EF! or actions/groups like 'Reclaim the Streets' demonstrate that Castells is right: radical eco-protest can be seen as a creative and potentially powerful response to changes in political structures in Western democratic nations that belie major shifts in the locations of power. The critical work of queer theory, which has as its starting point a question mark over 'legitimacy', which questions the very nature of identity, collectivity and politics, is a useful tool for understanding these connected processes in eco-politics. It may seem, at first glance, 'unnatural' to pair eco-activism and queer theory, but doesn't this just emphasise the constructedness of our political conceptions?

Eco-activism; identity-formative, a unity in flight, a politics of the 'postmodern age', is a mutable and contingent thing, but it is all the more significant for this. Or, to put it another way: the 'cultural figure' of the eco-activist, as one anti-roads activist suggested, is 'more possible than you can powerfully imagine'.

Notes

1   This assertion is at odds with that of a number of 'postmodern' thinkers, e.g. Frederic Jameson and Jean Baudrillard, who argue that the present period marks a major demise in politics. I have contested the 'demise' of politics elsewhere (Maples 1998); suffice here to say that groups like EF! and RTS are good evidence of an active political strain in the current historical moment.
2   Szerszynski is here developing an argument made by Alberto Melucci.
3   Seidman argues that identity formations, such as homosexuality, must be seen not merely as a matter of individual expression, repression, etc., but instead as a 'cultural figure or category of knowledge' (Seidman 1995: 128, citing Sedgwick).
4   Stuart Hall makes the important point, in regard to 'cultural identity', that the author, 'the "I" who writes here must ... be thought of as, itself, "enunciated". We all write and speak from a history and a culture which is specific. What we say is always "in context", positioned' (Hall 1990: 222). So, to indicate my own position: my long-term interest in environmental concerns was maintained in my twenties and early thirties with an involvement in both mainstream and radical eco-activist groups. In the early 1990s I was involved with EF! in the UK. Though I have largely turned towards more mainstream green politics, and my activisms are deeply circumscribed by academic

employment, I still occasionally take part in protests such as Reclaim the Streets actions.

5   Other – non-queer – theorists writing on 'identity' have also explored the processes by which legitimacy is conferred upon some identities over others. Stuart Hall (1990, 1997) and Paul Gilroy (1993), for instance, write convincingly about the challenges posed by 'hybridity' and 'diasporic' identities. Other theorists have discussed, for instance, femininity or masculinity and have argued that neither 'identity' is established by a 'natural' subject position (see, for example, Segal 1990; Kaplan and Rogers 1990), but are instead socially and culturally constructed. Hetherington (1998) explores a range of factors contributing to the establishment of a non-essentialised view of identity and is keen to consider this in relation to groups which fall outside of the 'class, gender, race' 'mantra', including environmental groups.

6   In part, 'queer' may be used as 'a shorthand to cope with the lengthening list of sexual/political articulations – lesbians, gays, bis, transgendered people' (Phelan 1997: 3) – but is also a politicised term, one that reclaims and rearticulates a politically loaded, derogatory or punitive word. This move to reclaim a language of debasement is important in that it implies the ability actively to set out an identity that challenges dominant ideologies.

7   Butler discusses the concept of 'constitutedness' thus:

> In a sense, the subject is constituted through an exclusion and differentiation, perhaps repression, that is subsequently concealed, covered over … . The subject is constructed through acts of differentiation that distinguish the subject from its constitutive outside, a domain of abjected alterity … . There is no ontologically intact reflexivity to the subject which is then placed within a cultural context; that cultural context, as it were, is already there as the disarticulated process of that subject's production, one that is concealed by the frame that would situate a ready-made subject in an internal web of cultural relations… . [T]o claim that the subject is constituted is not to claim that it is determined; on the contrary, the constituted character of the subject is the very precondition of its agency.
>
> (Butler 1992: 12)

8   For an interesting discussion of this notion, see Hall, 1997.

9   Stuart Hall describes the extreme expression of the stereotype's 'binary structure' which, he argues 'traps' its subjects. In discussing the ways in which stereotypes of blacks work on a variety of levels, Hall explains the real consequences of representations for black identity:

> the problem is that blacks are trapped by the binary structure of the stereotype, which is split between two extreme oppositions – and are obliged to shuttle endlessly between them, sometimes being represented as both of them at the same time. Thus blacks are both 'childlike' and 'oversexed', just as black youth are 'Sambo simpletons' and/or 'wily, dangerous savages'.
>
> (Hall 1997: 263)

10   There have been serious as well as more trivial attempts to ally EF! with the Wobblies, including the borrowing of the International Workers of the World's title, 'The Little Red Songbook'. 'The Little Green Songbook' was one of the first items publicised for sale in the US EF! newspaper.

11   Though in a clearly divergent context, Manuel Castells proposes that it is this 'fragmentary' formation, at the heart of the radical environmental movement that is exceedingly powerful in the face of the dominant forces of the 'network society' (Castells 1997: 360–362).

12   As promoted on a leaflet advertising the action.

13 Substantially more could be said about Bristol, but for my purposes these are some of the more salient points.

14 For an interesting discussion on the distinction between location and place, see Nigel Thrift (1997:196–197) who draws on the important work of Doreen Massey regarding the ways in which 'places' are locations 'made meaningful' through use.

15 'No M11' was a series of protests and urban encampments which sought to delay the construction of the M11 – a new thoroughfare through East London which led to the destruction of innumerable homes, trees and, some would argue, whole communities.

16 Hetherington (1998: 72, citing Keith and Pile) argues that 'sites of social centrality [may] become sites of resistance'. For RTS it is certainly important to address 'spaces that come to symbolise the socially central values of a society' (ibid.).

17 Personal communication with Phil McLeish, Reclaim the Streets, November 1997.

18 It was an aim of the party's 'hosts' that the protest be non-violent. The conclusion of the day was regarded as a 'disaster' (informal interview with Anonymous, 1997).

19 Aronowitz describes the scene when New York's Mayor Giuliani sought to close down the Department of AIDS Services in the city's fiscal interest:

> The leading AIDS activist movement, ACT-UP, swung into action against the proposed shutdown … . Activists staged a series of confrontations with the mayor; noisy demonstrations at public events … a lie-in across the Brooklyn Bridge … . After four months of press attention and disruptions promulgated by a small group of relentless activists, the city administration quietly dropped its proposal … . Where unions representing tens of thousands of municipal employees has failed, a relatively small, but highly vocal, social movement succeeded.
>
> (Aronowitz 1995: 359)

Bibliography

Anon. (1997) 'Earth First! – but what next?', *Do or Die – Voices From Earth First!*, 6: 18–20.

Anon./Reclaim the Streets (1997) 'Reclaim the streets!', *Do or Die – Voices From Earth First!*, 6: 1–6.

Aronowitz, S. (1995) 'Against the liberal state: ACT-UP and the emergence of post-modern politics', in L. Nicholson and S. Seidman (eds) *Social Postmodernism: Beyond Identity Politics*, Cambridge: Cambridge University Press.

Butler, J. (1990) *Gender Trouble*, New York and London: Routledge.

—— (1992) 'Contingent foundations: feminism and the question of "postmodernism"', in J. Butler and J. Scott (eds) *Feminists Theorize the Political*, New York and London: Routledge.

—— (1996) 'Gender as performance', in P. Osborne (ed.) *A Critical Sense: Interviews with Intellectuals*, London: Routledge.

Castells, M. (1996) *The Rise of the Network Society*, Oxford: Blackwell.

—— (1997) *The Power of Identity*, Oxford: Blackwell.

Doty, A. (1995) 'There's something queer here', in C. Creekmur and A. Doty (eds) *Out in Culture: Gay, Lesbian and Queer Essays on Popular Culture*, London: Cassell.

Eco, U. (1986) 'The multiplication of the media', in *Travels in Hyper-reality*, London: Picador.

Foreman, D. (1991) 'Second thoughts of an eco-warrior', in M. Bookchin and D. Foreman, *Defending the Earth*, Boston: South End Press.

Fraser, N. (1993) 'Rethinking the public sphere', in B. Robbins (ed.) *The Phantom Public Sphere*, London and Minneapolis: University of Minnesota Press.

Gilroy, P. (1993) *The Black Atlantic: Modernity and Double Consciousness*, London: Verso.

Hall, S. (1990) 'Cultural identity and diaspora', in J. Rutherford (ed.) *Identity: Community, Culture, Difference*, London: Lawrence & Wishart.

—— (1997) 'The spectacle of the "Other"', in S. Hall (ed.) *Representation: Cultural Representations and Signifying Practices*, London: Sage.

Hetherington, K. (1998) *Expressions of Identity: Space, Performance, Politics*, London: Sage.

Kaplan, G. and Rogers, L. (1990) 'The definition of male and female: biological reductionism and the sanctions of normality', in S. Gunew (ed.) *Feminist Knowledge: Critique and Construct*, London: Routledge.

Maples, W. (1998) 'It's no wonder people end up in trees': radical environmental activism in a postmodern age', unpublished PhD thesis, Birmingham University.

Phelan, S. (ed.) (1997) *Playing with Fire: Queer Politics, Queer Theories*, New York and London: Routledge.

Scott, A. and Street, J. (1999) 'New politics in old practices', paper presented at 'A New Politics? Representation, Mobilisation and Networks in the Information Age' conference, University of Birmingham, 16–17 September.

Segal, L. (1990) *Slowmotion: Changing Masculinities, Changing Men*, London: Virago.

Seidman, S. (1995) 'Deconstructing queer theory or the under-theorisation of the social and the ethical', in L. Nicholson and S. Seidman (eds) *Social Postmodernism: Beyond Identity Politics*, Cambridge: Cambridge University Press.

Szerszynski, B. (1998) 'Action's glassy essence: the dramatics of environmental protest', paper presented to the Annual Conference of the Royal Geographic Society with the Institute of British Geographers, Kingston University, 5–8 January.

—— (1999) 'Performing politics: the dramatics of environmental protest', in L. Ray and A. Sayer (eds) *Culture and Economy After the Cultural Turn*, London: Sage.

Thrift, N. (1997) '"Us" and "Them": re-imagining places, re-imagining identities', in H. Mackay (ed.) *Consumption and Everyday Life*, London: Sage.

Woods, C. (1995) *State of the Queer Nation: A Critique of Gay and Lesbian Politics in 1990s Britain*, London: Cassell.

Young, I.M. (1995) 'Gender as seriality: thinking about women as a social collective', in L. Nicholson and S. Seidman (eds) *Social Postmodernism: Beyond Identity Politics*, Cambridge: Cambridge University Press.

8   Swampy fever

Media constructions and direct action
politics[1]

Matthew Paterson

Introduction: Swampy fever

In early 1997 British politics produced a most unlikely hero, known as Swampy.
For the first few months of that year, Swampy was one of the most talked about
figures in British political debate, and his popularity endured throughout 1997.
Swampy was one of five protesters against a road-building scheme on the A30 in
Devon who managed to get themselves down an extensive network of tunnels
they and others had constructed when their protest camp, Fairmile, was evicted.
Swampy was the last of the tunnelling protesters to be pulled out of the ground
by 'rescuers' employed by the bailiffs to clear the way for the road, seven days
after the five had gone underground.

Swampy certainly had his fifteen minutes of fame:

> The Fairmile five are media darlings. Frost wants them, Lawley wants them,
> Sky, The Big Breakfast, Radios 1, 2, 3, 4, 5, Reuters, the Germans, Aussies
> and Czechs want them. Poised in the wings are film, record companies and
> chat-shows.
>
> (Vidal 1997b)

Swampy had, for nine weeks, his own column in the *Sunday Mirror*.[2] He appeared
on the TV news quiz comedy show 'Have I got News for You'. Some of the
more bizarre episodes included the *Daily Express* paying for a photo shoot with
Swampy dressed in Armani and Paul Smith suits (*Express*, 3 February 1997), a
(failed) attempt to get him to record 'I am a mole and I live in a hole' ('Pass
notes', *Guardian*, 18 March 1997) for a record company, and a rumoured plan to
make a film about Swampy, starring Matt Dillon (on the last of these, see *Sunday
Mirror*, 30 March 1997). Swampy became a byword for environmental direct
action and youth disaffection from formal politics, often being used in headlines
where he, as a person, never appeared in the articles.[3] He also became a particular sort of sex symbol, with *Just 17* (a teenage girl's magazine) proclaiming him
'alternative totty' (Bellos 1997) and *Cosmopolitan* editor declaring him to be 'so
much more sexy' than 'lads' (Raven 1997). He was the subject of the *Independent*'s
dilemmas page, where parents write in about their worries concerning their

children. In one week, the contributor had a daughter who 'has a crush on Swampy', and wanted to go to Manchester to join the anti-second runway protest (Ironside 1997). The Manchester Airport protest camp had a sign saying what was not wanted, which included 'Swampy groupies' (ibid.). Swampy's name was trademarked by a Hull businessman keen to cash in on Swampy's fame (and lack of interest in matters entrepreneurial) (Penman 1997). Later, in 1998, a character in the soap *Coronation Street* (Spider) was based on him (Wall 1999: 3). Swampy's reported blunt response to his fame was: 'Bollocks!' (quoted in Gibbs 1997; 'Pass notes', *Guardian*, 18 March 1997). The commercialisation of Swampy and the other A30 activists was satirised in *Do or Die* (the Earth First! UK magazine) with a cartoon advertising a 'Swampy Action Figure'™ with 'realistic digging hands', 'authentic iron-on Fairmile mud', and concluding with a quote from Muppet Dave, one of the others of the 'Fairmile five', saying 'When I'm worried about being turned into a youth icon I ask them if they know about DBFO. They vanish!' (*Do or Die*, No. 6: 142, see Figure 8.1).[4]

Although a certain proportion of the media construction in the A30 case was negative, portraying the protesters as unemployed outsider activists rejecting the values of 'normal' people,[5] what was interesting about this case was that in most of the British press and TV discourse the coverage was largely positive. The predominant image was constructed through discourses of youthful active heroic idealism, as widely noticed both by activists themselves, and by other journalists (e.g. Vidal 1997a). This marked a significant change in the constructions of protesters in previous actions at Twyford Down, Solsbury Hill, the M11 Link road, the M77 extension, and others. In these cases, most media construction was negative – of a small minority of extremists rejecting 'normal' society's values undermining democratically approved decisions. While there the press had focused on instances of violence, trying to associate the violence with the protesters; by the time of the A30 protest, we are shown photos of a protestor 'tickling' a climber trying to bring her down from a tree (O'Neill 1997).

Wall (1999: 131) suggests that the failure to portray the protesters successfully as violent was one factor in the shift in construction as outlined here. My argument is that central to the construction of the protesters was a process of normalisation; that the protesters were normalised through various means. Given the clear popularity of the A30 protesters, the tabloid press were faced with a need to be able to accommodate the popularity of the protesters, but this had to be done within the discursive frames available both to them and their audiences. The effect was to 'normalise' the protesters, to construct them as normal, regular members of society – in other words, to make them 'safe for *Express* readers'.[6]

What was perhaps bizarre was this construction reaching the staunchest of right-wing newspapers (Bellos 1997), notably the *Express*. This paper gave the protesters easily the most coverage of the UK tabloids.[7] One commentary by Radio One DJ (and regular *Express* columnist) Mark Radcliffe stated: 'I'm speechless with admiration for Swampy' (*Express*, 1 February 1997: 9). The paper also included an article by Bel Mooney, prominent protestor at an earlier protest against the Batheaston bypass over Solsbury Hill in 1994, entitled, 'Right or

Figure 8.1 'Swampy's grotto'

Source: *Do or Die* 6: 142, © Gavin Burrows

wrong, the young at least show some guts' (Mooney 1997). (Of course, while the young may have guts, youthful idealism is often easily understood as 'just a phase', again making it safe.)

The normalisation process in the *Express*'s construction is fairly overt. A leader entitled 'suburban guerrilla' on the day the paper had him dressed in designer clothes sums up the construction well:

He went from Swampy to Smoothie in a few short minutes. Britain's favourite anti-roads protestor was transformed from sweaty guerrilla to male model with surprising ease.

Perhaps this is why so much of the country – especially the furry-animal-loving vegetarian section – has taken him to its bosom. They could already see what we [the *Express*] have now proved. Beneath the encrusted grime and matted hair beats a respectable suburban middle-class heart.

(Express, 3 February 1997: 10)

It is extremely difficult to conceive of the *Express,* or other conservative newspapers, approving of actions such as those involved in the roads protests. Their capacity to make such actions acceptable in their eyes occurs in the articles through a combination of discourses of family, class and nation.[8] Use of these themes permitted the papers to make the protesters appear familiar, safe. The *Daily Mail's* main coverage was a page long article on Animal, the next most famous of the five tunnellers after Swampy (Mollard 1997).[9] They made much of Animal as a 16-year-old young woman. We are informed that Animal is 'the eldest daughter of middle-class, if unconventional parents, [who] gained good grades in 10 GCSEs last summer', and is 'a member of MENSA'. The *Mail* continues:

So why has this talented and articulate young woman decided to risk her life in a smelly tunnel?

What is the attraction when your parents have a perfectly nice semi-detached home, albeit with cabbages growing in the front garden?

(Ibid.)

Clearly, the *Mail* cannot quite bring itself to normalise her fully, harping on as it does about her 'unconventional' parents, the cabbages in her front garden, and the use of 'smelly' invoking notions of femininity which, in the *Mail's* view, Animal was transgressing (boys are allowed to be smelly, not girls). But the support of her parents is crucial in the way that the *Mail* communicates to its readers the acceptability in its eyes of her actions, and takes up much of the rest of the article. And the references to class, both direct and through the emphasis on her membership of MENSA, also serve to make her feel more familiar to aspirant middle-class readers. The *Mirror* also expressed it in similar ways in its portrayal of 'Animal Magic' (29 January 1997: 4–5), homing in on Animal's statements that her parents were proud of her, as well as on her MENSA membership. The *Mirror's* profile of Animal was on the 'Mirror Woman' page, and emphasised Animal's gender (it talked about her blushing when asked about boyfriends) and her being a teenager, implicitly underlining the importance of family (teenagers become relevant in part by reference to their relationship to their parents). At the other end of the journalistic spectrum, the *Guardian* also made similar constructions of Animal with a lengthy article on its 'Parents' page on Animal's parents, illustrating the importance of familial support to enable journalists' or popular support for the protesters to be given (Brooks 1997).[10]

Family and class are also important in the *Express*'s construction of Swampy, where he is pictured predominantly with his mother, under headlines such as 'Short history of Swampy, a nice middle-class boy' (*Express*, 1 February 1997: 20–21).[11] Again, this goes across the spectrum. Take this extract from the *Independent*: 'Daniel Hooper, aka Swampy, ... kisses his mother, Jill, after a court fined him £500 for damaging equipment at the Newbury bypass last May. "I support Daniel all the way", she said. "He deserves to be a hero." '[12] The editorial in the *Sunday Mirror* on the first day of Swampy's column in the paper also emphasised the family theme: 'Today on PAGE 9 he starts his eco-diary. But leaves one vital question unanswered: Does an eco-warrior give flowers on Mother's Day? I certainly hope I get MY bunch of daffs!' (*Sunday Mirror*, 9 March 1997).

The other major normalising theme in the coverage was that of nation. The construction was that of patriotic heroes saving the British (sometimes explicitly, English) countryside. This occurred more prevalently in the broadsheets, particularly in the *Guardian* and *Independent*.[13] The *Express* did regularly refer to Swampy as 'Britain's favourite anti-road protestor' (e.g. *Express*, 3 February 1997: 10). But in the broadsheets, more was made of the theme. The *Independent* had a leader entitled 'The nation digs you, Swampy' (30 January 1997), followed by a series of letters headed 'Why we should hail Swampy and friends as patriotic heroes' (*Independent*, 1 February 1997). Their actions were, in the words of one letter 'a spirited defence of our land, our country' (ibid.). John Vidal, in the *Guardian*, suggested that they should be thought of as doing 'active citizen service' (and invoked, as elsewhere, notions of 'Middle England' (Vidal 1997a)). Radio 4, appealing to a similar audience as the broadsheets, referred to him as a 'symbol to crystallize the nation's changing mood' (Vidal 1998).

In relation to this theme, the protesters themselves complied with the construction, by and large, fairly actively. Populist/nationalist expressions abound in their public proclamations (or at least how they were reproduced in newspapers themselves, the assumption that this is a reasonable representation of what they said being a rather problematic one). Muppet Dave (a former soldier) said 'I will continue in my efforts to fight against the needless destruction of my country' (quoted in Jury 1997a). Swampy, in various parts of his 'The World according to Swampy' columns in the *Sunday Mirror*, made similar populist appeals. 'Police helicopter circled camp for four hours. What a waste of taxpayers money', he wrote on 16 March, and on 23 March wrote 'My bail conditions are outrageous. I shall ignore them. The police should be catching muggers, burglars, murderers and crack dealers.' I will argue below that such a construction, and particularly the protesters' active participation in it, is politically problematic in terms of environmentalist strategy.

Perhaps the starkest image of normalisation in the whole construction is the Armani suit episode (*Express*, 3 February 1997: 4–5). The piece is a two-page spread, with a general headline 'Look what emerged from the Swamp'. On the left-hand side there is the caption 'From this: Swampy the eco-warrior', alongside a photograph of him in stripy jumper and baggy trousers tucked into wellington boots. On the right, three photographs, surrounded by the caption

'To this: Swampy in designer Armani', dominate the page, with Swampy's hair neatly groomed and him adopting men's clothing catalogue poses (presumably as directed by the photographer) – for example, one with legs apart, one hand in pocket, one adjusting his tie. In a small box at the bottom the ubiquitous interview with his mother has her stating that the transformation 'just goes to show that underneath he's a normal lad from a normal family' (*Express*, 3 February 1997: 5). Middle-class clean normal masculinity was literally inscribed on Swampy's body, leading him to express feeling 'like a model, or worse, like I was selling my body' (quoted in Griffiths 1997a), and that it was 'pornographic' (Vidal 1997a).

In a wonderful piece called 'Performative States' (Weber 1998), Cindy Weber analyses an advert for the US edition of *Men's Health* in the business section of the *New York Times* which involved a full-length photo of drag artist RuPaul in a leotard with a Stars and Stripes flag design, juxtaposed with the byline of the magazine, 'Tons of Useful Stuff for Regular Guys'. Weber uses the work of Judith Butler (1990; 1993, see also Maples, this volume), particularly the notion of performativity – 'the ways that identities are constructed iteratively through complex citational processes' (Weber 1998: 79; Parker and Kosofsky Sedgwick 1995: 2) – to show that it is precisely the discursive construction of RuPaul's body which helps to reproduce hegemonic forms of heterosexual masculinity. In other words, rather than understand the identity of 'Swampy' as pre-existing the media constructions of him, his identity is produced through those discursive constructions. As with RuPaul, clothing is important in this construction. It is the business suit that is attached in the article to the 'natural' Swampy existing 'underneath' (to use the phrase attributed to his mother) his more common appearance. Weber emphasises how processes of normativity are bound up with performance and performativity, but that this involves 'processes whereby "regular subjects" and "standards of normality" are discursively co-constituted to give the effect that both are natural rather than cultural constructs' (1998: 81). Thus the construction of Swampy dressed in particular clothing was important to the way in which the *Express* could normalise him. Swampy in the suit is presented as the 'natural' Swampy, while Swampy in boots and grimy jumpers is 'performing'. Rather, following Weber and Butler, we should regard his identity as being one which is continuously performed, but one which needs to be stabilised in order to make him conform to particular 'standards of normality'.

The 'Swampy case', the media, and radical environmentalism

> News is fundamentally a discourse of morality, procedure and hierarchy, providing symbolic representations of order.
>
> (Ericson *et al.* 1991, cited in Anderson 1997: 128)

I want now to draw out a number of points about what this says about the

relationship between the media – particularly in its role as a predominant repro-
ducer of hegemonic cultural norms – and practitioners of green politics.

Most work on the mass media and environmental politics concentrates on the
processes surrounding particular environmental issues. The intention in general
is to understand the way in which relationships between the media and environmental groups facilitate or hinder processes of mobilisation and resolution of
particular environmental problems (see, for example, the various contributions to
Hansen 1993, or Anderson 1997). Social constructionist analysis is prevalent,
focusing on the discursive constructions of 'nature', particular places, embedded
in news media and environmentalist discourse. In this case, however, the form of
media content is rather different since the focus of coverage was not an environmental issue, but rather the people involved in environmental protest and their
personalities. I would argue that the political dynamics of the coverage are thus
rather different.[14]

Tabloid journalists in particular are apt, as evidenced above in this instance,
to cover such protests in terms of the people engaged in protest, rather than the
issues raised by such protests. The protest became a human interest story with
much of the coverage involving biographies of the protesters, particularly
Swampy and Animal. Even much of the *Guardian* coverage was of a primarily
human interest type of story. While there was much more coverage of the issues,
such as DBFO, etc., there was also a great deal of 'profiling' of protesters as
individuals and fascination with the practical aspects of tunnelling. One episode
illustrates this nicely: 'When he [Swampy] wakes, he starts to describe life underground. "We did some interviews for radio people when we were down the
tunnels and we said, 'We want to talk about the road scheme.' They said, 'So
what's it like down there?' We said, 'We want to talk about the road scheme.'
They said, 'So what's it like down there?' 'We're drinking our own piss, what do
you think?'" He pauses. "And they believed us." ... So what's it like down there?'
(Griffiths 1997a). The *Guardian* journalist can't help asking the same human
interest question he knows Swampy has been trying to avoid answering to
tabloid journalists.[15]

For the media, the intention is to produce a 'symbolic package' (Anderson
1997: 35). Such packages operate within prevailing cultural 'frames'. 'In
choosing among possible stories, journalists, sources and consumers reveal the
cultural templates of their understanding' (Ericson *et al.* 1991: 356, quoted in
Anderson 1997: 124). Such frames are not fixed, and shift over time and across
different media sources, but are also not completely fluid 'since they are
constrained in important ways by the market and format considerations'
(Anderson 1997: 124). There are already a number of such packages ready-
made with which to construct environmentalists – gloomy scientists, scruffy
hippies, technocrat hustlers, to name but three. Constructing the protesters
within these frames means that whatever else covering the protests does, in terms
of helping to set political agendas surrounding road building, it will also play a
part in social reproduction by stabilising norms about 'normal' people, giving the
readers a clear sense of who they are by defining who they are not. What is

interesting here, of course, is that journalists predominantly chose to construct Swampy *et al.* as 'us', not 'them'.

Part of this is because of dynamics specific to print journalism. As Anderson makes clear, print journalists are often much closer to their audiences than are TV journalists; in part due to the function of letters pages (1997: 174), which provide for two-way communication between readers and editors/journalists. Anderson specifically quotes a *Daily Express* journalist in this regard. In addition, readership of daily newspapers is significantly more homogeneous in its social make-up than are audiences for television, with readers being familiar with the attitudes and politics of the paper(s) they read.[16] The result of this is that print journalists would have reasonably clear notions of the sorts of interpretive frames their readership would want to see, and thus that Swampy *et al.* were not viewed unfavourably by their readership. The *Mirror* conducted its own reader survey on the question, and stated that 80 per cent of its respondents supported the protesters (*Mirror*, 30 January: 11); however imperfect their survey methods might be from an academic point of view, this clearly gave their editorial line the appropriate push (see also Longrigg 1997).[17] This created incentives to produce the sort of interpretation outlined above. However, it does not produce the specifics of that interpretation. Swampy *et al.* still had to be 'made safe for *Express* readers', to be made to appear as 'normal'. This is where discourses of family, class, nation come in to make the protesters' lives appear familiar to the papers' readerships.

The effect of such a framing of the roads protest is clearly not wholly positive from the environmentalists' point of view. While clearly the positive construction of the protesters in terms of youthful idealism – 'at least the young have guts' – undoubtedly reinforced a broad public understanding that opposition to road-building programmes was legitimate, and therefore perhaps contributed to the scaling back of the road programme,[18] it has had other not so positive conse-quences. The connections between road building and broader social and political questions, and thus deep opposition of the road protesters to modern forms of social organisation and power, is erased. The question of contemporary legal reforms, notably the 1994 Criminal Justice and Public Order Act, one of whose (implicit) targets was roads protesters, was absent from tabloid discussions of the protests; thus contradictions in the views of *Express* readers and journalists were ignored (as Carey 1998 shows, these papers provided much of the moral panic around protesters, squatters and travellers which facilitated the passage of the CJA).

Fundamentally perhaps, there is a contradiction between the *Express*'s construction and radical environmentalists' self-constructions. Like the media, environmentalism is heavily dependent on symbols. In Melucci's words:

> Contemporary movements operate as signs, in the sense that they translate their actions into symbolic challenges to the dominant codes ... . In this respect, collective action is a *form* whose models of organization and soli-darity deliver a message to the rest of society ... . Contemporary social

movements stimulate radical questions about the ends of personal and social life.

(Melucci 1989: 12; Anderson 1997: 207)

The symbolic codes of radical environmentalists – and thus forms of collective action and preferred social organisation, or 'the ends of personal and social life' – are however fundamentally at odds with those of tabloid newspapers and (their assumptions about) their readership. In the particular constructions made by those newspapers of environmental protest, such contradictions are discursively erased and the challenge posed by green politics is neutralised.

The media is widely acknowledged by environmental groups as vitally important for their political tactics, if not strategy.[19] As Gitlin puts it:

Mass media define the significance of movement events or, by blanking them out, actively deprive them of larger significance. Media images also become implicated in a movement's self-image ... . The forms of coverage accrete into systematic framing, and this framing, much amplified, helps determine the movement's fate.

(1980: 3)

This was clearly understood by the protesters in the A30 protest. Swampy, in his *Sunday Mirror* column, wrote that despite misgivings about journalists 'the attention is welcome so we can raise and discuss the issues and the environmental damage done in the name of "progress"' ('The World according to Swampy', *Sunday Mirror*, 9 March 1997: 9). But if the media is important in this way, then so is appreciating the effects of mediated messages if we are to understand how they can (or cannot) be used easily for environmentalist purposes.

Some of the dynamics of the movement's dependence on the media in order to communicate its message(s) to a broader public are widely acknowledged: the reliance on stunts as pioneered, in particular, by Greenpeace, in order to create 'newsworthy' copy for newspapers and broadcasters, and the tendency (again exemplified by Greenpeace) towards professionalism, increased wearing of suits, reliance on science, and so on. Such a development has, in part, been produced by the assumption that to get the message across to 'normal' people, adopting hegemonic norms of a business culture (symbolised, not unimportantly, by suit-wearing) would be necessary to be regarded as 'serious' – an assumption, in part, produced by the normalising effects of media coverage, which denigrated environmentalists as 'scruffy' – and by implication 'disorganised' – and thus not to be relied on for 'serious' arguments.

For environmentalists, stunts have been a mainstay of getting issues onto the political agenda. The roads protests have been the latest in a long line of such tactics. Although in general, the advocates of direct action in the 1990s have tended to argue that action is not about media coverage (see conclusion below), in this case Swampy was clear concerning the advantages of such an approach in his widely cited quote on emerging from the 'Big Momma' tunnel: 'It is the only way to get a voice these days. If I had written a letter to my MP, would I have achieved all this? Would you lot be here now? I think not' ('Leader', *Independent*, 2 February 1997; Jury 1997a; 1997b).

But what the above analysis of press coverage of (one of) these protests suggests is that the coverage is never *only*, if it is at all, about the issues which campaigners want to see covered and promoted, but always interpreted in the light of prevailing frames of understanding that the journalists have, the interests of the owners of the paper or TV station, the assumptions about the readership, and so on. As already suggested, in this case it seems to have been more about neutralising the critique offered by Swampy *et al.*, by showing them in fact to be 'normal' middle-class suburbanites whose mums love them. The issue at hand for the media is not the pros and cons of 'Design, Build, Finance, Operate' (DBFO), or of the impact of road building on the environment – and is therefore an instance whereby the process of constructing the news 'contributes to *decontextualising* – or of removing an event from the context in which it occurs in order to *recontextualise* within news formats' (Altheide 1976: 179, quoted in Hannigan 1995: 60). Such a recontextualisation neutralises the impact of the protesters' intentions.

This recontextualisation entailed focusing on the lives and (media-constructed) identities of the people involved, rather than the political processes associated with road building and the environmentally and socially destructive nature of road-building schemes. Gitlin (1980: 146–179) shows how, in relation to the New Left in the US, the media converted leaders into celebrities, neutralising their political message in the process. In the A30, and in other direct action protests, certain people had to be converted first into leaders and then into celebrities, since roads protests have been organised on a direct action model which eschews divisions into 'leaders' and 'followers'. Organisations associated with roads protests such as EF! have deliberately tried to avoid a politics which promotes 'personalities' (Wall 1999: 92) on principle, but this intent has been effectively subverted by the media's need for such personalities on which to hang stories.

Environmentalist recognition of the importance of the media should therefore be tempered with an understanding that the media tends to reproduce existing forms of social power, not destabilise them. Owners of newspapers often regard this as an explicit part of their purpose in publishing newspapers, as is easily shown in the UK, and have routinely intervened in editorial policy to ensure a particular line is promoted (see, for example, Curran and Seaton 1997). But this reproduction does not simply involve promoting certain political agendas, it also involves governing by 'a specific, a permanent, and a positive intervention in the behavior of individuals' (Foucault 1988: 159), as evidenced here in the case of the A30.[20]

Conclusions

It is more the radical challenge to prevailing forms of social organisation offered by radical environmentalists that at root challenge class and family structures, among other things (although these are not specifically mentioned by Swampy *et al.*, they are lived through communal living practices, and assumed by association with travellers, commune dwellers, and so on). Such a critique is papered over partly by ignoring its content, but more by constructing the protesters as normal.

But the question for radical environmentalists is how to play this, given that this is one of the effects of media coverage of protests. The intention of much of the green critique is to subvert many of the 'symbolic packages', reproduced above, surrounding the family, class, the chauvinism and conservatism involved in notions of 'Middle England', and so on; but greens are unwittingly being drawn into the reproduction of such social structures through the media coverage of their actions.

In the direct action movement there are two sorts of responses that are made to this dilemma concerning the movement's relationship to the media. One is to argue for a need for alternative media sources which originate in the movement (e.g. Carey 1998; Harding 1998). A plethora of such fora have emerged during the 1990s in response to such a concern, notably magazines like *SQUALL*, *Pod*, *Aufheben*, and *Do or Die*, and video activists such as those associated with *Undercurrents*. The intention is to be able to connect with a broader public to spread the message without it being mediated through the frames of the main-stream media.

But others suggest that this is in itself problematic. Even for those involved in magazines such as *SQUALL* or *Do or Die*, there is a sense that there are tensions in their own media work, with dangers of becoming separated from the main part of the movement which is action-oriented. *Do or Die* (No. 7: 5–8) published an article arguing that the video activist organisation *Undercurrents* should be regarded with scepticism. It suggested that video footage taken by *Undercurrents'* camera operators was being given to mainstream media outlets too freely (on occasion being passed on to the police) and therefore was endangering actions and activists. It also stated that there have been occasions when video operators have attended actions claiming to be from *Undercurrents*, but such claims have been fraudulent and the videos were handed directly to the police. More gener-ally, it suggested that activists should be careful of the ways in which even alternative media outlets construct the actions, and that the internal organisation of *Undercurrents* meant that it was problematic in terms of promoting the move-ment's aims.

More deeply, the argument is that the focus on media distracts from the main purpose of direct action, which is, as it suggests, *direct* action. It is not primarily about 'changing public opinion', or 'influencing policy makers', but directly changing the way society operates and its ecological consequences. As *Do or Die* puts it:

> Actually taking part in direct action should come before the recording of the event for others. It should not be seen as a spectacle, but as the way to achieve results – people taking back control of their lives.
>
> (*Do or Die*, No. 7: 6).[21]

This is not suggesting, therefore, that no account of media should be taken by activists. But it does mean that they should not lose sight of the primary importance of the action itself, its direct ecological and political effects, and the empowerment and social change produced for the participants in the action. Perhaps the point to conclude on here is that despite the character and content of particular media constructions, one of the effects of press and TV coverage of protests like the A30 is that it can encourage others to visit sites and engage in action themselves. This is an unintended consequence of the coverage of the actions by the media, but nevertheless one which is important in helping radical environmentalists build the movement. Deep in the philosophy of direct action is the notion that engaging in action itself broadens the political consciousness of the participant. Hopefully, however, what this chapter has shown is that while this is undoubtedly the case, it does have to be tempered with the recognition of the importance of an ideological struggle, a counter-hegemonic project, associated with direct action, to highlight continually the deep political changes which such actions are designed to help bring about.

Notes

1   I am grateful for the contributions of many present at the conference on Direct Action and British Environmentalism at Keele in 1997. In particular, Bron Szerszynski and Chris Rootes made strong points on the original paper which I have tried to deal with in this revised version. Georgina Arnold sent me a copy of her undergraduate dissertation on the subject (Arnold 1998), and Erica Wirrman, also writing an undergraduate dissertation, gave me very helpful comments. Thanks to Brian Doherty for detailed feedback on the original paper and for suggesting a number of the references which I have included here. Thanks also to Jo VanEvery for discussions about, and references concerning, media studies. I should, however, perhaps apologise for any shortcomings in the paper which result from my interloping into media studies, which (as will be obvious to any specialist from what follows) is not my usual field. Hopefully, however, there is enough of interest to such a reader. The paper arose from more general work on the politics of the car, where in general I focus more on the (changing) cultural symbolism of the car and on the global political economy of the car (see Paterson 2000a, 2000b, for these other works).

2   According to Vidal (1998) this was ghost-written by a fellow activist at the Manchester airport protest, which immediately followed the A30 protest.

3   Just to take examples from the *Guardian*, see Bernard Crick (1997) proclaiming Swampy 'King, for a day', a review of A.N. Wilson's book about St Paul which suggests that the author 'downgrades Jesus to the role of first-century equivalent of Swampy, a flash-in-the-pan political activist within Judaism of symbolic rather than real significance' (Stanford 1997), or Andrew Moncur suggesting that Swampy should play rugby for England (1997). An interview with a professor of English at Liverpool University in *The Times Higher Education Supplement*, who writes about ecology and literature, was entitled 'Swampy's smart set' (Wallace 1997).

4   DBFO stands for Design, Build, Finance, Operate, and refers to the principles underlying road construction as organised through the Private Finance Initiative. The A30 scheme was one of the first constructed under this policy initiative, designed to bring in private finance to fund road schemes, criticised widely for involving a privatisation of the roads system which would ultimately be more expensive than direct building by the state.

5 'Adrian Rodgers, prospective Tory MP for nearby Exeter, is demanding that the tunnellers be "gassed out" or "starved"' (Vidal 1997b; Griffiths 1997b; 'Letters', *Guardian*, 8 May 1997: 18, letter from Addrian Hutson [Animal's father]). Later, during the Manchester airport protest, John Watts, Roads Minister, declared that he wanted to 'bury Swampy in concrete' (Margolis 1997; Brown 1997). Before its appropriation of Swampy as a popular hero, the *Express* had highlighted the way that the protesters were receiving social security benefits (criticised much more vehemently by Norman Tebbit in the *Sun* (see note 7)). Although less strident in their critique than Tebbit, both the *Express* and the *Telegraph* used the clearance of one camp on 24 January 1997, while protesters were in the pub spending dole cheques received that day, to portray protesters in a negative light – engaging in protest 'at the taxpayer's expense' in the *Express*'s words (Rees 1997; see also O'Neill 1997).

6 Although I do not develop the theoretical side of such a notion in this chapter, the notion of normalisation as used here comes out of a broadly Foucauldian understanding of the way power operates in modern societies. The way that people's bodies and identities are produced as useful to the state, through a combination of direct action by the state (surveillance, for example) and the development of academic disciplines (psychiatry, criminology, for example), is central to much of Foucault's work. For a short statement of this, see his 'The Political Technology of Individuals' (1988) which, although it does not use the phrase normalisation, reflects the understanding I have of the term. I develop this point to an extent later in the chapter.

7 The *Sun*'s only coverage was a Norman Tebbit column complaining about how it was they were able to claim social security benefits, and about the police and bailiffs being too liberal and 'making such a meal of clearing them out of the way' (*Sun*, 31 January 1997: 9). The *Daily Mail* gave only a small amount of coverage to this protest, compared to the *Express*. The *Mirror* gave more, and the *Sunday Mirror* featured 'The World According to Swampy' column, from March 9 to April 20.

8 I should perhaps at this point emphasise that I am not suggesting the journalists involved had sat down and consciously articulated these discourses, and this social construction of the protesters, as a deliberate strategy. Their intentions as they wrote the articles, and while various editors worked on them to give them a particular spin, is not particularly important to me. They may have been aiming simply to sell copy, to please their editors/proprietors, report 'objectively' according to their understanding of their professional code, or whatever. My aim is simply to offer a reading of the social/political symbolism embedded in the texts themselves. As Gitlin points out, hegemonic projects embedded in news discourse need not be consciously articulated by the journalists in order to operate as hegemony (1980: 257–258). I am grateful to Chris Rootes for raising this point, although I am not sure he will agree with this answer to his question.

9 The other three, who received less coverage, were Ian, Muppet Dave, and John Woodhams.

10 For similar accounts in the *Telegraph*, see O'Neill and Davies (1997), or Leonard and Barwick (1997). In the former of these, however, the *Telegraph* blacked out Animal's eyes. It claimed she could not be named for legal reasons because of her age. Whether or not this was correct (all of the other papers named her), the blackout of the eyes serves also to construct her as a subversive.

11 Alex Bellos picks up on this theme in his review of the 'Swampy fever' (1997).

12 The title of the article is worth quoting here: 'Swampy the digger fined £500, but his mum still loves him', *Independent*, 2 February 1997.

13 *The Times* had very little coverage of the protests or of 'Swampy mania'.

14 There are two aspects of the coverage highlighted in this literature, however, which would enhance the analysis offered here considerably. One is that audience reception studies, now a mainstream part of media studies, would reveal the ways in which the press coverage was read and understood by the variety of readers of the papers

covered. My reading of the coverage is, of course, in part produced by my own identity, social position, world view, etc., and it should not be assumed that this reading would inevitably be shared by others reading the articles (although that doesn't mean that I don't think the reading I offer here is persuasive). I am grateful to Bron Szerszynski for emphasising this point at the Keele conference. Second, there is a neglect here of the local press. As Burgess and Harrison point out (1993), local media often give distinctively different accounts of environmental controversies than do the national media, and the analysis would be made richer if local press could have been covered.

15 Jay Griffiths was also involved in the protest, as well as sometimes writing reports on them for the *Guardian*, perhaps complicating this point. I am grateful to Brian Doherty for this information.

16 'Politics' here should be read broadly – several studies show that readers often don't know which party their paper supports.

17 It is, however, also backed up by more systematic evidence. The British Social Attitudes survey of 1997 revealed a broader tolerance for protest than in previous years (Curtice and Jowell 1998). Vidal (1998) also suggests that this personalisation of the protest 'neutered or trivialized' it. He also shows the personal consequences for the person, Daniel Hooper, whose personal life was affected deeply by the unwanted attention he received.

18 This had, by and large, already occurred by the time of the A30 protest, in part due to earlier protests but also to other factors such as the Royal Commission on Environmental Pollution report on trunk road building, and financial considerations (see Robinson, this volume). Its effect appears to have worn off with the Labour government reviving some schemes such as the Birmingham Northern Relief Road.

19 On the importance of the media to environmental groups, see, for example, McKay (1998: 9), Negrine (1989: 163–178), Hansen (1993), Anderson (1997), Gamson and Wolfsfeld (1993). I use the term 'environmental groups' in its broadest sense, such that it could encompass everything from loose groupings of greens engaged in NVDA through to the CPRE or the National Trust. While there are obviously differences in how groups along this spectrum deal with the media, the point that the media is central to their tactics is still relevant. Where the differences between the groups will be relevant below, is that the tensions I discuss become more relevant the more one goes towards the radical end of the spectrum. Some in the Direct Action specifically reject the importance of the media, as will be discussed, because of these tensions. Of the works cited above, only Gamson and Wolfsfeld (1993: 116) recognise that not all social movements will rely on or advocate cultivating the mass media.

20 The media have thus become part of what Foucault – following the meaning which emerged in France and Germany in the sixteenth to the eighteenth centuries – refers to as 'the police'. This is a much broader set of practices engaged in by the state than that of the police as the term is understood in English, and explicitly includes the governing of the 'moral health' of the population, something which is easily understood as a practice carried out by the media in the late twentieth century.

21 I am grateful to Ben Seel for alerting me to this article. For a similar expression of scepticism towards either mass or alternative media, see also Aufheben (1998), especially at pages 115–116.

Bibliography

Altheide, D. (1976) *Creating Reality: How TV News Distorts Events*, Sage: Beverley Hills.
Anderson, Alison (1997) *Media, Culture and the Environment*, London: University College London Press.

Arnold, Georgina (1998) 'Representing resistance: radical environmentalism, the media and "Swampy"', undergraduate dissertation, Department of Geography, Newcastle University.

Aufheben (1998) 'The politics of anti-road struggle and the struggles of anti-road politics: the case of the No M11 Link Road campaign', in George McKay (ed.) *DiY Culture: Party and Protest in Nineties Britain*, London: Verso.

Bellos, Alex (1997) 'Swampy fever', *Guardian*, 12 May.

Brooks, Libby (1997) 'Cradle of the revolution', Parents page, *Guardian*, 11 June: 6–7.

Brown, Colin (1997) 'Politics: "Bury Swampy" remark fuels gaffe machine', *Independent*, 15 March.

Burgess, Jacquelin and Harrison, Carolyn M. (1993) 'The circulation of claims in the cultural politics of environmental change', in Anders Hansen (ed.) *The Mass Media and Environmental Issues*, Leicester: Leicester University Press, 198–221.

Butler, Judith (1990) *Gender Trouble: Feminism and the Subversion of Identity*, London: Routledge.

—— (1993) *Bodies That Matter: On the Discursive Construction of 'Sex'*, London: Routledge.

Carey, Jim (1998) 'Fresh flavour in the media soup: the story of *SQUALL* magazine', in George McKay (ed.) *DiY Culture: Party and Protest in Nineties Britain*, London: Verso.

Crick, Bernard (1997) 'Politics and the English language', *Guardian*, 29 March: 23.

Curran, James and Seaton, Jean (1997) *Power without Responsibility: The Press and Broadcasting in Britain*, 5th edn, London: Routledge.

Curtice, J. and Jowell, R. (1997) 'Trust in the political system', in R. Jowell, J. Curtice, A. Park, L. Brook and K. Thomson (eds) *British Social Attitudes, the 14th Report: The End of Conservative Values?*, Aldershot: Ashgate.

Ericson, R.V., Baranek, P.M., and Chan, J.B. (eds) (1991) *Representing Order: Crime, Law and Justice and the Mass Media*, Milton Keynes: Open University Press.

Foucault, Michel (1988) 'The political technology of individuals', in Luther H. Martin, Huck Gutman and Patrick H. Hutton (eds) *Technologies of the Self: A Seminar with Michel Foucault*, London: Tavistock.

Gamson, William A. and Wolfsfeld, Gadi (1993) 'Movements and media as interacting systems', *Annals of the American Academy of Political and Social Sciences*, 528: 114–125.

Gibbs, Geoffrey (1997) 'Swampy the star returns to his hole', *Guardian*, 4 March: 5.

Gitlin, T. (1980) *The Whole World is Watching: Mass Media in the Making and Unmaking of the New Left*, Berkeley: University of California Press.

Griffiths, Jay (1997a) 'Swampy's subterranean homesick blues', *Guardian*, 9 February: 1.

—— (1997b) 'Swampy: he went down the tunnel a nobody, and came back up a national hero', *Guardian*, 2 February: 10.

Hannigan, John A. (1995) *Environmental Sociology: A Social Constructionist Perspective*, London: Routledge.

Hansen, Anders (ed.) (1993) *The Mass Media and Environmental Issues*, Leicester: Leicester University Press.

Harding, Thomas (1998) '*Viva camcordistas!* Video activism and the protest movement', in George McKay (ed.) *DiY Culture: Party and Protest in Nineties Britain*, London: Verso.

Ironside, Virginia (1997) 'Dilemmas: my daughter wants to be with Swampy', *Independent*, 20 March.

Jury, Louise (1997a) 'One week on, Swampy comes out blinking into the television lights', *Independent*, 31 January.

—— (1997b) 'Swampy's University of Action', *Independent*, 1 February.

Leonard, Tom and Barwick, Sandra (1997) 'I'm proud of him, says mother of Swampy, the master tunneller', *Telegraph*, 1 February: 4.

Longrigg, Clare (1997) 'Swampy the subterranean star buries politicians in fame name poll', *Guardian*, 24 February: 4.

McKay, George (1998) 'DiY culture: notes towards an intro', in George McKay (ed.) *DiY Culture: Party and Protest in Nineties Britain*, London: Verso.

Margolis, Jonathan (1997) 'Theme of the week: twaddle', *Guardian*, 15 March: 2.

Melucci, Alberto (1989) *Nomads of the Present: Social Movements and Individual Needs in Contemporary Society*, London: Century Hutchinson.

Mollard, Angela (1997) 'At 16, the rebellious road of a girl they call Animal', *Daily Mail*, 29 January: 12.

Moncur, Andrew (1997) 'And another thing ... Name of the game', *Guardian*, 3 February.

Mooney, Bel (1997) 'Right or wrong, the young at least show some guts', *Express*, 1 February: 10.

Negrine, Ralph (1989) *Politics and the Mass Media in Britain*, London: Routledge.

O'Neill, Sean (1997) 'Police raid camp as bypass protesters spend dole at pub', *Telegraph*, 25 January: 6.

O'Neill, Sean and Davies, Caroline (1997) 'Girl called Animal tells of four days in protest tunnel', *Telegraph*, 29 January: 5.

Parker, Andrew and Kosofsky Sedgwick, Eve (1995) 'Introduction: performativity and performance', in Parker and Kosofsky Sedgwick (eds) *Performativity and Performance*, London: Routledge.

Paterson, Matthew (2000a) 'Car trouble', in *Understanding Global Environmental Politics: Domination, Accumulation, Resistance*, London: Macmillan.

—— (2000b) 'Car culture and global environmental politics', *Review of International Studies*, forthcoming.

Penman, Danny (1997) 'Swampy™: been there, dug that ... now buy the T-shirt', *Independent*, 10 August: 4.

Raven, Charlotte (1997) 'New lads out, new man Swampy in', *Guardian*, 22 April.

Rees, Alun (1997) 'Raid police dole out a surprise', *Express*, 25 January.

Stanford, Peter (1997) 'Second front: Jesus Christ's smarter brother', *Guardian*, 25 February.

Vidal, John (1997a) 'The scum also rises', *Guardian*, 29 January: 17.

—— (1997b) 'Gone to ground', *Guardian*, 22 February: 4.

—— (1998) 'Swampy goes to ground', *Guardian*, 1 April: G2, pp. 2–3.

Wall, Derek (1999) *Earth First! and the Anti-Roads Movement: Radical Environmentalism and Comparative Social Movements*, London: Routledge.

Wallace, Jennifer (1997) 'Swampy's smart set', *Times Higher Education Supplement*, 4 July: 15.

Weber, Cynthia (1998) 'Performative states', *Millennium: Journal of International Studies*, 27, 1: 97–118.

9   Friends and allies

The role of local campaign groups

Gill Cathles

Local campaigns have played a key role in all the major road protests of the 1990s. Their impact and input varies but, in almost all cases, without them the challenge mounted against government and contractors would have been very much less successful in terms of level of involvement, delay in construction and long-term changes in public opinion and government programmes. 'Direct action of itself has not stopped a road; and by themselves the direct action protesters ... would have been marginalised by the government. But, in conjunction with the 250 or so local groups ... a transport policy has been overturned' (Alarm UK quoted in Jacobs 1996: 107).

In the summer of 1998, among the many environmental protests taking place in the UK, one was trying to stop the expansion of a quarry in Bristol and another was fighting a proposed motorway in Birmingham; both were initiated by local campaign groups and later supported by direct action protest camps. The campaign to prevent construction of the 27-mile-long Birmingham Northern Relief Road (BNRR) was led by 'The Alliance Against the BNRR', an umbrella group representing up to twenty-six residents' groups in communities along the proposed route. A six-lane tolled motorway, running 'from the M6 south of the West Midlands conurbation to the M6 north of the conurbation', the BNRR would be Britain's first privately financed toll road. It was proposed by the Highway Agency and Midland Expressway Limited (MEL) – a private consortium of Kvaerner and Autostrada. Given the go-ahead in 1997, it would destroy twenty-seven miles of Green Belt and two SSSIs and pass through communities already significantly affected by major roads and motorways (Friends of the Earth West Midlands Transport Campaign 1997). In Bristol, the 'Friends of Ashton Court' organised themselves to defend a meadow, which formed part of Ashton Court, from Pioneer Aggregates, a subsidiary of an Australian owned company that in 1996 had been given permission to extend an existing quarry (Bristol Friends of the Earth 1997a). Ashton Court, an open green space to the north-west of Bristol, had been 'bought by the council for the people of Bristol in 1959, under the condition that no part of it should be set aside for works which detract from its value as a recreation ground or prejudice the enjoyment of the people' (Ashton Court Quarry Campaign 1998).

Both campaigns brought these issues to the attention of the community, the media and the wider environmental movement. Public meetings were organised, technical information researched, publicity produced, MPs lobbied and court cases prepared. For some, actions have stretched over more than ten years and many local campaigners have become experts on issues such as route planning, road surface construction, court processes, particulates and noise levels. Especially where legal challenges have been undertaken, the impact has also been a financial one, both for individuals and for the community as a whole. The level of risk sustained by individuals in mounting a legal campaign is considerable – for those who put their name to a High Court challenge, were costs to be awarded against them they would be personally liable and risk losing their homes and livelihoods. Local campaigners cannot pack up and move on and for many their involvement will also have long-term effects on their relationships with employers, customers, neighbours or families.

These activities and this level of commitment go largely unrecognised by commentators (e.g. McKay 1998) and by those within the direct action protest movement who recognise only direct action as a strategy for change. The activities of local campaign groups are often more difficult to uncover and are certainly less dramatic. The temptation for many recording and reporting protest is to concentrate on direct action. Emma Must, of Alarm UK, refers to the way in which coverage of direct action overshadows 'weeks or months of careful planning' and how 'direct action has dramatised and highlighted what is going on, but it is only the tip of the iceberg. Underneath there are 250 groups beetling away at a much earlier stage, before the bulldozers have moved in' (quoted in Brass and Koziell 1997: 42).

Tens of thousands of people living in towns and villages across the UK, not satisfied with accepting decisions affecting their environment made by local and national government, are involving themselves in local protest campaigns against housing developments, out-of-town shopping centres, GMOs, and other issues. Local campaigning provides access to protest to a much wider population than does direct action. Seeing friends and neighbours involved challenges the media stereotype and encourages others to join in (McLeod 1998: 351–352), and the nature of the protest allows them to take part at whatever level they feel able. The experience provides opportunities for people in their own communities to learn how to organise and campaign, to understand and use the decision-making processes which affect their lives, and to put their own experiences into a national and global context. Campaigns such as those led by 'The Alliance' and 'Friends of Ashton Court' demonstrate that the willingness to protest now goes well beyond the stereotyped image of young people with dreadlocks and dogs on string. As McLeod commented in relation to the protests in Brightlingsea against the transport of live animals (1998: 357), 'the activity of protesting has become increasingly acceptable socially – as a mechanism which enables "ordinary" members of the public to communicate and register their concerns to governmental bodies'. The media-styled 'Middle England' are the people who have raised large sums of money to support the campaign, who have waved banners in city centres, taken supplies to direct activists on protest camps and threatened, if all else fails, to join them up trees and down tunnels. It is this 'Middle England' which is now calling into doubt the process of government, challenging the claim that we live in a democracy and supporting and co-operating with radical activists.

The fact that 'ordinary people' are finding it necessary to make their views known by protesting has implications for the government and the democratic process. 'Feelings of political powerlessness' (Jacobs 1996: 109) may well encourage more people to become involved in more extreme and varied forms of protest, threatening to overwhelm the structures of law and order (King and Brearley 1996: 105). For some, the result may simply be indifference. In 1995, the Joseph Rowntree Reform Trust commissioned MORI to conduct a State of the Nation poll, which updated similar polls in 1973 and 1991 and 'revealed a high and increasing level of disillusionment with the processes of British politics'. In 1995, 76 per cent believed the present system of governing Britain needed 'a great deal of improvement' compared with 49 per cent in 1973 (Jacobs 1996: 106; MORI 1995). Local campaigns are being used by people as a means of making their views known; something which they feel is denied them by the established processes.

Local campaigns as part of the wider environmental movement

Local campaigns and direct action on environmental issues are part of a complex interaction of groups and individuals, which also includes national environmental organisations such as Friends of the Earth (FoE) and Wildlife Trusts and radical environmental groups like Earth First (EF!), as well as non-aligned individuals. Road Alert! (1997: 1) describes the 'stereotypical sequence' as being 'years of patient, energetic campaigning, lobbying and awareness-raising by dedicated locals; followed by a last-ditch, hectic and spectacular direct action frenzy as construction begins'. Having identified a possible threat to the environment – for example, an application for planning permission – residents and local groups raise awareness of the existence of the threat, both locally and nationally. Strategies to prevent development include petitions, letter writing, representations at public inquiries, legal challenges and demonstrations. It is usually when these have failed that direct action protesters set up protest camps (Doherty 1998: 372), occupying the site and preparing to resist eviction with tunnelling, 'lock-ons' and tree fortifications, etc. Strategies employed by the different groups involved vary, but tend to fall within certain parameters with each group being clear where their own boundaries lie. The use of these strategies by the groupings involved are summarised in Table 9.1 below.

Table 9.1 Protest strategies

	Identification of a risk to the environment	Objections and legal challenges (reformist)	Raising awareness	Direct action (radical)
Camp protesters	Camps are usually established at a much later stage	A strategy not usually used	Some information provided on site; information shared within protest community	The principal strategy, including occupation, tunnelling, 'lock-ons', etc.
Established environmental organisations	Regular monitoring and in a good position to alert the local community	Mainly at public inquiries	Information provided at national and local level	Individual members take part; administrative and organisational support
Local campaign groups	May pick up information within the community	Principal strategy; will involve fund-raising	Information provided for the local community	Depending on agreed aims/type of action/individual choice

Local campaigns and Friends of the Earth

This protest strategy matrix includes (as indicated in Table 9.1) established environmental organisations – mainly local branches of national organisations such as the World Wide Fund for Nature, Wildlife Trusts, Greenpeace and Friends of the Earth. At both Ashton Court and Birmingham it was local FoE groups which played a significant part in kick-starting the campaigns and which provided substantial, on-going support. Radical groups such as EF! have been very critical of what they see as FoE's reluctance to take part in direct action, evidenced particularly by their withdrawal from the Twyford Down protest following advice that assets could be sequestered if they continued (Doherty 1998: 371). Rootes (1997a: 16) maintains that FoE, hampered by lack of resources, has failed to meet local campaigners' needs and that the 'institutionalisation of environmental activism' (1997b: 3) has meant that it has become an increasingly marginalised player. This is a position not supported by events in Birmingham or Bristol. In Birmingham it was members of the local FoE group who first knocked on people's doors in 1991 and persuaded them to fight the road; in Bristol it was through contact with their FoE group that many local people were alerted to quarry extension plans. In these and other protests – for example, Manchester Airport (Griggs *et al.* 1998: 363) – FoE has remained actively involved throughout the campaign, providing practical support and resources, including office facilities, information and publicity, including detailed coverage on its web sites. An 'Alliance' supporter commented, 'We couldn't have done what we did in the beginning without them.' As Rootes (1997a: 18) admits, established environmental organisations like FoE 'may, potentially, serve both as nuclei around which local groups may form and as nodes for the formation of effective networks'. In providing information and publicising the protest, FoE has ensured that local campaigns are placed within a context wider than the immediate local issue. At the same time, it recognises the importance of a locally based and organised campaign and positions itself in a support role. A Bristol FoE spokesperson described FoE's role as being 'to empower people ... not to ensure that everyone joins FoE' (Bristol FoE, June 1998) and Birmingham FoE states that it 'campaigns at local level, to effect environmental change through non-violent direct action (NVDA), empowering people through participation and representation' (Birmingham Friends of the Earth 1999a). This is a position which fits with the wishes of both the campaign groups studied who, while recognising the contribution made by FoE and continuing to work with them, wished to be recognised as separate autonomous groups, believing that gave them more influence and credibility with the public and decision-makers.

Public inquiries

Both the Ashton Court and the BNRR campaigns followed the established route of objecting to plans through planning application procedures and public inquiries. This is a strategy rejected by direct activists and in fact has a poor history of success in terms of stopping construction. It has, however, had the positive effect of politicising those most closely involved, an experience replicating those of campaigners in other environmental protests (Griggs *et al.* 1998; North 1998).

In Birmingham, protest groups established when the road was first announced in 1984 made successful presentations at the first public inquiry in 1988, but in 1989 the route was again proposed, this time as Britain's first private toll road and in 1991 the concession to build the road was given to the Trafalgar House/Iritecna Joint Venture, Midland Expressway Ltd (MEL) (Trafalgar House was later taken over by Kvaerner and Autostrada International). A second public inquiry was set up, reporting in 1997, and, despite over 10,000 registered objections and the longest ever road inquiry, the road was approved (FoE West Midlands Transport Campaign 1998).

It was their experience of the second inquiry which dismayed and incensed campaigners and which led them to question the democratic process. The chair of 'The Alliance', speaking at a public meeting at Water Orton in July 1998, described it as 'a sham' and the ensuing report as 'a travesty of justice' and gave the reason for the need for the campaign against the road as being 'because democracy has let us down'. Another speaker described the evidence used in support of the road as 'obscene in its inaccuracies', and many of those who presented objections are very bitter about the way in which they feel their views were ignored. One resident, living in the village of Gilson in one of the houses nearest to the planned BNRR route, remarked, 'We were bulldozed over' (Anon.

Gilson, July 1998) and another that 'they don't listen to you' (Anon. Gilson, July 1998). The conclusion of many objectors was that the decision to build the road had already been made. As one campaigner concluded: 'What a waste of time – they were going to do it anyway' (Anon. Warwickshire, July 1998).

In Bristol, it was the action of local government which created similar disillusion and disgust. The Ashton Court Estate is owned by Bristol City Council, but until 1996 was located in the county of Avon. In 1985, Bristol City Council granted an option to Pioneer Aggregates allowing them to lease the meadow for quarrying and in 1994 the company submitted a planning application. The application was opposed by a petition from 16,000 local residents, supported by protesters from the Solsbury Hill road protest, near Bath. The City Council decided it could not support Pioneer's application, but the company made a further application for a reduced area to Avon County Council in 1995, which was passed to North Somerset District Council when Avon was abolished. North Somerset Council, despite further objections, granted planning permission in July 1996 (Bristol Friends of the Earth 1997a). The actions of both Bristol City Council and North Somerset District Council have been severely criticised by all the groups involved in the protest. A spokesperson from Avon Wildlife Trust described Bristol City Council as having been 'almost criminal in their negligence' and as making 'a nonsense of the idea of democratic rights' (Avon Wildlife Trust, June 1998). A Bristol FoE spokesperson similarly described the process as 'undemocratic' and as one that has been 'completely disempowering' (Bristol FoE, June 1998). 'Friends of Ashton Court' was set up immediately following the granting of planning permission by residents of Clifton, one of the areas of the City closest to Ashton Court, and a founder member explained how members were 'horrified that it was happening without anyone realising and without anyone having been consulted' (Anon. Bristol, June 1998). She, and others involved, repeated the comments of an elected member of North Somerset District Council, who was reported as having said that even if 99 per cent of the population of Bristol was against the quarry expansion, that was not grounds for planning refusal.

Similar experiences are described by Griggs *et al.* in the campaign against the M77 (Griggs *et al.* 1998: 369) and by North (1998) in the Solsbury Hill campaign, going 'some way in explaining the identification of many residents with the new forms of protest action' (Griggs *et al.* 1998: 369). The response of BNRR campaigners was 'to fight on', a spokesperson adding, 'Who knows what battles we might be able to fight in the future?' ('Alliance' public meeting, Water Orton, July 1998). Whatever their level of participation in future actions, their 'rapid disillusionment' (Griggs *et al.* 1998: 369) with the democratic process is not something which can be unlearned and is a permanent radicalising legacy of the campaign.

Court actions

Both 'The Alliance' and campaigners in Bristol, having lost their argument at the planning stage, became involved in court actions, a strategy which led to further disillusionment, but also to the further politicisation of campaigners. In

Bristol, two residents applied independently to seek a judicial review on the basis that North Somerset District Council's decision was 'based on misguided information and assumptions' (Bristol FoE 1997c). However, the applicants had to prove that they had *locus standi* (sufficient standing) and Mr Justice Popplewell ruled that this was not the case (Bristol FoE 1997c). One of the applicants commented, 'The court is saying two people who live in the area and use the park cannot have *locus standi* ... . It is like the people of Bristol's opinion doesn't count. If we don't have *locus standi* I don't know who can have' (Gibb 1997). This refusal by the courts to recognise members of the local community as stakeholders, combined with lack of resources, establishes a marked disparity in power between campaigners and the construction companies. 'Friends of Ashton Court' considered mounting a High Court challenge, but, concerned about personal liability for damages, did not pursue the idea.

In Birmingham, the legal battle was much longer and more intense. Following John Prescott's decision to allow plans for construction of the road to go ahead, 'The Alliance' went to the courts. On 1 May 1998, a legal challenge was mounted by 'The Alliance' to gain access to information contained in the Concession Agreement between the Department of the Environment, Transport and the Regions (DETR) and MEL concerning high cancellation charges, which 'The Alliance' believes is the reason the Labour Government failed to cancel the programme. The DETR had attempted to prevent access to this secret agreement claiming 'commercial confidentiality' (Friends of the Earth West Midlands Transport Campaign 1998). On 29 July 1998, the High Court ruled in favour of 'The Alliance', quashing the decision by the Secretary of State for Transport and the Environment to refuse to make the concession agreement public, and ruling that the definition of commercial confidentiality as argued by MEL was too wide (Alliance against the BNRR 1998b). This was a significant victory for 'The Alliance' and provided an important boost to morale and an incentive to continue to pursue their challenge to the construction of the road. It will also have consequences far beyond the campaign: it 'will establish case law that will have far reaching effects for many Private Finance Initiative (PFI) projects, of which the BNRR is a flagship ... it will stop the practice of secret private/public contracts being concocted' (Alliance against the BNRR 1998c) and 'the case has already forced the DETR to stop the practice of Government and private business using mutually self-declared secrecy as a smoke screen to hide PFI deals behind' (Alliance against the BNRR 1998a).

'The Alliance' also took their case to the High Court to stop the road being built. However, after two years, court action 'had to be abandoned when it became clear that mounting costs could bankrupt the eight applicants who had financially guaranteed the lawyer's costs' (Alliance against the BNRR 1999b). As with the Public Inquiry, 'The Alliance' felt the process was one which always worked to their disadvantage and the experience reinforced their disillusion with, and distrust of, government and the decision-making process. This lack of comparable financial resources marks a further, apparently insurmountable, obstacle for campaigners. One 'Alliance' member described the whole system as being 'loaded against' the campaigners, those objecting to the scheme having had to raise tens of thousands of pounds in order to present their case at the High Court, while MEL were 'represented by two full-time QCs', supported by experts from the Highways Agency – meaning the campaigners were, in effect, 'up against a government-backed private scheme' (Anon. Warwickshire, July 1998). The experience provided local campaigners with an insight into the role of 'big business' and multinational corporations, their impact on local issues and their connections with local and national government. As observed by Rootes (1999: 298) in relation to campaigns against waste management schemes, 'Local concerns thus came to be identified with global issues and local campaigns with the global phenomenon and so were seen to be in *everybody's* backyard.

The processes of mounting a campaign and preparing for public inquiries and legal challenges meant that campaigners also rapidly educated themselves about the technologies involved in their opponents' industries. This is an experience also noted by McLeod (1998: 355) in relation to live animal exports and Rootes (1999: 298) in relation to waste management. At Ashton Court, campaigners informed themselves about rock formations and primary aggregates, and at the BNRR protest about, for example, light and noise pollution, road surfaces and emissions. Often better informed than the politicians and corporations they were dealing with, this was knowledge which led them to question the information they were given by 'experts' and the rationale provided for the development, and to establish connections with wider environmental issues. Local groups also distribute this information within their community. This leads at least some residents – a source of what McLeod describes as 'potential protesters' – to 'challenge the status quo' (McLeod 1998: 354) by joining campaigns and, in some cases, taking part in direct action protest.

Local campaigns and protest camps

As well as working with established environmental groups, campaigners in Bristol and Birmingham – as in many other protests (Twyford Down, M11, Manchester Airport, etc.) – worked with direct action protesters living on protest camps. The major difference between local campaigners and camp protesters (e.g. Doherty 1998; North 1998) is the adoption by those living on protest camps of an alternative lifestyle, posing 'a cultural challenge to mainstream society which makes people question the existing way of life' (Doherty 1998: 382). However much their experience has changed their attitudes, the reality is that most local campaigners will not adopt this lifestyle, suggesting a major limitation on the process of radicalisation and establishing a clear divide between local campaign groups and camp protesters.

The term NIMBY ('Not In My Back Yard') is often used (e.g. Rootes 1997a; Robinson 1998; North 1998) in discussions of residents' groups motives and strategies. Locals' determination to protect their 'quality of life and material interests' is contrasted with the eco-radicals' 'ideological commitment' and altruistic desire to protect the environment (Griggs *et al.* 1998: 367), or NOPE ('Not On Planet Earth') (Robinson 1998: 3). Although collaboration and understanding between local campaigners and camp protesters is acknowledged, it is principally the local campaign groups whose motives are explored. This polarisation of NIMBY and NOPE and concentration on the values and motives of local campaign groups is problematic in that it creates artificial and unjustifiable divisions. It gives the moral high ground to eco-radicals and patronisingly presents local campaigners as having to be educated by camp protesters before they can be regarded as members of a global environmental movement. In reality, there are differing levels of understanding of local issues and awareness of wider global issues among both groups, and there are members of both whose motivations are personal as well as political. Local campaigners are often very well informed about issues and the wider implications (Griggs *et al.* 1998: 360) and do not necessarily start from the classic NIMBY position. 'The Alliance against the BNRR', for example, campaigned right from the beginning not that the road should be built in someone else's backyard, but that it should not be built *at all – anywhere*. Camp protesters do, very effectively, introduce new strategies and tactics of direct action and expose local campaigners to an alternative lifestyle and worldview. It would be a loss to the environmental movement, however, to regard the profitable exchange of views and strategies as an entirely one-way process. The strategies of local campaign groups effectively enable people living in a community to take part in environmental protest and their involvement prevents eco-radicals from becoming isolated from the values and lifestyles of the communities in which they are based.

At Ashton Court, after strategies to stop the quarry had failed, a protest camp was set up by the Ashton Court Quarry Campaign, a group led by local protesters and supported by Bristol FoE. The protesters styled it very deliberately as a camp run by local people for local people and, although it attracted some support from other sites, there was always a strong local presence. The on-site protesters made considerable efforts to involve other locals and to break down barriers, welcoming visitors to the camp, providing information and arranging picnics and parties to which locals were invited. At the same time, they did endeavour to place the campaign within the wider context of government strategy – for example, encouraging supporters to write to their MP demanding a tax on primary aggregates (Ashton Court Quarry Campaign, undated). Protesters made strenuous efforts to portray themselves as local activists rather than 'eco-warriors', describing their action as being about 'local people fighting for their open space', not 'hippies in woods getting sentimental over a bunch of flowers' (Ashton Court Quarry Campaign 1998). Locals did support the camp, keeping them supplied with food and resources – one man, for example, bringing water to the camp almost daily. Some locals, like those at Solsbury (North 1998) and the M77 protests (Griggs *et al.* 1998) stayed at the camp intermittently. Support for the picnics, however, declined and comments made by those who did turn out suggested that, although there was a general concern about the loss of the meadow, it was one of many competing local issues (including, for example, the Avon Ring Road) and not necessarily the most urgent or important. There was also a lack of focus, with people commenting that they would like to do something, but they were not sure what action to take. This may have been because, with the 'Friends of Ashton Court' no longer very active at this stage, there was no base within the local community from which to co-ordinate activity. Although the 'Friends of Ashton Court' stated that they were 'not into throwing ourselves in front of quarry lorries' (Anon. Bristol, June 1998), they supported the camp in principle, recognising that protesters were taking up a fight the 'Friends' were unable to continue. The boundaries between local campaign and direct action camp were thus blurred to some extent by the emphasis placed by camp protesters on the local context.

Those who set up the Birmingham camp had been protesters at Newbury and were later joined and replaced by activists from other road protest sites. Local campaigners welcomed them and were keen to provide support. 'In the early days', a resident at the northern end of the route explained, 'we collected equipment – tarpaulins, tents, pots and pans. I kept bags in my hall for people from the village to put things in and then I took them up to the camp' (Anon. Staffordshire, July 1998). A campaigner from another part of the route described how he still went to a cash-and-carry every fortnight and took 'catering packs of soup and baked beans' up to the camp on his way home (Anon. Warwickshire, July 1998). Other residents made frequent visits to the camp and helped protesters out with, for example, lifts to benefit offices and GPs and let them use their homes for baths and 'time out'. Talks with protesters on site and discussions about tactics and progress led to mutual respect, lasting friendships, and a willingness by local campaigners to consider adoption of their direct action tactics. One member of 'The Alliance' announced at a public meeting that if construction began she would chain herself to a bulldozer, and a local minister – known as 'the manic tree preacher' – promised that he would D-lock himself up a tree. This was a level of support which camps at both Bristol and Birmingham often experienced difficulty in attracting from other eco-radicals, apparently affected by a perception within the radical environmental protest movement that road protest camps had outlived their usefulness and that, the battle over roads having been won, the focus for action lay elsewhere in, for example, the campaigns against GMOs and green belt housing.

Although for most local campaigners adopting the eco-radicals' lifestyle was not an option, the extent of collaboration and contact undertaken by many leads to a shift in their attitudes, a development observed by Griggs *et al.* (1998: 368) and Doherty (1998: 372) in other protests. A member of 'The Alliance against the BNRR' explained how when she first met protesters from Newbury, 'I nearly died when I saw them; I felt quite intimidated … but I've never met such a bunch of intelligent people. My views changed overnight, I tell you' (Anon. Staffordshire, July 1998). Perhaps because of the relatively low numbers and because the camps were well away from residential areas, neither attracted the hostility described by North at Solsbury Hill (North 1998: 6), where locals felt increasingly resentful of, and threatened by, protesters.

The relationship is not, however, entirely unproblematic. North (1998: 4) describes how at Solsbury Hill, the media-popular coming together of 'Locals in green wellies and tribal Dongas' turned out to be only 'a temporary alliance', and there is some evidence that residents' groups deliberately establish and maintain a separate identity. In the M77 protest, local people lived, took part in and supported the Pollok Free State, but some also set up a separate protest camp, expressing the need to be seen fighting their own battles (Robinson 1998: 17). Campaigners at both Ashton Court and BNRR expressed some anxiety about what they perceived to be the negative impact of the camp protesters' image on public opinion and with what a Friends of Ashton Court supporter described as 'the powers that be'. The Friends of Ashton Court, while wishing protesters 'Good Luck', did not become involved and viewed the camp as something quite separate. They were anxious to be regarded by the Council as a residents' group and not part of the site protest group, which a spokesperson felt the Council might regard as 'a rabble' (Anon. Bristol, June 1998). Some members of 'The Alliance' worried that the BNRR camp projected 'the wrong image' – 'People from the camp sometimes attend "Alliance" meetings. But the meetings are primarily about fund-raising and the problem is that some people won't give money if they think it's going to the camp' (Anon. Warwickshire, July 1998). Others felt that the camp had begun to attract the 'wrong kind of people'.

It is interesting that even when there is a 'twin-track approach' (North 1998: 21), as in the BNRR campaign, with court action and direct action happening simultaneously, it is the local campaign group which is inevitably seen as being in the 'support' role – a view which reinforces the belief that it is direct action that is the more credible strategy. However close their collaboration with campaigners, there are many direct activists who still express the view that they hold the moral high ground and that it is local campaigners' timidity and failure to make the ultimate sacrifice which prevents them from joining. This insistence on direct action as the purest form of demonstration has also led, within protest camps, to a macho approach that has discriminated against women (Anon. 1998: 10). The almost exclusive concentration on the need to construct defences has allowed the often predominantly male communities to ignore the fact that, while men are chopping wood and climbing trees, it is almost always the women who are doing the washing up and cooking, a support role not dissimilar to that assigned to campaign groups (e.g. 'The Mobberley Mums' (Griggs *et al.* 1998: 368) at the Manchester Airport protest). Women living on both the Birmingham and Ashton Court sites complained that their concerns had been dismissed by the men as unimportant and that attempts to address these issues either with them or in women's groups had been resisted.

Despite these problems, it is clear that direct action protest is regarded by most local campaigners as complementary to their own activities, providing a welcome boost to publicity and injecting energy and enthusiasm into campaigners tired and isolated after years of battling through public inquiries and the courts. Although campaigners expressed a willingness to join protesters in direct action if all else failed, the view most often expressed was that the camp protesters employed a *different* set of strategies from mainstream or local campaign groups. As one member of 'The Alliance' said: 'I've tried all the legal ways and I support these people. They do what they do. The Eco-warriors are doing what they're best at and the people in suits are doing what they're best at' (Anon. Warwickshire, July 1998).

Visiting and supporting protest camps, observing and taking part in direct action have exposed local campaigners not only to an alternative lifestyle and to another form of protest, but also to the reaction that it provokes from the authorities and construction companies, an experience which for many has reinforced their low opinion of those responsible for the planned developments. In May 1998, it was suggested to protesters at the BNRR site that they could be the subject of charges under the Prevention of Terrorism Act and in July 1998 the police presence became far more intimidating, with a police helicopter tailing visitors across the field to the site and hovering daily over the camp. In addition, a notice was displayed at the entrance to the field, which has to be crossed to reach the camp, advising people that: 'This land or building is being unlawfully occupied by trespassers in order to prevent a proposed road scheme' and that by being on the land 'as a trespasser' and reading the notice people 'can be assumed to be personally aware' that 'tunnels, shafts, fortifications are being constructed'. It warned that 'Any person shown to have carried out such works or to have incited, conspired towards or aided and abetted such works would be liable to arrest and prosecution' (Justice? 1998). According to the *SchNEWS* report, Staffordshire police warned at a press conference that if the building occupied by the protesters was evicted and 'anyone, be they a protester, a bailiff or the police was injured during the eviction, all those on site would be arrested and charged with "conspiracy to commit murder"'. These warnings made it clear that anyone visiting the protest site or doing anything to support the protesters could be liable to criminal charges. This could include residents who visited the site and brought food or other supplies and possibly even those who produced pamphlets or supported the protest in other ways. Members of 'The Alliance', already identified on numerous occasions in the local press and by police, did not appear to be intimidated by this threat, but local residents with less experience are more likely to have been deterred.

At Ashton Court, Pioneer Aggregates employed Pinkerton Security (a global security operation with its headquarters in the United States) to guard their site. The protesters made an official complaint following an incident when they claimed that guards trampled across their tents one night in May 1998 during a 'dawn raid' (Murphy 1998) and at a picnic on the meadow later that month parents of a group of young girls objected to guards driving a Land Rover at speed close to the girls and shouting at them not to touch the fence. There was, in addition, considerable evidence of surveillance, security guards regularly being observed videoing those attending events. Anyone accessing the Bristol FoE Internet web site on the Ashton Court Quarry Campaign was also, apparently, being watched, the site warning that: 'These web pages are being visited by North Somerset District Council and Pioneer Aggregates and were used as evidence against campaigners at the recent High Court hearings. Reading this material could therefore result in the forces of destruction bringing charges against you for conspiracy' (Bristol Friends of the Earth 1997b).

King and Brearley (1996: 104), commenting on the use of surveillance, wonder how 'otherwise "respectable" demonstrators will view the prospect of being the subject of police surveillance and by implication "suspect"'. An FoE spokesperson reported that some locals were frightened of direct action following the conspiracy charges laid against protesters at Whatley Quarry (in the Mendips, south of Bristol) and that FoE had run training sessions in an attempt to address the problem.

Conclusion

The success of environmental campaigns cannot be measured only in terms of preventing construction. In Bristol, neither the Friends of Ashton Court nor the Ashton Court Quarry Campaign succeeded in stopping Pioneer Aggregates and, once quarrying was under way, the protest by local campaigners and camp protesters came to an end. 'The Alliance' has been more successful in that construction of the BNRR, originally planned for 1996, has been considerably delayed by their actions. Although 'The Alliance' has been forced to abandon its challenge in the courts, they view their campaign as far from over. With Birmingham Friends of the Earth they planned 'a mass rally to be held by communities against the BNRR' in September 1999, asking people to 'come along and show that there is a campaign which is not going away' (Birmingham Friends of the Earth 1999b). A campaign has also been mounted to put pressure on companies financing the BNRR, bolstered by the reported financial problems of the construction company, Kvaerner Corporate Developments (KCD) (Alliance against the BNRR 1999a). Rootes (1997a: 12) suggests alternative measures of success can be found, not only in practical environmental outcomes, but in changes in public policy. Certainly, in terms of practical achievements 'The Alliance', in its successful challenge to contract secrecy, has secured a ruling which could strengthen future environmental campaigns and which has demonstrated the ability of campaigns to challenge governments and multinational corporations successfully.

The Ashton Court campaign illustrates the difficulty of sustaining opposition to relatively small developments. The BNRR, in contrast, will, if built, affect the lives of tens of thousands of people and, although it is not always easy to persuade people that the new motorway would not relieve their problems of traffic congestion on major roads, those living along the route are more easily persuaded of the risks of pollution, noise and increased heavy vehicle use of roads through their communities. These factors have made the argument put by 'The Alliance' much stronger and more persuasive than that put by Friends of Ashton Court, where no residents were directly affected, the quarry was already in existence and the extension affected what was perceived to be only a small part of the Ashton Court area, with minimal effects in terms of traffic and pollution. It was notable that at the Ashton Court Community Festival in July 1998, although the Ashton Court Quarry Campaign was there to publicise their action, very little notice was taken of the eight-foot high security fences around the meadow area and no obvious protest made by the thousands of people visiting. Rootes (1997a: 3) suggests that the skill of campaigners forms a major contribution to their success and the Ashton Court and BNRR campaigns illustrate the importance of a group which can act as a focus for action and mobilisation of local support. The decline of 'Friends of Ashton Court' meant that opposition to the quarry could only be expressed by individuals. This left people wanting to take some action but lacking collective organisation. The BNRR campaign, in contrast, has benefited from the formation of 'The Alliance', a strong campaign group which has successfully fulfilled its role as an umbrella organisation for the number of smaller, local groups scattered along the twenty-seven-mile route and which revitalised the campaign at a crucial point. Driven by a small core group, the success of 'The Alliance' in keeping the campaign going, pursuing action through the courts, maintaining its profile and raising hundreds of thousands of pounds supports the contention that the continued presence of a group of determined, resourceful and skilled campaigners is of crucial importance.

In the long term, success has also to be judged by the contribution made to the environment movement as a whole, not only through changes in national and international policy and practice, but also in the extent to which people's attitudes are changed in a way which will inform their actions in the future (Rootes 1997a: 18). Evidence has been provided from a number of campaigns to support the belief that for those most closely involved in local campaigns, it is an educational and politicising experience (McLeod 1997; Griggs *et al.* 1998; Doherty 1998; North 1998; Robinson 1998; Rootes 1997a). Engagement with government, democratic and judicial systems has led people to change their attitudes and to question the motives and claims of the organisations and institutions involved. Camp protesters are involved in a similar learning process, their attitudes changing as the result of contact with other activists and their engagement with the authorities. With both groups, it is extremely difficult to gauge the long-term effect of these changes. As local campaigners may give up, move on or forget, so may those living on protest camps.

Each of the different groups involved in a protest have clear aims and objectives and are aware of their own boundaries, often taking deliberate steps to establish themselves as separate and different from other groups. They are at the same time keen to work together and value each others' contributions to the overall campaign. It is perhaps in this growing recognition and respect that the strength of the environmental movement lies, rather than in arguments about which strategy, on its own, is more likely to succeed. The BNRR and Ashton Court campaigns demonstrate the importance of a strong, committed, campaigning local group which can mobilise people and resources, and it is quite clear that without the collaboration of local residents, protest camps would not survive. Local campaign groups successfully establish local networks, raise funds, research technical information and organise publicity – all strategies which enable the protest to continue, both in the community and on the protest camps. They also provide an important access point for members of the public who are affected by the proposed construction and who want to find out more, but who would not visit a protest camp. There are growing numbers of those who, like the 'West Country Activist Network', are attempting to maintain and strengthen links between actions and people and work against 'Artificial divisions such as "front-line hardcore" and "part-timer" ', which they believe 'have turned people away from what could be a mass movement' (West Country Activist 1998). The discussion about protest based on the division of protesters into 'NIMBY' and 'NOPE' has accentuated this divide. By concentrating on an examination of the motives and aspirations of NIMBYs, set against an uncritical acceptance of those of NOPEs, the strengths and achievements of those living and protesting in their own community have been under-valued. As has been illustrated, the levels of commitment and of personal risk taken by protesters and local campaigners are comparable and, whatever their tactics, both inevitably find themselves directly confronting the establishment, whether it is police and bailiffs, or the High Court.

Bibliography

Alliance against the BNRR (1998a) 'Landmark legal judgement on BNRR decision day'. Available online at: http: //ds.dial.pipex.com/beep/bnrlegal.htm (9 November 1999).

—— (1998b) 'Residents win court battle over Midlands toll road, 29 July'. Available online at: http://ds.dial.pipex.com/beep/bnrr/bnrlegal.htm (9 November 1999)

—— (1998c) 'Judge orders discovery of secret BNRR deal, 2 June'. Available online at: http://ds.dial.pipex.com/beep/bnrr (9 November 1999).

—— (1999a) *Who owns the BNRR???*, Birmingham: The Alliance against the BNRR.

—— (1999b) 'Motorway madness: the Birmingham Northern relief road'. Available online at: http://ds.dial.pipex.com/beep/bnrr.

Anon. (1998) 'No escape from patriarchy: male dominance on site', *Do or Die; Voices from Earth First*, 7: 10–13.

Ashton Court Quarry Campaign (1998) *They Want to Dig Up Our Park – LET'S STOP THEM!*, Bristol: Ashton Court Quarry Campaign.

—— (no date) sample letter to Gordon Brown, MP.

Birmingham Friends of the Earth (1999a) *Home Page*. Available online at: http://ds.dial.pipex.com/beep (9 November 1999) .

—— (1999b) *Action Briefing: Stop the BNRR*. Available online at: http://ds.dial.pipex.-com/beep/newslet/news0899/story10.htm. (9 November 1999).

Brass, E. and Poklewski Koziell, S. (1997) *Gathering Force: DIY Culture – Radical Action for Those Tired of Waiting*, London: The Big Issue Writers.

Bristol Friends of the Earth (1997a) 'Ashton Court Quarry Campaign – a brief history'. Available online at: http://www.joolz.demon.co.uk (9 November 1999).

—— (1997b) 'Ashton Court Quarry Campaign'. Available online at: http://www.joolz.-demon.co.uk (9 November 1999).

—— (1997c) 'Ashton Court: the legal case against the quarry'. Available online at: http://www.joolz.demon.co.uk (9 November 1999).

Doherty, B. (1998) 'Opposition to road-building', *Parliamentary Affairs* 51, 3: 370–383.

Friends of the Earth West Midlands Transport Campaign (1997) *Six Reasons Why the Birmingham Northern Relief Road Should Not Go Ahead*, Birmingham: West Midlands Friends of the Earth.

—— (1998) *BNRR Legal Briefing*, April. Available online at: http://ds.dial.pipex.com-/beep/bnrr/bnrlegal.htm (9 November 1999).

Gibb, F. (1997) 'High Court clears way for quarrying in public park', *The Times* 25 March. Available online at: http://www.joolz.demon.co.uk (9 November 1999).

Griggs, S., Howarth, D. and Jacobs, B. (1998) 'Second runway at Manchester', *Parliamentary Affairs* 51, 3: 358–369.

Jacobs, M. (1996) *The Politics of the Real World*, London: Earthscan.

Justice? (1998) 'Ashton Court' in *SchNEWS*, issues 172 and 173, 24 June.

King, M. and Brearley, N. (1996) *Public Order Policing: Contemporary Perspectives on Strategy and Tactics*, Leicester: Perpetuity.

McKay, G. (ed.) (1998) *DiY Culture: Party and Protest in Nineties Britain*, London: Verso.

McLeod, R. (1998) 'Calf exports at Brightlingsea', *Parliamentary Affairs* 51, 3: 345–357.

MORI (1995) 'MORI State of the Nation survey for the Joseph Rowntree Reform Trust', *British Public Opinion* (MORI newsletter), June.

Murphy, M. (1998) 'Quarry camp "dawn raid" sparks fury', *Bristol Evening Post*, 6 June.

North, P. (1998) ' "Save our Solsbury!": the anatomy of an anti-roads protest', *Environmental Politics* 7,3: 2–23.

Road Alert! (1997) *Road Raging: Top Tips for Wrecking Roadbuilding*, Newbury: Road Alert.

Robinson, A. (1998) 'From NIMBY to NOPE: building eco-bridges', in C. Barker and M. Tyldesley (eds) (1998) *Alternative Futures and Popular Protest Conference Papers*, Vol. 2.

Rootes, C. (1997a) 'From resistance to empowerment: the struggle over waste management and its implications for environmental education', paper presented to the Sixth IRNES conference, Imperial College, London, Canterbury: University of Kent.

—— (1997b) 'The transformation of environmental activism: activists, organisations and policy-making', paper prepared for the conference of the European Sociological Association University of Essex, Canterbury: University of Kent.

—— (1999) 'Acting globally, thinking locally? Prospects for a global environmental movement', *Environmental Politics* 8, 1: 290–310.

West Country Activist (1998) 'Building the network', *West Country Activist* Issue 6, April/May.

10 The vitality of local protest

Alarm UK and the British anti-roads protest movement

Wallace McNeish

Introduction

Almost all of the academic literature which has been produced thus far on the phenomenon of the anti-roads protest movement in Britain during the 1990s has concentrated upon the direct action specialists linked to the deep Green (dis)organisation Earth First! or anarchist/social ecology groups like Reclaim the Streets! (e.g. McKay 1998; Plows 1995; 1997; Routledge 1997; Seel 1996; Wall 1999). The anti-roads protest movement was however characterised by an alliance between direct action groups such as these and local residents and community groups rooted in the areas which would potentially suffer negative effects from the building of a new road or motorway (Doherty 1996). This chapter sets out partially to redress the balance by examining and exploring a number of the key organisational, sociological and political dimensions of Alarm UK, which between 1991 and 1998 operated as the national umbrella organisation for local groups opposing road and motorway schemes. Weaving together extracts from interviews with leading Alarm UK activists, and quantitative data drawn from a postal survey of the social and political attitudes of Alarm UK supporters, this chapter will argue that this organisation and the local groups affiliated to it made a vital contribution to the overall development of the anti-roads protest movement. Indeed this contribution was so vital that without it the protest movement simply would not have achieved its aims.

Research methodology

The research presented in this chapter was conducted as part of an ESRC-funded PhD on the anti-roads protest movement in Britain in the 1990s. During 1996 a series of recorded semi-structured in-depth interviews with leading Alarm UK activists based in London were undertaken alongside a number of informal meetings with Alarm UK activists based in local groups around the country. In September 1996, with the generous aid of activists based in Alarm UK's London office, this researcher was able disseminate a survey consisting of 500 anonymous questionnaires by post which aimed to build up a social and political profile of Alarm UK's support base within its affiliated local groups.

The questionnaire was distributed in a single mailshot from London by Alarm UK national organisers in order to protect the anonymity of respondents and the confidentiality of the organisation's mailing list. According to the Alarm UK organisers, half of the questionnaires were mailed directly to individual Alarm UK activists who were subscribers to *Alarm Bells* (Alarm UK's newsletter), while the other half were sent out in small batches to the chairpersons of affiliated local anti-roads action groups throughout England and Wales for distribution to activists at meetings. A single reminder letter was sent out at the beginning of October 1996 and by the end of November the last batch of questionnaires was returned. Out of the 500 questionnaires, 236 (47 per cent) were returned completed and 50 were returned blank by the chairpersons of local action groups who had either failed to, or declined to distribute them.

The response rate is indicative of the problems of distribution and of the fact that Alarm UK was a campaigning organisation whose membership was organised in a very loose, fluid and decentralised manner (see next section). The organisers were however aware of the importance of getting a representative sample of affiliated activists and gave assurances that they tried to distribute the questionnaires in such a manner as to achieve this aim. On being sent the results of the postal survey (initially in a brief descriptive form and later again in more detailed form after having employed SPSS as an analytical tool), the national organisers of Alarm UK expressed their general agreement with the research findings. The reliability of the survey results was further tested by comparing them with those of similar surveys of environmental/campaigning organisations which have already been published, while their validity was tested by a process of piloting and refining the questions asked. As with all social surveys, error and bias cannot be ruled out; however, the quantitative research on Alarm UK was supplemented by a number of qualitative interviews which complement and sustain the research findings.

The questionnaire itself was designed to build up a sociological and political profile of Alarm UK's activist base amongst affiliated local groups and individual supporters; thus it included standard questions relating to occupation, income, class, age, gender, ethnicity, housing, and education, together with more complex questions that related to political attitudes, environmental issues, membership of other organisations, lifestyle, types of activism and reasons for activism. The questionnaire also included a revised version of Inglehart's test (1977, 1990) for post-materialism and questions taken from recent British Social Attitudes surveys which are useful for the purposes of comparison. Due to the demands of space and cogency only selected survey results are presented in this chapter; the full results will be published by the University of Glasgow in 2000 as part of the PhD for which the research has been conducted.

Alarm UK: aims, organisation and structure

Growing out of Alarm, the London-wide alliance of local residents associations, environmental and public transport pressure groups, which had successfully campaigned against the road plans included in the *London Assessment Studies* (1988), Alarm UK was launched in 1991 as an umbrella body for the national alliance of grassroots local community action groups opposing the schemes announced in the government's 1989 £23bn *Roads for Prosperity* road-building programme. It was run entirely on a voluntary basis from an office in south London and relied entirely on donations and subscriptions to its newsletter *Alarm Bells* for funding. In 1995, Emma Must, a leading Alarm UK activist did however win the prestigious Goldman Foundation International Award for environmental activism due to her considerable work and personal self-sacrifice in the protests against the M3 extension at Twyford Down in 1992. Aside from carrying the same acclaim and recognition as Oscars do in the world of film, this award carried with it the monetary value of $50,000, a sum which was vital to sustaining the Alarm UK organisation in subsequent years.

Alarm UK's main function was to provide a co-ordinating support network that supplied well researched technical information, relevant tactical advice and both human and material resources in order to increase the effectiveness of local campaigns and aid the development of sustainable transport alternatives. In an interview, John Stewart, the chairperson, described the organisation's role in terms which can perhaps be seen as taking advantage of what social movements theorists call an opening in the political opportunity structure (e.g. Tarrow 1994).[1]

> What Alarm UK set out to do was to change transport policy – it filled a certain niche which was badly needing filled – I mean there are groups like Transport 2000 who are very good, who produce good transport documents, and who think radically and are very good at high level lobbying and that's their role – that's the 'respectable side' ... but I think there was definitely – and out of our London experience we saw this – there was a niche for getting together a grassroots organisation – Stephen Joseph (director of T2000) himself will say that when he goes to speak to senior civil servants they take more notice of his arguments now because there are all these groups ... most of them Alarm groups, around the country saying 'we want change'. So we clearly set out to build this coalition to be a part of changing transport policy and I think that was fairly clear from the beginning.
>
> (John Stewart, 12 July 1996)

The Alarm UK coalition was built around a highly decentralised structure which allowed each local campaign group affiliated to it complete autonomy of action. The aim was to stop roads before public inquiries took place, and before even the statutory consultation period, through the encouragement of local oppositional self-activity which bypassed legal institutions and the due processes of law. In the area of transport policy this constituted an entirely new form of campaigning:

We are there to assist our local groups oppose roads and that is fundamentally what we do – of course it is in a more radical way than they normally
would do so they don't have any belief in public inquiries or the courts
doing them wonders – in many ways that is our biggest contribution to our
local groups – so they don't have any faith in the structures.

(John Stewart, 12 July 1996)

In terms of organisational structure a written constitution was eschewed in
favour of a commitment to just five simple 'guiding principles' that were
designed to focus the aims of affiliated groups in their campaigning:

Halt and ultimately reverse growth in car and lorry traffic.
Encourage people out of their cars and onto their feet, bicycles and public
transport.
Switch freight from lorries to rail and water.
Oppose any more growth in road capacity.
Reduce the need to travel by locating life's essentials (healthcare, employ-
ment, shops, etc.) near to where people live.

(Stewart 1995 13: 4)

Alarm UK did not conform to any of the other usual bureaucratic trappings
associated with formal organisation. Thus there were no leaders as such, only
'organisers' or what might be termed facilitators, and there were no AGMs and
hence no votes, resolutions or centralised decision-making mechanisms to grind
out policy or fix a 'party line'. Once or twice yearly there were, however,
roundtable meetings of a loose 'steering group' made up of between fifteen and
twenty prominent anti-roads and public transport activists from around the
country and numerous meetings of a similar nature occurred more regularly on
a regional basis. These groups met in order to learn from the experiences of
others, to discuss transport policy and to co-ordinate future strategy. National
conferences were also organised every couple of years or so (1993, 1995, 1996),
which, aside from engendering further opportunities for the establishment of
solidarity networks, provided workshops on campaigning techniques and wide-
ranging debate and discussion on relevant issues. When questioned in interviews
about the lack of democracy in Alarm UK, leading activists did not deem this to
be a problem because all key decisions regarding campaigns were taken at a local
level where groups organised according to their own preferences in a variety of
different ways. Organisation at the local level, therefore, ranged from highly
structured groups with formally elected office bearers through to the loosely
structured informal activist network favoured by the Alarm UK organisers themselves. Describing the organisational set-up one leading activist said:

to be quite honest there has not been all that much democracy in Alarm –
somebody called it 'virtual democracy' … it is a coalition, there is some sort

of steering, the members are a sounding board but there is also a very small group of people who have given it direction.

(Anon. London, 12 July 1996)

The lack of a formalised structure with no defined leadership or hierarchical chain of command was held by the organisers to be a tactical advantage in pursuing Alarm UK's aims:

what they (*the government and media*) is obsessed by is the question of who are the secret leaders, who is pulling the strings and they couldn't work out that the movement didn't have leaders – we'd often meet journalists with the same sort of mindset as MI5 and they would ask 'who are the leaders? are you the leader?' 'hardly hardly' – 'what are the various journals we should be looking at?' – 'none' – and they just couldn't understand this lack of structure – now it really did throw them – when the M11 was on they hired Grays (a private security agency) to take pictures of everyone involved and what they were partly trying to do I think was to build up cases so they could bring charges after the event – it was also though to pick out who the leaders were.

(Anon. London, 13 December 1996)

One of the most significant aspects of Alarm UK's role in the mobilisation against road building was that NIMBYism (Not in My Back Yard-ism) was strongly discouraged by Alarm UK's organisers in favour of a NOPE (Not on Planet Earth) philosophy. The term NIMBY, as commonly used in relation to planning issues, connotes a narrow, particularist self-interest which, although generally accepting the need for development – in this case roads and motorways – seeks to shift the spatial location of that development to another community/area in order to avoid the potential costs that the development will engender. In the case of roads and motorways, the locational burden might include quality of life costs like noise, pollution and loss of environmental amenity or more material costs like the loss of value of property. Robinson (1998) describes NIMBYism as 'the rational response of people concerned that the impact of an environmentally damaging development, which they support in principle, will be confined to their locality whilst benefiting other areas and in this sense NIMBY protests are essentially concerned with distributional issues' (Robinson 1998: 3). Alarm UK sought to combat NIMBYism by taking a stance against *all* road building and by encouraging networking and solidarity between the different local groups opposing roads. In an interview, the chairperson of Alarm UK indicated that, although NIMBYism may have been an initial factor in mobilising affiliated local anti-roads groups, it is a mobilising factor which decreased in significance as the Alarm UK network developed:

Our biggest problem in the early days when we started nationally and in London as well was NIMBYism ... to combat this Alarm in London had only one rule – the rule was that the groups, local residents etc had to say 'no roads anywhere in London' and then they could join Alarm. With Alarm UK – although we try to encourage the same ethos we have never really said no to any group … its the angle people were coming in from – there needs to be a little bit of self-interest, its not just altruism … now on the whole things have expanded tremendously since then and individuals grow with campaigns, but that (*NIMBYism*) was a driving force initially.

(John Stewart, 12 July 1996)

This extract also illustrates a recognition that values often change through the experience of taking collective action – i.e. that what often starts out for an individual as a sectional or particular interest develops into an engagement with more universalist concerns. In fact, postal survey evidence indicates that a significant minority of Alarm UK's support base were involved in opposing roads which would not impact in the area where they were living (42 per cent of respondents) and therefore the term NIMBY cannot be applied to them.

A mark of the intensity of disquiet with the government's plans in potentially blighted areas of the country is that within the first year of its existence Alarm UK had attracted the affiliation of approximately 100 new local action groups, a figure which grew to almost 300 in the mid-1990s when opposition reached a peak. These groups were mostly concentrated in and around Greater London, East Anglia and the south of England, where most of the government's plans centred, although there was also a scattering of affiliated groups throughout all the other parts of the United Kingdom. Groups could have anything between 10 and 1,000 members and the Alarm UK organisers in London usually estimated membership on the basis of each group averaging 100 members. Thus, although an exact figure cannot be arrived at, it is possible that, at its height, there were up to 30,000 members and supporters participating in one way or another in the local action groups affiliated to Alarm UK.

The socio-political dimensions of participation in Alarm UK's local groups

Postal survey data (as illustrated in Table 10.1), reveals that the typical member/supporter of a local group affiliated to Alarm UK broadly conforms to the socio-demographic picture of such activists painted by the theoretical literature on the class nature of 'new' social movements. This literature posits that adherents to contemporary social movements are in general relatively affluent, highly educated and rooted in the professional new middle class (Eder 1993; Habermas 1987; Inglehart 1990; Melucci 1989; Offe 1987; Scott 1990; Touraine 1988). The figures also display a consistency with empirical research carried out in the UK on the memberships of anti-nuclear and environmental organisations, which reinforces the above thesis (Parkin 1968; Cotgrove 1982; Porritt and Winner 1988; Mattausch 1989; Bennie, Rudig and Franklin 1991).[2]

Table 10.1 Socio-demographic characteristics of Alarm UK supporters

Variable	Description of key frequencies
Ethnicity	95% white European
Age	25% under 35, 59% under 45, 81% under 54. The median age group is 40–44
Sex	69% male, 31% female
Marital status	44% married, 42% single, 18% cohabiting
Educational attainment	68% hold a university degree, 25% hold a higher degree or professional qualification
Employment	22% higher professional, 22% lower professional, 10% self-employed in technical/consultancy/creative services, 10% self-employed in small business, 5% routine manual/non-manual, 12% retired, 11% unemployed, 8% students
Union membership	36% are or have been members: 19% in teaching unions (AUT, NUT, etc.), 14% in UNISON. 16% are or have been members of professional associations.
Household income	26% under £10,000 per annum, 14% above £45,000 per annum. The median income bracket is £15,000–£24,999
Housing	71% privately owned, 21% privately rented, 3% council tenants, 5% other

What is particularly noteworthy about the statistics pertaining to the socio-demographic profile outlined in Table 10.1 is the almost complete absence of both routine manual and non-manual workers, who together make up only 5 per cent of the total, and the fact that Alarm UK was an overwhelmingly 'white' organisation. One key reason for this is that the government's road-building programme was largely centred upon the shires of central, and southern England where working-class and ethnic-minority populations are far less concentrated than in the urban environment. The predominance of male respondents should also be highlighted as the survey results also suggest that Alarm UK was a very male-dominated organisation. This, however, would be misleading because as a leading activist said in an interview:

> In Alarm … once you get out to the groups it is the women that are in posi-tions of influence and power and the men tend to be sleeping members which is the reversal of most organisations – it is excellent and it's all about our style of campaigning.
>
> (Anon. London, 13 December 1996)

Thus, according to the quoted activist, what the survey bias in favour of men reflects is the support base of Alarm UK at a particular level, i.e. the less active supporters as opposed to the most active supporters, tend to be the chairpersons or office bearers of local action groups. This answer was in fact confirmed by an earlier small-scale pilot questionnaire disseminated at the Alarm UK national conference in February 1996, which revealed that among core activists there was greater gender parity with the split 55–45 in favour of men.[3] Leading activists also confirmed in interviews that on the 'steering' group there was a similar 'rough' parity between women and men (Anon. London, 13 December 1996).

From the statistics in Table 10.1, a demographic profile of a typical member/supporter of a local group affiliated to Alarm UK can be constructed. This member/supporter is a white, middle-aged home-owning male who is highly educated and does professional white-collar work which is relatively well paid in the public sector. Table 10.2 reveals what political values this member/supporter is likely to hold and what political activities he is likely to be engaged in.

Politically, the survey data indicates that the local groups affiliated to Alarm UK had a support base which was broadly homogeneous and moderately left wing in its ideological orientation. Statistics from questions which asked respondents to locate themselves on a left–right scale through to those which were concerned with party membership, voting intentions and political activism each indicate a broadly leftist political outlook. Questionnaire responses to a modified version of Inglehart's test for post-materialism (Inglehart 1990: 74–75), also constitute evidence to support this thesis in that respondents consistently chose to give priority to options that pertained to 'quality of life' issues as opposed to those linked to material acquisition.[4]

Table 10.2 Political values and political activism of Alarm UK supporters

Variable	Description of key frequencies
Self-placement on a left/right scale	47% centre left, 20% centre, 13% far left, 12% deny the validity of the categorisation
Political self-description	29% green, 28% socialist/green socialist, 12% liberal/green liberal, 9% conservative/green conservative, 12% non-political. 61% of total use the term 'green'
Key political issues	64% environment, 30% transport, 30% social justice, 28% democracy, 21% unemployment, 14% health, 12% education
Voting intentions (general election)	30% Labour, 17% Green, 16% Liberal Democrat, 5% Conservative, 23% undecided, 7% not-voting
Activism in political parties	35% are party members. 15% in Green Party, 11% Labour, 6% Liberal Democrats. 20% were party members in the past
Activism in campaigns/pressure groups	62% are members of FoE, 44% T2000, 32% Greenpeace, 24% CND, 24% Anti-CJA, 20% Earth First!, 18% Animal Rights

It is important to note, however, that despite this general left-wing orientation, respondents did not define either themselves or their political concerns in a traditionally left-wing manner (i.e. as socialists with socialist concerns) as the prominence of the self-description label 'Green' and a prioritisation of the environment as the number one political issue illustrates. Nevertheless, for Alarm UK supporters, to be Green and to place the environment at the top of the political agenda clearly entails an identification with the left.

Alarm UK supporters also expressed a high level of interest in politics because, in response to a survey question designed to measure such interest, three-quarters of respondents indicated that their interest was 'a great deal' (45 per cent) or 'quite a lot' (38 per cent) as opposed to the 14 per cent who indicated 'some interest' and the 3 per cent who answered 'not much' or 'none'. The British average for the first two categories combined is only 32 per cent (Brook *et al.* 1992: 49). Alarm UK respondents were clearly then much more 'political' than the wider population, and this supports the thesis advanced by Witherspoon and Martin (1992) through their empirical research that 'political interest levels have a large and consistently positive impact on the main dimensions of environmental concern' (ibid.: 14–15). One of the key findings of the survey in relation to the politics of Alarm UK respondents was, however, that a high proportion translated their 'environmental concern', their political beliefs and interest in politics into forms of political action not only through their involvement in anti-roads campaigning, but also through membership of political parties and/or a variety of campaigning pressure groups.

Taken together the findings outlined above suggest that the local groups affiliated to Alarm UK contained many experienced political/social movement activists who already had a left/green identity of one type or another prior to their involvement with anti-roads activism and could bring campaigning skills and organisational experience to bear in the context of such activism. Indeed, from the research it can be surmised that these skills coupled with the resources of education and finance which the professional new middle class possesses played an important role in facilitating the mobilisation and in determining the overall success of the anti-roads protest movement. In pointing to the left/green identity of Alarm UK supporters and the multi-dimensionality of their environmental activism, the research is also suggestive of the way in which the mobilisation and success of the anti-roads protest movement was bound up with the longer-term evolution and impact of the wider Green movement.

Alarm UK's early campaigns and the impact of Twyford Down

In 1991–1992, Alarm UK affiliated groups recorded a number of small-scale successes in Birmingham, Yorkshire, Woodstock and Exeter. Road schemes costing several hundred million pounds in total were abandoned before construction began after local people mobilised quickly and engaged in well organised and highly focused protest campaigns designed to embarrass and pressure their local councils into capitulation. These campaigns involved a mixture of innovative publicity stunts, demonstrations, mass letter-writing and the circulation of alternative sustainable transport plans and counter-information to the media. Survey data reveals that activists in Alarm UK's affiliated local groups engaged extensively in the following types of 'traditional' activism: letter-writing (86 per cent), petitioning (54 per cent), demonstrations (54 per cent), organising public meetings (50 per cent), campaign fund-raising (41 per cent). In the summer of 1992, however, pivotal events occurred in the campaign to stop the M3 from being built through Twyford Down, which were to have a profound impact on the future direction of Alarm UK, the growing anti-roads protest movement, and indeed on the wider environmental movement in general.

At the Twyford Down construction site, after lengthy planning and legal processes had been exhausted, significant numbers of objectors from local action groups, joined the young 'deep-green' activists of the Donga Tribe and the newly formed British wing of the radical environmental 'disorganisation' Earth First! in collective non-violent direct action (NVDA) protests involving tree-sitting, obstruction of machinery and mass trespasses, which flouted the law and led to physical confrontations with security guards, and large-scale arrests from the police. Naturally these events brought an intense media presence to the protest site, beginning a trend of media interest which was to persist throughout the 1990s. Although the battle at Twyford Down was eventually lost, the protests succeeded in adding a substantial figure to the final costs of construction. It is estimated that Tarmac, the construction firm, ran up a bill of £267,000 with Brays, its security contractors, simply for surveillance of the protesters, while in 1993 the Department of Transport (DTp) began legal processes to claim damages of £1.9 million (rising eventually to £3.5 million) from those activists who played a key role in delaying the motorway construction. The DTp was eventually forced to drop its case in 1995 (Rowell 1996: 336–337). The protest also succeeded in bringing the issue of road building into the wider public arena for the first time in a very dramatic manner. Of more significance, though in terms of the overall 'war' against the government's road construction plans, was the positive experience of the local groups working together with Alarm UK, as the national umbrella organisation, and the 'eco-warriors' (as the press had now branded them). This cemented a new alliance which, although fragile and at times highly tense due to very real philosophical and tactical differences, was nevertheless sustained throughout the protests of subsequent years.[5]

Bridging the gap between moderates and militants

Alarm UK as the national umbrella organisation for local anti-roads action groups played a crucial role in maintaining the anti-roads alliance by supporting the NVDA tactics favoured by the eco-warriors from the outset, even if it meant breaking the law. At Twyford Down, Alarm UK lent its active support to the direct action protests through the local objectors groups and donated £7,000 of its Goldman prize money towards supporting the Road Alert! organisation, which had a specific remit to concentrate on educating protesters in NVDA skills. Such a firm stance stood in direct opposition to established environmental groups like the CPRE (Council for the Protection of Rural England), who opposed the roads programme but also opposed direct action, or Friends of the Earth who vacillated on the question until the Newbury protests of 1995. Alarm UK's positive position vis-à-vis direct action is made clear in the following interview extract:

> we have no problem with breaking the law, no problem with direct action, in fact we actively support direct action – I think what we would say is that it is sensible to try to stop a road before it gets to direct action – most of our groups do not want some great political battle – they want to stop a road – but if the bulldozers are coming then we have absolutely no problem at all … . Some groups, traditional groups like FoE and the CPRE have got into a hell of a mess as to whether they should break the law and support direct action – for us it was never an issue. Now in some ways we are therefore tarred by officialdom because what we are doing is seen to be so dramatic or what is seen as a big step in breaking the law – they can just about under-stand colourful protests but once you take the step of breaking the law you are suddenly beyond the pale … you're M15 fodder … so we would get our phones tapped in the way that the CPRE would never get theirs tapped, but also we wouldn't be invited to – say there was some big roundtable discus-sion on transport – on the whole we wouldn't get an invite because we're tarred with breaking the law.
>
> (Anon. London, 13 December 1996)

Data from the postal survey reveals that a significant minority in Alarm UK's local groups also had 'no problem' with taking direct action in that a third (33 per cent) claimed to have taken part in NVDA and almost three-quarters (74 per cent) agreed that law-breaking was legitimate in certain circumstances.

As the above interview extract also illustrates, this positive stance on direct action meant that Alarm UK paid certain penalties in terms of its relationships with established environmental organisations and with government officials. However, on the other hand, such a stance also enabled it to draw both a high degree of respect (which the established organisations had forfeited) and support from militant groups such as Earth First! Indeed as the survey data in Table 10.2 indicates, Earth First! made up a small but significant layer of Alarm UK's membership in the local action groups. It is notable, however, that the highest proportions in terms of organisational crossover are from FoE and Transport 2000, something which reflects the wish among the grassroots in these organisa-tions to be more pro-active on the roads issue. Alarm UK should therefore be viewed as performing a vital bridging role for the wider anti-roads protest move-ment in bringing together, and in creating solidarity and dialogue between, a wide array of activists from different backgrounds, age groups and perspectives upon politics and the environment.

At times, however, the role which Alarm UK played was very much like that of a tightrope walker who has to maintain a very singular focus in order to get to the other side of a chasm. Alarm UK thus took a radical stance in opposition to road building and in its advocacy of sustainable transport policies, but in order to keep the coalition together it did not directly engage in overtly 'political' activities or, for most of the 1990s, widen its brief to take on other social and environmental issues. Leading activists certainly saw their own activities as being highly political, but deliberately set out to cultivate an apolitical image for Alarm UK so as to not alienate any of its supporters in the coalition. On this subject a leading organiser said:

> we're highly political but we don't give that image … the image that Alarm UK is giving is to be non-party political which is fairly standard amongst the pressure groups but I think that some of us who are centrally involved see it as much more political than some of our member groups would do.
>
> (Anon. London, 12 July 1996)

Another leading activist argued how important it was to stay focused on the issues of roads and transport and how other campaign issues that she had clear sympathy with had to be excluded in order to maintain the coalition:

> it is this focused thing – otherwise we'll fall apart – even with leaflets and things it's difficult – I've got this leaflet against the arms trade and we cannot put it in our Alarm Bells newsletter because its too confrontational and it's not a transport issue – it offends me greatly but we've got to stick to our guns.
>
> (Anon. London, 12 July 1996)

Despite this will to 'stay focused' and to stick to its transport–roads remit, Alarm UK did nevertheless begin to redefine its agenda in the mid-1990s. In 1996, Alarm UK joined the 'Real World Coalition' of thirty NGOs, voluntary organisations, campaigning and pressure groups that aimed to put the issues of environmental sustainability and social justice onto the party political agenda (Jacobs 1996). Its acceptance by the Real World was a sign of its growing mainstream 'respectability' and importance as a campaigning network. In October 1997, Alarm UK also published a report entitled *Poor Show* (Stewart *et al.* 1997) that criticised new Labour's transport policies for failing the poor and made a number of recommendations which linked the needs of social justice with sustainable transport alternatives.

Evaluating the role of Alarm UK and the local action groups

The anti-roads protest movement in Britain during the 1990s constituted what was perhaps the most widespread expression of radical environmentalism this country has yet seen. Through the mobilisation of numerous local protest groups a mass protest movement came into being that was prepared to challenge the government in the area of its transport and environmental policies in an often very direct and confrontational manner. By the late 1990s that challenge had proven largely successful in that the government's roads programme had been cut to less than one-third of its original £23 billion projection, while environmental, transport and traffic issues had been pushed to the top of the policy agenda.[6]

This U-turn in government policy and policy making, beginning with the Tories at the end of their long period in office and continuing under 'new' Labour, can be explained by looking to the inter-related factors of a change in public opinion resulting in political pressure, the spiralling costs of policing road construction sites and the fiscal desire to cut public spending (but see Robinson, this volume).[7] The former, however, is the most important of the three factors: first, because the policing of contentious constructions such as nuclear facilities of both military and civilian usage has always been expensive, but there has always been a political will to do so since opposition has come from only a minority of the public; and, second, because the desire to cut public spending is something which has been a constant wish of successive governments for the last couple of decades and is therefore nothing new. What best explains this change, therefore, is that government's political will to drive ahead with its roads programme simply evaporated after it became increasingly clear that a significant and steadily growing proportion of public opinion was no longer on its side. This change is directly attributable to the actions of Alarm UK affiliated local groups and the eco-activists which formed the partnership integral to the anti-roads protest movement. In taking such a militant stand against this particular area of government policy, the activists involved in this partnership combined 'traditional' and more 'direct' methods to fight individual roads, and to publicise and raise the profile of the wider environmental–social issues involved. In turn, this generated the conditions for a wide-ranging public debate which has significantly altered social attitudes.[8]

Had the partnership at the heart of the anti-roads protest movement not existed and each wing acted autonomously, then it is difficult to see where success in stopping the roads programme could have come from. The local groups would probably have taken legal processes to their limits, lobbied through the usual channels and perhaps even have disrupted public inquiries, as some did in the 1970s (Tyme 1978), but would not have gone much further. On the other hand, the eco-activists would no doubt have made their moral point by taking direct action, but, lacking in material and financial resources and in large-scale support on the ground, it is likely that they would have been suppressed by the state and marginalised by a hostile media. In contrast, the partnership created a protest movement that was focused, innovative, dynamic and well supported, with each wing complementing the other. In this partnership Alarm UK played the vital bridging role of facilitator, thus enabling something akin to what Habermasians call a 'communicative dialogue' (Habermas 1987) to take place among the different social interests and diverse environmental and political groupings involved. The success of the protests against road building is such that

by April 1998 the organisers of Alarm UK viewed themselves as having essentially achieved what they set out to do in 'winning the argument against the
government', and therefore folded their national organisation. Many of Alarm
UK's local groups continue though to operate through regional networks
campaigning on transport and developmental issues.[9]

Notes

1   Tarrow (1994) defines these structures as the 'consistent – but not necessarily formal,
     permanent or national – dimensions of the political environment which either
     encourage or discourage people from using collective action' (Tarrow 1994: 18).
2   The age breakdown of the Alarm UK respondents and the referenced studies which
     contain data on the age profiles of other British social movement organisations do
     however differ significantly from the assertion of European 'new' social movements
     theorists that activists are primarily young.
3   In February 1996 a small-scale pilot questionnaire was disseminated amongst the
     eighty or so core activists attending Alarm UK's national conference in Nottingham.
4   Respondents were asked to prioritise the following ten categories in order of impor-
     tance to them politically. Five of these Inglehart defines as materialist and five as
     post-materialist: fighting crime, protecting the environment, fighting inflation,
     creating a less impersonal society, maintaining order within the nation, the protection
     of civil liberties, creating more beautiful cities, maintaining economic growth, giving
     people more control over their own lives and maintaining strong defence forces. Of
     the values which Inglehart defines as materialist, only 'fighting crime' made it into the
     top five priorities chosen, with 47 per cent choosing it as their fifth option – what this
     reflects perhaps is the very real fear of crime which many people living in the UK
     currently experience.
5   By the late 1990s direct action protests against roads and motorways on the 'British
     model' had spread to the European continent, particularly to France, Luxembourg
     and Germany where construction schemes posed a threat to the future of ancient
     forests. During this period Alarm UK also sent representatives to Poland and
     Hungary, where environmentalists had requested advice to further their cause against
     road developments engendered by post-'communist' industrial 'modernisation'.
6   The budget of November 1996 was the decisive turning point because it reduced the
     number of planned road schemes from the 600 included in the original 1989 plans to
     150. Of these, 144 were to be publicly funded and 33 were to be privately funded
     DBFOs (Design, Build, Finance, Operate) (Stewart 1997: 1).
7   In mid-1995, the National Audit Office predicted that it would cost £26 million to
     guard road construction sites before the government's road programme was
     completed – at this high point of protest £575,000 per month was being spent on
     security at these sites (Rowell 1996: 352).
8   The British Social Attitudes Survey (1998) found that in terms of commonly
     perceived threats to the countryside 'the greatest change in recent years – especially in
     just the last three years – has been the rapid increase in concern about roads and
     traffic' (*British Social Attitudes* 1998: 115). Trends of concern about the related areas of
     traffic congestion and pollution were also significantly upwards in the mid- to late
     1990s, while, as a solution to personal travel and mobility problems, support for
     improving all areas of public transport outweighs 'building more roads' by more than
     a factor of two and a half (*ibid.*: 115–127). On the issue of direct action tactics, survey
     figures such as those produced by Gallup in 1995 showed that 68 per cent of the
     adult UK population would be willing to consider civil disobedience in favour of a
     cause that they believed in – this was up 14 per cent from a similar poll carried out in
     1984 (Porritt 1996: 302).

9 Of those roads currently at the planning stage, the £250 million M74 Northern
Extension, which has been routed to cut a swathe through the south side of Glasgow,
is probably the most controversial – this road is being resisted by a new umbrella
organisation called JAM74 (Joint Action Against the M74) that was set up in August
1998 and which consists of local objectors, public transport pressure groups and environmental organisations who aim to stop it before it reaches the construction phase.
However, if unsuccessful in this JAM74 will encourage NVDA against it.

Bibliography

Bennie, L., Rudig, W. and Franklin, M.N. (1991) *Green Party Members: a Profile*, Glasgow:
Delta Publications.

Brook, L., Jowell, R., Prior, G. and Taylor, B. (eds) (1992) *British Social Attitudes – the 9th
Report*, Aldershot: Dartmouth Publishing Company.

Cotgrove, S. (1982) *Catastrophe or Cornucopia*, London: Wiley.

Doherty, B. (1996) 'Paving the way: the rise of direct action against road-building and the
changing character of British environmentalism', in, C. Barker and M. Tyldesley (eds)
Alternative Futures and Popular Protest Conference Papers, Vol. 2, Manchester: Manchester
Metropolitan University Press.

Eder, K. (1993) *The New Politics of Class*, London: Sage.

Habermas, J. (1987) *The Theory of Communicative Action*, Vol. 2, London: Beacon Press.

Inglehart, R. (1977) *The Silent Revolution: Changing Values and Lifestyles amongst Western Publics*,
Princeton/London: PrincetonUniversity Press.

—— (1990) *Culture Shift: Change in Advanced Society*, Princeton: Princeton University Press.

Jacobs, M. (ed.) (1996) *The Politics of the Real World*, London: Earthscan.

McKay, G. (ed.) (1998) *DIY Culture: Party and Protest in Nineties Britain*, London: Verso.

Martin, J. and Witherspoon, S. (1992) 'What do we mean by Green?', in L. Brook, R.
Jowell, G. Prior, and B. Taylor (eds) *British Social Attitudes – the 9th Report*, Aldershot:
Dartmouth Publishing Company.

Mattausch, J. (1989) *A Commitment to Campaign: A Sociological Study of CND*, Edinburgh:
Edinburgh University Press.

Melucci, A. (1989) *Nomads of the Present*, Philadelphia: Temple University Press.

Offe, C. (1987) 'Challenging the boundaries of institutional politics: social movements
since the 1960s', in C.S. Maier (ed.) *Changing Boundaries of the Political*, Cambridge:
Cambridge University Press.

Parkin, F. (1968) *Middle Class Radicalism*, Manchester: Manchester University Press.

Plows, A. (1995) 'Eco-philosophy and popular protest: the significance and implications of
the ideology and actions of the Donga tribe', in C. Barker and M. Tyldesley (eds) *Alternative Futures and Popular Protest Conference Papers*, Vol. 1, Manchester: Manchester
Metropolitan University Press.

Porritt, J. (1996) 'Twyford Down: the aftermath', in B. Bryant (ed.) *Twyford Down: Roads,
Campaigning and Environmental Law*, Aldershot: Earthscan.

Porritt, J. and Winner, D. (1988) *The Coming of the Greens*, London: Fontana.

Robinson, A. (1998) 'From NIMBY to NOPE: residues of reform on Glasgow's Southside', in C. Barker and M. Tyldesley (eds) *Alternative Futures and Popular Protest Conference
Papers*, Vol. 2, Manchester: Manchester Metropolitan University Press.

Routledge, P. (1997) 'The imagineering of resistance: Pollok Free State and the practice of
postmodern politics', *Transactions of the Institute of British Geographers* 22, 3.

Rowell, A. (1996) *Green Backlash*, London: Routledge.

Scott, A. (1990) *Ideology and the New Social Movements*, London: Unwin Hyman.

Seel, B. (1996) 'Frontline eco-wars! The Pollok Free State road protest community: counter-hegemonic intentions, pluralist effects', in C. Barker and M. Tyldesley (eds) *Alternative Futures and Popular Protest Conference Papers*, Vol. 2, Manchester: Manchester Metropolitan University Press.

Stewart, J. (ed.) (1995) *Alarm Bells* No. 13 June.

—— (ed.) (1997) *Alarm Bells* No. 19 January.

Stewart, J., Miles, N. and Connolly, P. (1997) *Poor Show*, London: Alarm UK.

Tarrow, S. (1994) *Power in Movement: Social Movements, Collective Action and Politics*, New York: Cambridge University Press.

Touraine, A. (1988) *Return of the Actor*, Minneapolis: University of Minnesota Press.

Tyme, J. (1978) *Motorways Against Democracy*, London: Macmillan.

Wall, D. (1999) *Earth First! and the Anti-Roads Movement: Radical Environmentalism and Comparative Social Movements*, London: Routledge.

11 The politics of the car

The limits of actor-centred models of agenda setting

Nick Robinson

Introduction

> It must be considered that there is nothing more difficult to carry out, nor more doubtful of success, nor more dangerous to handle, than to initiate a new order of things. For the reformer has enemies in all those who profit by the old order, and only lukewarm defenders in all those who would profit by the new order, this lukewarmness arising partly from fear of their adversaries, who have the laws in their favour; and partly from the incredulity of mankind, who do not truly believe in anything new until they have had actual experience of it.
>
> (Machiavelli 1513: 21)

The explosion in the number and diversity of actors involved in the conflict over road building is one of the most significant changes since the end of the Thatcher era. At one extreme the 'traditional' transport groups with a long history of transport campaigning, such as Transport 2000 and Alarm UK, have been joined by the direct action movement, which has operated outside the established policy making arenas through their occupation of the road construction sites. At the other extreme, the period has seen the increasing involvement of 'moderate' mass membership campaigning organisations such as the RSPB and the National Trust, which, due to the nature of their membership, enjoy quasi-insider status (Young 1993: 20–21).

It is a common hypothesis within the political science literature that changes to the nature of the opposition to a policy are often an instrumental precondition for changes to the agenda (see in particular Dudley and Richardson 1995, 1996 and 1998 for analysis with reference to the roads issue). This chapter argues that agency-based accounts such as these, while useful, are too simplistic to account fully for the political conflict surrounding the roads issue in the Major era. In fact, in order to explain the apparent impact of the direct action movement at this time, it is essential to look both at the impact of their activity (as agents) and the effect of changes to the political landscape which have enabled these groups to become more effective.

Part 1 of this chapter thus examines the impact of the activity of the direct action movement on the political handling of the roads issue. It argues that the

legacy of exclusion from the formal policy process led the direct action movement to search out alternative policy arenas (such as the media and the
construction sites) in order to influence the policy agenda and overcome the
institutional bias of the road lobby. (For an exposition of this approach in the
roads case, see Dudley and Richardson 1996, 1998.) I examine the view that
such action has indeed led to significant change to the policy agenda, arguing
that physical occupation of the construction sites enabled the direct action movement increasingly to influence the media agenda, dramatically changing the
perception of the roads issue (Anderson 1997: 122; cf. Paterson, this volume).

But while acknowledging that the direct action movement has become
increasingly sophisticated at exploiting such arenas in order to pressure government, I argue in the remainder of this chapter that much of the apparent success
of these groups has been conditional on luck, resulting from changes to the political landscape which have occurred independently of their actions.

First, the government itself has been implicated in a number of policy disasters which have 'unwittingly' aided the anti-roads groups. In particular, I argue
that the government's 1989 *Roads for Prosperity* programme (Cm 693), intended to
overcome the problem of congestion, was totally inadequate for the task. This
enabled the anti-roads groups to question the entire rationale behind the government's policy of accommodating projected traffic growth through road building.
Second, the problems (and, crucially, the perception of the problems) associated
with transport have got worse: congestion is rising, ambient air quality is deteriorating, global warming has been 'discovered'. Third, the relatively small majority
of the Major government gave relative power to the 'Not In My Constituency'
campaigns of Conservative MPs attempting to secure local support in the face of
the party, which were an important factor in the cancellation of the proposed
M25 widening and in the cancellation of a series of bypasses. The actions of
these MPs were not indicative of any sea-change in government policy, nor did
they reflect the actions of the direct action movement; instead, they were based
on short-term perceptions of electoral gain. And, finally, the anti-roads groups
have benefited from a number of systemic developments (Sabatier and Jenkins-
Smith 1993) which have reduced the control of the Department of Transport
(DTp) over policy. These have resulted from four main sources: the European
Union, the Department of Environment, global environmental forums (in particular surrounding the Climate Change Convention), and the Treasury.

Thus, in order to offer a genuinely comprehensive account of political change
in the roads case it is not sufficient to focus *just* on the activities of the anti-roads
groups – it has to be acknowledged that changes to the political landscape have
been instrumental in enabling these groups to become more effective.

Alternative policy arenas and the anti-roads groups

Here, in the first part of this chapter, I look at the capacity of the direct action
movement to change the policy agenda. Dudley and Richardson's work on
policy change and British trunk roads policy provides a useful starting point for

exploring the role of outsiders such as the direct action movement on the agenda-setting process (Dudley and Richardson 1995, 1996, 1998). These studies have been motivated by a desire to 'reconcile the tendency of established policy communities to create conditions of stability, or even inertia, with powerful dynamics which can produce significant change both in the network of actors involved and in policy itself' (Dudley and Richardson 1996: 63).

They argue that, historically, roads policy has been dominated by a core network involving an 'alliance' between the road lobby and Department of Transport, which excluded the anti-roads groups (1996: 64; see also Hamer 1987; Dudley 1983). However, since the 1970s the anti-roads groups have been able to overcome the institutional bias of the core network by infiltrating arenas which the pro-roads groups have less control over: 'It is of crucial importance, therefore, to recognise that, although an interest may be apparently excluded from a core policy community, by selection of the correct arena for its activity, and effective transmission of its message, it may by indirect means have a signifi-cant effect on the policy network and policy itself' (Dudley and Richardson 1996: 75).

A key method by which these groups have affected policy by *indirect means* reflects the interaction between the image of a policy and the arena in which it is discussed. Policies that are discussed in the core arena will be dominated by the institutional bias of the actors which are involved within that arena: they will dominate the nature of discussion and, in normal circumstances, will be able to maintain control over the image of policy. In contrast, when policy is discussed in an arena outside the core, outsider groups are able to exercise more influence over the nature of the conflict between actors and, hence, the policy image of an issue (Baumgartner and Jones 1993: ch. 2 and 1991: 1045–1047).

Dudley and Richardson have described a number of arenas which the anti-roads groups have successfully infiltrated in order to change both the discourse conducted between actors involved in, and the policy image of, the transport issue. Of particular importance to the opponents of roads has been, in the 1970s, the highway inquiry process (see Dudley and Richardson 1998: 6–15), and, in the 1990s, the road construction sites (see Dudley and Richardson 1996: 78 and 1998: 18–21). Thus, change to the policy agenda has resulted from the anti-roads groups' strategy of operating in alternative arenas using a variety of tactics, of which the most innovative has arguably been extra-legal activity in the form of occupation of the road construction sites.

The media and the politics of direct action

A number of studies of the politics of transport have focused on the effect of the interaction between direct action and the media on the policy agenda (Anderson 1997; Paterson, this volume; Doherty 1997; Dudley and Richardson 1996; Young 1993). In the 1970s, conflict centred on the highway inquiry process, being explicitly designed to disrupt its operation and thus gain widespread coverage in the mass media (Tyme 1978: 40; Levin 1979: 27). By the 1990s, however, the intensity of the conflict between rival interests had increased dramatically. Significant sectors of the anti-roads 'alliance' had lost faith in the highway inquiry process, resulting in a new form of transport protest focused on disruption and physical obstruction of the road construction sites. As was the case in the 1970s, the protests were conducted in ways guaranteed to secure extensive coverage in the media (Doherty 1997: 154).

Doherty argues that these new kinds of anti-roads protests have taken on the character of 'a form of siege warfare', in which the occupiers build defences in trees, tunnels and houses and the 'besiegers outnumber the occupiers and have greater resources' (1997: 150). In spite of the imbalance of resources between these groups, the protesters have had considerable success in maintaining media interest in the protests through a process of ongoing technological innovation in the nature of the tactics which they have used. The most significant of these innovations have been lock-ons, walkways, tripods and tunnels, all of which depend for their success, and their high media profile, 'upon the risks taken by the protester. By making themselves vulnerable, they require the evictors to take extra care and time, to avoid injury' (Doherty 1997: 153). Protesters have thus been able to sustain the interest of the media in the conflict over roads.

The impact of these tactics on the media's handling of the transport issue has been considerable. In an interview, Keith Harper, transport correspondent for the *Guardian* newspaper, suggested that they were instrumental in changing the perception of the transport issue from that of a technical and specialist issue to an emotive and public one. The protests at Twyford Down, in particular, were extremely important: for the first time the act of protest became news in, and of, itself. Editors began to report the protests as general news stories, and through association a number of hitherto specialist transport stories gained an emotive aspect and a higher media profile (Interview, 8 May 1996).

At one level, the impact of direct action has been considerable. First, it is not governed by rules of engagement which can be controlled by the pro-roads groups. While highway inquiries, by their nature, restrict the scope of the opposition to a particular road scheme – it is not possible to question the need for a road in the first place or to request that a single road proposal be looked at in relation to the strategic plan for the whole network (Levin 1979: 23–31) – in contrast, the direct action arena enabled the anti-roads groups to gain institutional advantage in their conflict with the road lobby for the first time. The culture of the road lobby means it is unlikely to deploy outsider tactics in order to get its message across, but for 'outsider' groups direct action is a much more rational tactic. It is highly confrontational, and frequently extralegal, thus appealing to groups which have little to lose in alienating mainstream political opinion.

Second, the insider groups' traditional methods of lobbying increasingly failed to interest news editors, at the same time as the direct action groups gained unprecedented media access. Thus an important line of communication between the pro-roads groups and the public was progressively restricted during the Major era, to the advantage of the direct action movement.

However, although these changes have had a significant effect on what Schattschneider (1960) would term the 'public' perception of the transport issue, they have had less effect on the 'private' consideration of the issue, which remains closed to the direct action movement. From their outsider perspective, policy making is still characterised by frequent contact between government bureaucrats and the pro-roads groups in a core policy community. Overall, the effect of the media interest in direct action has been double-edged: while it has enabled anti-roads groups to gain access to public opinion, it has also led to concerns amongst government policy makers over the capacity of these groups to engage in conventional dialogue.

An actor-centred account of agenda setting in the transport area hinges on two key premises: that the strategies of the outsider groups have opened new arenas to the anti-roads groups, thus creating opportunities for them to challenge the dominance of the pro-roads lobby; and that these changes, in a causal sense, explain the transformation of the transport agenda in the Major era. The preceding analysis has shown that the activities of the anti-roads groups have indeed opened a number of new arenas of political conflict in this period, in particular through the relationship between the media and the direct action protests at construction sites. However, as I will now argue, it is important not to overstate the impact of direct action: the transformation of the transport agenda has, at least in part, been down to 'luck'.

Luck and the direct action movement

In the Major era the direct action movement was the beneficiary of significant good fortune in four key ways. First, these groups benefited from a number of policy disasters by central government. Second, transport increasingly came to be seen as a policy problem on the basis of congestion and vehicle-related air pollution. Third, the relatively small parliamentary majority of the Major government following the 1992 election left the road programme vulnerable to local constituency campaigns. And, finally, a number of systemic developments reduced the control of the Department of Transport over policy.

This section of the chapter explores the impact of these changes, arguing that they have significantly altered the political landscape, and so benefited the direct action movement. However, these changes have occurred largely independently of the activity of the anti-roads groups, and without them those groups would have had much less impact on the political agenda, regardless of the ingenuity or innovation of their political activity.

Policy disasters and luck

The 1989 *Roads for Prosperity* (Cm 693) initiative was a public policy disaster. It was developed in response to the *National Road Traffic Forecasts* of 1989, which predicted that traffic levels would grow by between 83 per cent and 142 per cent by the year 2025 (DTp 1989). Government itself was thus instrumental in outlining the nature of the problem of congestion; in response to these figures it launched an expanded roads programme, *Roads for Prosperity* (Cm 693), presented as the solution designed to overcome the problem.

However, it became clear almost immediately that the scale of the congestion problem outlined by the government's traffic projections could not be solved by *Roads for Prosperity*. In particular, studies by Friends of the Earth (FoE) and the British Road Federation (BRF) aimed at evaluating the extent to which future road provision would accommodate the projected growth in road traffic reached very similar conclusions.

The FoE study examined the effect of the projected rise in UK traffic levels on the motorway network (McLaren and Higman 1993 cited in Cm 2674: 6.26–6.27). It focused on 'the situation at the automated national traffic census points ... which are selected to represent free-flowing traffic conditions and do not therefore include the most congested sections of the motorway' (Cm 2674: 6.26). According to the FoE survey, even at these points there was considerable congestion at 14 of the 29 census points in 1989. Furthermore, by 2025, even assuming that all of the extensions to the road network envisaged in *Roads for Prosperity* were fully implemented, 'there would be chronic congestion at all but one of the 29 points' (Cm 2674: 6.26). Calculating the scale of extensions to the road network which would be necessary in order to accommodate the projected traffic increases and ensure that chronic congestion was prevented, it concluded that on the M1 between Luton and the M25, to take the most extreme example, the road would need to be widened to ten lanes in each direction (Cm 2674: 6.27). Thus the programme of road building outlined in *Roads for Prosperity* was insufficient to sustain the predict and provide orthodoxy in the long term.[1]

The BRF was also concerned with the capacity of the trunk road network to accommodate future traffic growth (Centre for Economics and Business Research 1994). 'The conclusion reached was that, if expenditure on the trunk road programme continues at the present level, congestion will increase by 14 per cent between 1993 and 2010 and the average speed of traffic will fall by 5 per cent. Even with a 50 per cent increase in expenditure on the trunk road programme, it was calculated that congestion would increase by 7 per cent and speeds fall by 3 per cent' (Cm 2674: 6.28). Thus, both studies illustrated that the expansion of the road programme envisaged in *Roads for Prosperity* was insufficient to accommodate predicted traffic growth, posing a serious challenge to the long-term stability of the predict and provide orthodoxy.

The *Roads for Prosperity* initiative can be described as a 'policy disaster' (see Dunleavy 1995 and Grant 1997). According to Dunleavy, a policy disaster can be identified as 'a large scale, avoidable policy mistake' which is 'eminently foreseeable – but decision-makers systematically choose to ignore an abundance of critical or warning voices in order to persevere with their chosen policy' (Dunleavy 1995: 52).

The simultaneous publication of the *National Road Traffic Forecasts* and the government's *Roads for Prosperity* initiative conform to Dunleavy's criteria. First, it is reasonable to assume that policy makers should have been aware that the proposed road programme would not be able to ameliorate the anticipated growth in road traffic: it was clear that the proposals were inadequate to solve the problem.

Second, it should have been clear to policy makers that the shortfall was such that the anti-roads groups would inevitably derive great benefit politically. Government decision-makers should have foreseen that *Roads for Prosperity* would strengthen the campaigns of the anti-roads groups, enabling them to argue that it was impossible to accommodate the government's own projections within a sustainable expansion of the road network:

> I think the government at that particular moment saw there to be votes in roads, so they had the biggest programmes that they'd ever had, but the reality was that they'd already had a fairly substantial road programme, they always knew those things were going to require attention, they just hadn't ever, perhaps, published them in quite the same way with quite so much attention. So, yes, I think the government's own pride in it made it a very tempting target.
>
> (Interview, Paul Everitt, BRF, 21 August 1996)

Thus, the government's own forecasts, and its proposed solution, unwittingly aided the opposition of the anti-roads groups. The anti-roads groups were further aided by the publication of the BRF report, which compounded the sense that *Roads for Prosperity* (Cm 693) was a government-instigated policy disaster. According to Phil Goodwin of the SACTRA committee, the conclusions of the BRF report:

> [were] interpreted by the BRF at the time as being a very powerful argument in favour of additional road building because if one didn't have a very big, much expanded road programme, congestion [would get worse which would] affect economic growth and so on. What actually the report demonstrated though, was under the *Roads to Prosperity* roads programme, still extant at the time, congestion would actually get a bit worse every year. And even if the roads programme were increased by 50 per cent ... congestion would still get a bit worse every year; though not so quickly on their calculations. ... Now, the fact that it was the British Roads Federation demonstrating that the largest conceivable roads programme wasn't actually going to make congestion better (was only going to slow down the pace at which it got worse) was an absolutely decisive part of the argument in then casting doubt on the whole strategy of which capacity construction was a core.
>
> (Interview, 20 June 1997)

The events surrounding the publication of *Roads for Prosperity* (Cm 693) were thus important in providing the basis for the conflict which would develop in the Major era, providing the first element of the good fortune which would subsequently aid the activities of the direct action movement.

Policy problems: road transport, public health and luck

In the Major era transport came to be seen as a policy problem on the basis of both public health and congestion.

First, transport was identified as a significant contributor to deteriorating public health. Knowledge of the effects of transport emissions on public health increased significantly: research was produced in the 1990s which clearly identified the impact of emissions on the respiratory system, the functioning of the brain and the development of leukaemias and cancers (Cm 2674: 3.20–3.30 and Cm 3587). Second, a number of studies established that 'in many areas, particularly urban, they [road vehicles] have become the predominant source of many pollutants', accounting for over 75 per cent of all emissions (Cm 3587: 43). These findings had a very powerful effect on the policy agenda with considerable public attention focused on the perceived link between vehicle emissions and increasing levels of asthma.

A common trend throughout the developed world has been an increase in both the *prevalence* of asthma (i.e. the number of registered asthmatics) and the *incidence* of asthma (i.e. the number of recorded asthma attacks), particularly among children. In the UK there has been a fivefold increase in both the prevalence and incidence of asthma since the mid-1970s (cited in Cm 2674: 3.23 and DoH 1995a: 2). These increases are important in explaining the rise of transport as a policy problem, as both public and media became convinced that they could be explained by rising vehicle emissions (Grant 1995: 172), although the argument that such emissions are responsible is in fact far from certain: the findings of a number of scientific studies suggest that factors such as deteriorating indoor air quality and increases in the numbers of household dust mites are a more likely explanation (see, in particular, DoH 1995b; see Cm 2674: 3.23–3.30 for an overview). In spite of this uncertainty, however, both the public and the media remain convinced of the link, perhaps because of the public's reluctance to admit that personal lifestyle choices could also explain increasing levels of asthma:

> People always latch on to things that they don't have to do something about. One of the other frustrating things that we have to deal with, when we are under constant pressure to improve air quality, is that people think that it's the government's responsibility to improve air quality. Now most people spend at least 50, 60, 70 per cent of their time indoors, and mothers or fathers with young children spend up to 90 per cent of their time indoors. Indoor air quality is another issue altogether. And the factors affecting indoor air quality are actually quite different from outdoor air quality, but they're much more difficult to control. But people focus on the outdoor air quality because it's something that someone else is responsible for.
>
> (Interview, Tim Barraclough, DoETR,
> Air Quality Division,
> 4 September 1997)

So in spite of considerable uncertainty within the scientific community, both the media and the public remained convinced that vehicle emissions were causing a rise in the number of asthmatics and that the problem would become worse in the future. Thus, the direct action movement was once more the beneficiary of luck: for at a time when vehicle emissions (particularly from new cars) were declining and having less effect on public health, the public perception remained that they were increasing and causing significant damage to public health (for data on the decline in vehicle emissions see Cm 2674: 289–300). Such a perception significantly eroded the policy image of motor vehicles, with great benefit to the activities of the direct action movement.

Policy problems: congestion and luck

Second, transport came to be seen as a policy problem on the basis of congestion. In particular, increasing traffic congestion led to concerns over its effect on economic development, with a survey by the CBI in 1989 estimating it was costing the UK economy £15 billion per annum (cited in CBI 1995b: 38). With the discrediting of the predict and provide orthodoxy in the Major era, the CBI was particularly concerned that the government had failed to develop any alternatives:

> Demand on parts of the network is effectively being rationed by the economically and environmentally inefficient tool of congestion. The Government's wish to see a shift in traffic from road to rail as one way of relieving pressure on the road network, for environmental reasons, is welcome and well documented; but neither the size of shift which government believes feasible is clear, nor the mix of policies needed to achieve it.
>
> (CBI 1995a: 80)

Transport was also identified as a significant problem as a result of the publication of the report, *Trunk Roads and the Generation of Traffic*, by the Standing Advisory Committee on Trunk Roads Assessment (SACTRA) in 1994, which aimed to evaluate the efficiency and accuracy of the traffic forecasting models used by the DTp and to examine the impact of infrastructure developments on traffic generation (SACTRA 1994: i).

Given the long-term strategic nature of transport infrastructure, planning the role of forecasting is very significant (SACTRA 1994: 2.06–2.07). In the light of this, the report was concerned to note that the existing forecasting system did not consider that expansion in capacity could generate additional traffic, a fact which it found surprising:

> Every scheme involves the investment of a large sum of public money, and can also imply large private sector investment. Highway development can have a profound and long-term effect not only on the fabric of the nation,

but also upon regional and local land-use patterns, the environment and the way in which people conduct their business and personal lives.

(ibid.: 2.02)

The DTp argued that this omission could be justified 'on the grounds that any estimates of generated traffic would be very uncertain and (for the most part) would have a very small effect on traffic flows' (ibid.: 2.11). Whilst SACTRA acknowledged that research into induced traffic was complex, its conclusions contradicted those of the DTp, finding that induced traffic was in fact extremely important: new, or improved, trunk roads actually contribute significantly to the generation of traffic (ibid.: ii).

The impact of this report on the agenda-setting process was considerable. In a political climate in which the roads programme was under sustained pressure generally, the SACTRA report further discredited the roads for prosperity orthodoxy, legitimising the anti-roads groups' criticisms of the capacity of the predict and provide orthodoxy to accommodate increases in traffic. Once more the direct action movement were fortunate.

In the Major era, transport thus became a policy problem on the basis of congestion due to a combination of factors: the legacy of the policy disaster which resulted from the *Roads for Prosperity* programme in 1989; growing opposition both to the effects of congestion on quality of life and on economic development and the legacy of the SACTRA report. Together these developments eroded the predict and provide orthodoxy. But they did not lead to a significant change in policy: the nature of the orthodoxy on which policy was based shifted only slightly from predict and provide to *restrict and provide*. This new orthodoxy acknowledges that is not possible to provide sufficient infrastructure to accommodate the predicted growth in traffic. A mechanism, such as road pricing, must be introduced which manages demand on the road network, so maintaining network efficiency.

Overall, therefore, while the direct action movement has been the beneficiary of good fortune this has not been sufficient to gain control over the pattern of policy making which still remains dominated by policy insiders and the government.

Parliamentary politics and luck

The direct action movement also benefited from the pattern of parliamentary politics which developed in the Major era. Following the 1992 general election the parliamentary majority of the Major government was reduced to 21, further decreasing during the lifetime of the government. The effect of Major's small majority was variable: in general terms, 'the drop in the majority ... represented more of a potential than an actual threat' to Major's administration, but on certain policy issues, ministers 'had to make concessions to their own backbenchers' in response to a threat of rebellion by a group of MPs (Riddell 1994: 49; see also Ludlum 1996: 117–125). One such issue was the road programme, with back bench rebellion leading to the cancellation of a number of proposed schemes within the government's *Roads for Prosperity* programme (Cm 693).

The centrepiece of backbench opposition in the roads case related to a series of schemes proposed in the south-east of England, with the proposal to widen the M25 between the M3 and the M4 to 14 lanes (DTp 1994: 18, 50–53) providing the principal focus of conflict. This, together with other proposals within the government's roads programme, provided the impetus for a group of MPs to come together and co-ordinate their opposition (BBC 1994). A BBC *Panorama* programme, *Nose to Tail* (1994), identified ten MPs who were instrumental in leading parliamentary opposition to three principal schemes: the widening of the M25 and the M62, and a proposed east–west route from Harwich to South Wales through Buckinghamshire.

Opponents of the road schemes in parliament were joined by local government representatives, similarly concerned about the electoral implications of widespread road building. In the South East, the local authorities affected by the government's road proposals formed an alliance (SERPLAN) under the leadership of the transportation director of Surrey County Council, Geoffrey Lamb, in order to lobby the government for alternative solutions (BBC 1994). Once again the sheer scale of the proposed widening of the M25 provided the focal event for the opponents of further road building:

> If you look at some of the things that were proposed: the sections through Surrey. If it had been done incrementally then probably no one would have noticed ... [Laughter] ... . That sounds a bit stupid I know. They blew up this huge political balloon and someone was bound to try and prick it. It was just too tempting ... . And then when you have the stalwarts of the Tory heartland come out against it: counties like Surrey who are very, very powerful. The war they can rage against proposals like that is pretty substantial. They are not ALARM or even Friends of the Earth, they can mount a terrific campaign. And of course all the others joined them.
>
> (Interview, Richard Davies, Mott Macdonald, 27 February 1996)

The importance of this combined opposition in south-east England was considerable, but had little to do with the actions of the direct action movement. Opposition to the government's road schemes was motivated, for the most part, by short-term electoral considerations, not in response to the direct action movement's demands:

> My feeling is that this change, certainly in a lot of this grass roots protest, would not have been successful if it had merely been a few people throwing themselves in front of bulldozers in Twyford Down, or what-have-you. They would have been marginalised. It's been successful because it's had, what I called, I rather like the phrase so I'll use it again, 'the voting classes' behind it.
>
> (Interview, John Stewart, Alarm UK, 23 November 1995)

The anti-roads groups thus benefited from the support of public opinion, but, in relying on the support of such public opinion in order to influence the policy agenda, their ability to effect change is restricted. For public opinion on the roads issue is subject to high levels of internal inconsistency: while road users oppose the building of new roads and show high awareness of the environmental impacts of motor vehicles, they are unwilling to reduce their reliance on the car to reflect this environmental consciousness.

The cuts to the roads programme in the period 1995–1998 can, therefore, only really be explained as a pragmatic reaction to pressure by governmental actors operating within the parliamentary arena. This pressure resulted from the contradictory demands of the 'voting classes', combined with the need to reduce public expenditure (for the latter, see below), rather than any fundamental change to the priorities of government as a result of the activity of the anti-roads groups. In fact, a focus on the parliamentary arena reveals that outsider groups are still heavily reliant on influencing public opinion at 'arm's length'. Parliament remains an unstable arena for the anti-roads groups, motivated, as it is, by ambiguous public opinion, trying to balance short-term environmental and revenue saving concerns with future demands by the public for further road building.

Exogenous political pressure and luck

Finally, the anti-roads groups have benefited from a number of changes to the external environment in which roads policy is formulated. As Sabatier argues, such changes 'can dramatically alter the composition and the resources of various coalitions and, in turn, public policy within the subsystem' (1993: 19). This has proven to be true in the roads case as overspill pressures resulting from global environmental forums (in particular, surrounding the Climate Change Convention), the European Union (EU), the Department of Environment (DoE), and the Treasury have significantly reduced the control of the DTp over policy.

First, transport has increasingly come to be seen as a problem in global environmental terms. In the past twenty years the nature and magnitude of the problems associated with transport have changed from concern over local environmental effects, such as noise and emissions of pollutants such as lead and black smoke, to the impact of transport on trans-boundary environmental problems, such as acid rain and global warming (Button 1995: 173). This change has been very important in further eroding the positive policy image of the car with considerable benefit to the direct action movement.

While the problems of acid rain and global warming both became identified as problems associated, in part, with the car, their effects on the policy process have been quite different. In the case of acid rain, increased knowledge has resulted in significant policy change. The effects of acid rain resulting from vehicle emissions can be largely ameliorated by a technical fix in the form of a catalytic converter; the implementation of such solutions was supported by the government as they do not rely on any significant changes to transport behaviour. In contrast, global warming, which requires significant changes to behaviour, has had less impact on policies. Government has proved reluctant to implement policies such as road pricing or planning restrictions, which could significantly change behaviour, and so reduce the contribution which road vehicles make to greenhouse gas emissions (see Robinson 2000: Chapters 6 and 3 for a discussion of road pricing and the planning issue respectively). Consequently, initiatives have focused on policies such as the fuel duty escalator and 'tax breaks' for small cars which, critics argue, will have little impact on transport behaviour and hence emissions of the principal greenhouse gases (see, for example, Maddison and Pearce 1995: 135).

Second, during the Major era the EU has achieved progressively more prominence as an actor in transport policy, which has served both to aid and to undermine the activities of the direct action movement.

On the one hand, EU activism has helped the direct action movement by opening an alternative arena to the direct action movement which appears superficially sympathetic to their aims. This was illustrated during the conflict over the M3 extension through Twyford Down when the European Commission launched enforcement procedures against the UK government in October 1991, arguing that it had failed to undertake adequately an Environmental Impact Assessment and had thus broken Community law (Kunzlik 1996: 257–258).

At one level, the intervention of the then EU Environment Commissioner, Di Meana, was of great benefit to the direct action movement, threatening, as it did, to stop the construction of the M3 extension and commanding extensive coverage in the media. However, at another level, the legacy of the conflict 'sparked an immediate crisis in relations between the Commission and the government' (Kunzlik 1996: 256), which served to harden the attitude of the UK government towards Europe. The conflict over Twyford thus became caught up in the wider conflict between Britain and Europe surrounding the negotiation of the Maastricht treaty, which was in progress at that time, with the result that the government could not and would not back down in the conflict over Twyford (Kunzlik 1996: 257; see pp. 287–288 (note 56) for an overview of the reaction of the government).

On the other hand, EU activism has restricted the capacity of the direct action movement to affect policy change through the development of a closed system of policy making surrounding the 1993 'Auto-Oil' programme which consciously excluded the anti-roads groups. The 'Auto-Oil' programme marked 'an unprecedented three-year collaboration' between vehicle manufacturers, the oil industry and the Commission with the aim of finding proposals to reduce vehicle emission levels and removing the need for vociferous lobbying by vehicle manufacturers and the oil industry (*Financial Times* 26 June 1996: 20).

The strategy of incorporating the oil and vehicle manufacturers in a technical network designed to 'identify which new measures may be required to meet rational air quality objectives in the most cost effective way, derived from scientifically sound data' served to exclude the opponents of road-based transport from the policy process and to avoid the lifestyle implications of rising traffic volumes on transport's contribution to air pollution. Thus EU policy aimed to manage the challenge of the anti-roads/environmental groups by invoking technical solutions to manage the political agenda.

Third, during the Major era, the DoE and DTp became increasingly divided and this served to reduce the operational autonomy of the DTp.[2] In particular, at this time the DoE became progressively concerned with the impact of the deregulated emphasis of transport policy on issues such as land-use planning, deteriorating ambient air quality and sustainable development. The nature of this division was well illustrated by the conflict over out-of-town shopping that developed between the DoE and DTp in the mid-1990s when a number of documents published by the DoE questioned the predict and provide ethos of transport and the impact of the car on traditional town centres (see, for example, DoE 1994). This conflict reflected a more widespread division between the DTp and DoE over the basic philosophy of transport policy, with the DTp continuing to emphasise a market-driven ethos for transport and planning policy, while the DoE emphasised a need for greater direction, regulation and guidance of the transport and planning systems. Such conflicts reduced the autonomy of the DTp, again benefiting the direct action groups.

The final way in which the direct action movement has benefited from overspill pressures relates to the activity of the Treasury. As Dudley and Richardson point out, during the Major era 'pressure to reduce public expenditure yet again left the trunk roads programme an exposed target for cuts' (1996: 80), with the 1994 budget setting out a reduction of trunk roads expenditure from £2.1bn in 1994–1995 to £1.7bn by 1997–1998. They argue that the activities of the direct action movement at this time helped to erode the hitherto positive policy image of roads, reducing public support for them and helping to legitimise Treasury cuts to the programme as a whole. This suggests that, far from being the beneficiaries of luck, the direct action movement was instrumental in changing the parameters of the agenda by focusing the Treasury's attention on cutting back expenditure on the road programme in the light of broader macro-economic priorities (1996: 79).

While it is true that the actions of the direct action movement were important in this regard, in this area too the role of luck in explaining the apparent capacity of these groups to affect such change must be acknowledged.

The cuts to the road programme which were authorised in the mid-1990s have to be seen in the context of the economic recession which occurred in the early 1990s (Bonefeld *et al.* 1995: ch. 4). Such was the depth of the recession that the economy did not return to the level of output reached in early 1990 until the end of March 1994 (Jay 1994: 170–171). According to Jay, the legacy of the recession combined with the desire by the new chancellor, Kenneth Clarke, to 'portray himself as a stern and sound financier' (ibid.: 192) resulted in simultaneous increases in taxation and reductions in public expenditure in both the 1993 and 1994 budgets. Thus, the cuts to the road programme must be seen as a product of the 'fiscal crisis' prevalent at the time.

In addition, the cuts authorised in the mid-1990s were not unique, reflecting instead a long-standing pattern in which expenditure on the trunk roads programme has risen and fallen across time. Painter shows that during the 1970s total expenditure on trunk roads fell from £383.1m in 1970/1 to £313.6m in 1971/2, rising to £386.2m in 1972/3 before going into gradual decline during the next five years to reach a figure of £281.6m in 1977/8 (1980: 166; figures at 1975 prices). The relatively low support which the DTp has enjoyed historically within the cabinet and with the electorate has always left the roads budget relatively vulnerable to changes of political emphasis by government (Finer 1958: 54). Thus, the direct action movement were lucky in that their activity was targeted at such a programme.

Furthermore, initiatives at the EU level also exerted pressure on the Treasury to reduce state spending on the domestic road programme. Leibfried and Pierson emphasise that in a number of the Community's member states the desire to participate in EMU served to legitimise cuts in state spending, resulting in reductions to a number of social and infrastructure plans (Leibfried and Pierson 1996: 202). In particular, the conditions for entry into EMU (the convergence criteria) were 'quite explicit' in concentrating 'exclusively on monetary variables' (Tsoukalis 1996: 295), placing considerable pressure on the spending plans of the member states to converge in line with other Community countries. Although the Major government had no commitment to join EMU at this time, it, along with all of the other member states in the European Union, has adopted macro-economic policies in line with these objectives, further serving to legitimise a reduction in spending on the road programme.

Finally, the European Union promoted a transnational emphasis on private finance for the funding of its own infrastructure proposals, very much in line with that being proposed by the Major government domestically through the private finance initiative. Hence, developments at the European level and within macro-economic policy domestically both served to legitimise reductions in state spending by the Treasury on the road programme.

Thus, once again, although the activity of the direct action movement has been important in legitimising cuts to an unpopular area of public policy, they have relied on the fact that the road programme itself enjoys relatively low priority with policy makers domestically and on changes to the external environment within which the roads issue has been processed. It is these latter factors, rather than the former, which have been instrumental in legitimising cuts to the road programme.

The direct action movement and luck: can protesters make their own luck?

To conclude this consideration of the role of luck on the success of the direct action movement, it is important to ask whether protesters can make their own luck: can they generate good fortune by exploiting the events which have occurred such as increased congestion and the linkage of cars to deteriorating public health?

On the one hand, the activities of the direct action movement could have produced the conditions which enabled reports such as the SACTRA report or the public health issue to have a greater effect. From this perspective, the protests gave reports such as SACTRA greater force as they changed the nature of the media coverage of the transport issue from a technical to an emotive one. So, although the protests were relying on other, more mainstream, groups such as the National Trust for their legitimacy and access to decision-makers, they were important as members of an alliance which was designed to effect change.

On the other hand, in focusing on the example of congestion one could argue that the publication of the SACTRA report itself was the decisive event. From this perspective, the impact of the report stemmed primarily from the legacy of the policy disaster which the Thatcher government unwittingly began in 1989 with *Roads for Prosperity*. Furthermore, any focus on the role of groups in the conflict over congestion emphasises the key role played by business groups such as the CBI and 'middle-class' groups such as the National Trust – the former strongly critical of the capacity of predict and provide to accommodate future traffic growth, while the latter's involvement was decisive in opening up the parliamentary arena to the knowledge that road building was electorally unpopular. While the National Trust might perhaps be responding to the activity of direct action protests such as those at Twyford, I contend that, in the main, they were not. At Twyford, for example, the protests were led from the outset by local middle-class NIMBY groups, with the direct action movement, in the form of the Dongas, late (though important) additions to the protests.

Overall, however, the precise impact of the protests is not an issue which is of primary concern to this chapter as the key point is to emphasise the *principle* that a number of events occurred outside the activities of the direct action movement which helped them appear more important than they would otherwise have been. Direct action is important, but events must also be taken into account if an accurate account of the politics of the car is to be offered.

Conclusion

This chapter has considered the common hypothesis within the political science literature that changes to the nature of the opposition to a policy are often instrumental in changes to the policy agenda. Applied to the transport policy arena, such an account rests on two central premises: first, that the increasing diversity and scope of the opposition to the road programme has led to the increasing salience of the transport issue, and, second, that the anti-roads groups have used and exploited a number of alternative arenas in order to pressure government and promote their objectives. Although both of these developments have occurred and are significant, this chapter has argued that they do not alone provide a sufficiently comprehensive explanation.

A genuinely comprehensive account of political change needs to acknowledge that changes to the political landscape have been instrumental in enabling the anti-roads groups to become more effective. These have occurred on a number of levels. First, the government's own *Roads for Prosperity* programme instigated a policy disaster which unwittingly aided the activity of the direct action movement. Second, the problems associated with transport have worsened: congestion is rising, ambient air quality is deteriorating, global warming has been 'discovered'. Third, Major's small parliamentary majority and the opposition of a number of MPs to the road programme changed the nature of parliamentary politics, enabling the direct action movement to benefit from that opposition. Finally, a series of overspill pressures have reduced the operational autonomy of the pro-roads groups.

This chapter has argued that all of these changes have been instrumental in enabling the direct action movement to become more effective: without them a very different pattern of policy making would have developed.

Notes

1 The predict and provide orthodoxy refers to the view that government ought to accommodate projected increases (or indeed decreases) in future transport demands through investment to expand (or reduce respectively) the capacity of the infrastructure network. In the case of the road network, this orthodoxy has been used historically to justify expansion, while it has been used to reduce the size of the public transport network (in particular, rail).

2 The DoE and DTp merged in 1997 to form the Department of the Environment, Transport and the Regions (DoETR). However, a number of interviewees working in the new department have suggested that conflict is still extensive within it over the priorities of transport policy.

Bibliography

Anderson, A. (1997) *Media, Culture and the Environment*, London: UCL Press.

Baumgartner, F.R. and Jones, B.D. (1991) 'Agenda dynamics and policy subsystems', *Journal of Politics* 53, 4: 1044–1074.

—— (1993) *Agendas and Instability in American Politics*, Chicago: University of Chicago Press.

Bonefeld, W., Brown, A. and Burnham, P. (1995) *A Major Crisis: The Politics of Economic Policy in Britain in the 1990s*, Aldershot: Dartmouth.

British Broadcasting Corporation (1994) *Panorama: Nose to Tail*.

Bryant, B. (1996) *Twyford Down: Roads, Campaigning and Environmental Law*, London: E. & F.N. Spon.

Button, K. (1995) 'UK environmental policy and transport', in T.S. Gray (ed.) *UK Environmental Policy in the 1990s*, London: Macmillan: 173–188.

Centre for Economics and Business Research (1994) *Roads and Jobs: The Economic Impact of Different Levels of Expenditure on the Roads Programme*, study undertaken on behalf of the British Road Federation, London: British Road Federation.

Cm 693 (1989) *Roads for Prosperity*, London: HMSO.

Cm 2674 (1994) Royal Commission on Environmental Pollution, *Eighteenth Report, Transport and the Environment*, London: HMSO.

Cm 3587 (1997) *The United Kingdom National Air Quality Strategy*, London: HMSO.

Confederation of British Industry (CBI) (1995a) *Missing Links: Settling National Transport Priorities – A CBI Discussion Document*, London: CBI.

—— (1995b) *Moving Forward: A Business Strategy for Transport*, London: CBI.

Department of Environment (DoE) (1994) *Vital and Viable Town Centres: Meeting the Challenge*, London: HMSO.

Department of Health (DoH) (1995a) *Asthma: An Epidemiological Overview*, London: HMSO.

—— (1995b) *Asthma and Outdoor Air Pollution*, London: HMSO.

Department of Transport (DTp) (1989) *National Road Traffic Forecasts (Great Britain) 1989*, London: HMSO.

—— (1994) *Trunk Roads in England: 1994 Review*, London: HMSO.

Doherty, B. (1997) 'Direct action against road-building: some implications for the concept of protest repertoires', in J. Stanyer and G. Stoker (eds) *Contemporary Political Studies 1997*, 1: 147–155.

Dudley, G.F. (1983) 'The road lobby: a declining force?', in D. Marsh (ed.) *Pressure Politics*, London: Junction Books: 104–128.

Dudley, G.F. and Richardson, J.J. (1995) 'Explaining policy change: adversarial communities, policy arenas, and the development of UK trunk roads policy since 1945', unpublished paper.

—— (1996) 'Why does policy change over time? Adversarial policy communities, alternative policy arenas, and British trunk roads policy 1945–95', *Journal of European Public Policy* 3, 1: 63–83.

—— (1998) 'Arenas without rules and the policy change process: outsider groups and British roads policy', draft paper submitted to *Political Studies*.

Dunleavy, P. (1995) 'Policy disasters: explaining the UK's record', *Public Policy and Administration* 10, 2: 52–70.

Finer, S.E. (1958) 'Transport interests and the road lobby', *Political Quarterly* 29: 47–58.

Grant, W. (1995) *Autos, Smog and Pollution Control: The Politics of Air Quality Management in California*, Aldershot: Edward Elgar.

—— (1997) 'BSE and the politics of food', in P. Dunleavy, A. Gamble, I. Holliday and G. Peele (eds) *Developments in British Politics 5*, Basingstoke: Macmillan.

Hamer, M. (1987) *Wheels Within Wheels*, London: Routledge and Kegan Paul.

Jay, P. (1994) 'The economy: 1990–94', in D. Kavanagh and A. Seldon (eds) *The Major Effect*, London: Macmillan/Papermac: 169–205.

Kunzlik, P. (1996) 'The legal battle: "an astonishing intervention"', in B. Bryant, *Twyford Down: Roads, Campaigning and Environmental Law*, London: E. & F.N. Spon.

Leibfreid, S. and Pierson, P. (1996) 'Social policy', in H. Wallace and W. Wallace (eds) *Policy-Making in the European Union*, Oxford: Oxford University Press: 185–207.

Levin, P.H. (1979) 'Highway inquiries: a study in governmental responsiveness', *Public Administration* 57, 1: 21–49.

Ludlum, S. (1996) 'The spectre haunting conservatism: Europe and backbench rebellion', in S. Ludlum and M.J. Smith (eds) *Contemporary British Conservatism*, Basingstoke: Macmillan: 98–120.

Machiavelli, N. (1513) 'The Prince', translation by L. Ricci, revised by E.R.P. Vincent in *The Prince and Discourses*, New York: The Modern Library.

McLaren, D.P. and Higman, R. (1993) 'The environmental implications of congestion on the interurban network in the UK', paper given to 21st PTRC Summer Annual Meeting, 1993.

Maddison, D. and Pearce, D. (1995) 'The UK and global warming policy', in T.S. Gray (ed) *UK Environmental Policy in the 1990s*, London: Macmillan: 123–143.

Painter, M. (1980) 'Whitehall and roads: a case study of sectoral politics', *Policy and Politics* 8, 2: 163–186.

Paterson, M. (1996) *Global Warming and Global Politics*, London: Routledge.

Riddell, P. (1994) 'Major and parliament', in D. Kavanagh and A. Seldon (eds) *The Major Effect*, London: Macmillan/Papermac: 46–63.

Robinson, N. (2000) *The Politics of Agenda Setting: The Car and the Shaping of Public Policy*, Aldershot: Ashgate.

Sabatier, P.A. (1993) 'Policy change over a decade or more', in P.A. Sabatier and H.C. Jenkins-Smith (eds) *Policy Change and Learning; An Advocacy Coalition Approach*, Boulder: Westview Press: 13–39.

Sabatier, P.A. and Jenkins-Smith, H.C. (1993) 'The advocacy coalition framework: assessment, revisions, and implications for scholars and practitioners', in P.A. Sabatier and H.C. Jenkins-Smith (eds) *Policy Change and Learning: An Advocacy Coalition Approach*, Boulder: Westview Press, 211–235.

Schattschneider, E.E. (1960) *The Semisovereign People: A Realist's View of Democracy in America*, Illinois: Dryden Press.

Standing Advisory Committee on Trunk Roads Assessment (1994) *Trunk Roads and the Generation of Traffic*, London: HMSO.

Tsoukalis, L. (1996) 'Economic and monetary union: the primacy of high politics', in H. Wallace and W. Wallace (eds) *Policy-Making in the European Union*, Oxford: Oxford University Press: 279–299.

Tyme, J. (1978) *Motorways versus Democracy*, London: Macmillan Press.

Young, S. (1993) *The Politics of the Environment*, Manchester: Baseline Books.

Index

A30 69, 122, 151, 152
acid rain 210
ACT-UP 144–5, 146
*Adbusters*105
affinity groups 129
agenda setting: and congestion 200; 204, 207–8; and external factors 200, 210–13; and luck 200, 203–13; and opposition of MPs to the road programme 200, 208–10; and policy arenas 200–1; and policy disasters 200, 203–5; and policy image 200–1; and policy problems 206–8; and public health 206–7; punctuated equilibrium model 200–1; and the Treasury 200
All London Against the Roads Menace (ALARM) 3, 8, 184–5
Alarm UK 8, 42, 81, 118, 168, 183–98, 209; aims 184–6; social bases of membership 3, 51, 188–91; structure 185–8
Alliance Against the BNRR 167–82
alternative policy arenas 200–3
anarchism 14, 44–5, 73, 87, 183; direct action as contemporary expression of 97–8; in Earth First! 114, 116, 123, 125, 126, 128–30; in J18 108; in RTS ideology 66–7, 82
Animal 154, 157
Animal Liberation Front (ALF) 80, 86–7, 127
animal welfare campaigns 28–31, 40–1, 45–6, 49
anti-capitalism 12, 51, 74, 88–9; in anticonsumerist movements 106; in Earth First! 114, 127–30; in RTS 67, 145
anti-capitalist protests 9, 12, 71, 82, 88–9, 108, 129; *see also* J18

anticonsumerism 51, 94, 99–100, 102–8, 145; and Christmas 103, 106
anti-nuclear movements *see* nuclear power, nuclear weapons
Areas of Outstanding Natural Beauty 65
arms sales/trade protests 72, 84, 108, 112, 114, 128, 194
Aronowitz, Stanley 134, 144–5
Ashton Court 167–82
asthma 206–7
Australia 8, 17, 52, 63, 68, 69, 73–4, 75, 105
Austria 15

Band of Mercy 86; *see also* Animal Liberation Front
bearing witness 2, 5, 84
Beck, Ulrich 12
Big Issue 125
biocentrism *see* deep ecology
Birmingham Northern Relief Road (BNRR) 167–82
Bookchin, Murray 94, 98–9, 101, 107, 114
Brewery Fields 122, 123, 124
British exceptionalism 15–17
British Road Federation (BRF) 204–5
Burbridge, Jake 8, 83
Butler, Judith 134, 137, 139, 141, 145–6, 156

capitalism *see* anti-capitalism
Carnival against Capitalism *see* J18
Castells, Manuel 11–12, 14, 20, 141, 147
Channel Tunnel 34, 47
cherry-picker cranes 65, 67, 69
civil disobedience 1–2, 104, 127, 146
Civil Rights Movement 63
CJA *see* Criminal Justice and Public Order Act

Claremont Road 67, 69; *see also* M11

class 3, 15, 135, 136–7; make-up of Alarm UK 189–91; in media constructions 154–5, 156

Cohn, Norman 94, 95–7, 99, 100

Confederation of British Industry 207, 214

congestion 179, 200, 204–5, 207–8

collective identity *see* identity

community, as ideal of protesters 12, 14–15, 66, 72, 101

Corporate Watch 113

corporations *see* multinational corporations

courts: and evictions 75; as means of stopping protests 68, 118; use by protesters for publicity 72, 83, 94, 107; use of to stop road schemes 119–20, 168, 172–4, 179, 180, 181

Council for the Protection of Rural England (CPRE) 7, 52, 193

counterculture 9, 15, 33, 51, 53, 73, 107; in the US 97, 102–3; *see also* New Left

counter-hegemony 130, 162

Countryside Movement/Alliance 29, 64, 89

Criminal Justice and Public Order Act (1995) (CJA) 21, 67, 68, 118, 144, 158; campaigns against 49, 104, 118, 143

Critical Mass 70–1

cross-national comparisons 15–19, 28, 51–3, 63, 73–4; *see also* diffusion, individual countries

cultural codes *see* symbolic politics

cycles of protest 32, 63–5, 73

Debord, Guy 102

deep ecology 74, 86, 87, 94–5, 114–5

deforestation *see* rainforest destruction

democracy, lack of, as reason for protesting 85, 169, 171–2

Department of Environment (DoE), conflict with Department of Transport 212

Department of Environment, Transport and the Regions (DoETR) 49, 173

Department of Transport (DTp) 192; and conflict with the Department of Environment 212; and historically low support from the Treasury 212; and the SACTRA report 207–8

Design, Build, Finance, Operate (DBFO) 152, 156, 160; *see also* Private Finance Initiative

development 15; in Earth First! ideology 104, 105, 106, 108; in anticomsumerist ideology 115, 120, 121, 123, 126; *see also* anti-capitalism

diffusion 18, 63–5, 72–5, 80, 90

Diggers 96

DIY culture 33, 107

D-locks 73, 176

Do or Die 65, 74, 88, 113, 152, 161; *see also* Earth First!

Donga Tribe 9, 81, 104, 122, 136, 177, 192; spirituality of 65

Dudley and Richardson 199, 200–1

Earth First! 3, 65, 72, 79, 81, 83–7, 104, 106, 112–32, 133, 144, 146, 147, 169, 183, 192; *Action Update* 75, 112; diffusion to other European countries 18, 74; Fisons action 140–2; founding of in UK 8–9; local groups 9, 112; national gathering 9, 114, 140–2; relationship to Alarm UK 193; repertoires of 42–5, 83–7; at Twyford Down 81; US 8, 52, 73, 75, 126; *see also* *Do or Die*

Earth Liberation Front (ELF) 80, 85–6, 87, 127

Earth Summit (UNCED) 7, 16

Ecodefense (Foreman and Haywood) 8, 73, 87, 119

eco-feminism 115

ecophilosophy 94, 114

eco-socialism 114

ecotage 85–7, 126–7; *see also* elving, pixieing

eco-villages 120, 129

elving 85–7; *see also* ecotage

empowerment 115, 122, 123, 126, 129, 137, 138, 162, 171

Enlightenment, the 96, 100

environmental movement organisations (EMOs) 6, 7, 16–21, 26, 29, 51, 63–4; professionalisation/ institutionalisation of 1, 7, 16, 18, 25, 53, 104, 117, 159; *see also* individual organisations

epistemologies of rule 99, 107

ethical shoplifting 38, 84

ethnicity 11, 135, 136, 137; of Alarm UK members 189

European Union 210–1; and 'auto-oil' programme 211; and conflict at Twyford Down 211; and EMU 213

Express 152–6

Fairmile 68, 69, 122, 151–2; *see also* A30,
    Swampy
family 160–1; in media constructions of
    protests 154–5; in utopian communities
    101
feminism 84, 115, 119, 139; *see also* family,
    gender
Finland 18
Fisons 85, 140
FoE *see* Friends of the Earth
Foreman, Dave 87, 119, 133
Foucault, Michel 100, 160
France 31–2
Friends of Ashton Court 167–182
Friends of the Earth (FoE) 1, 3, 7, 16, 51,
    80, 169, 193, 204, 209; and
    anticonsumerism 106; forms of protest
    42–6; founding of 4–6; membership
    growth 48; relationship with Earth
    First! 118–9, 141; Schweppes action 5,
    103; support for direct action 8, 20–1,
    81, 118, 170–1, 179

Gandhi 1, 84–5, 86, 88
gender 74, 97, 134–7; in media
    constructions 154–6; in millenarian
    movements 96; in protest camps 71, 72,
    177; of Alarm UK members 189–90;
    see also family, feminism
genetic modification 49–50, 79–92; crops
    19, 21, 49; food 9, 12, 21, 50, 71, 72,
    106; organisms (GMOs) 52, 168, 176
Genetics Engineering Network (GEN) 113
GenetiX Snowball 72, 82–3, 84
Germany 15, 18, 19, 26, 73, 74
Giddens, Anthony 12
global warming 14, 79, 200, 210–1
globalisation: as focus of protest 12, 104,
    145; and new social movements 12–3;
    see also anti-capitalism
GM *see* genetic modification
Golden Hill (Bristol) 79, 80–1
Goldman Foundation 185, 192
Green Anarchist 8, 87
green consumerism 104, 133, 138
Greenham Common 72, 83, 84
Green Line 8
Greenpeace 1, 7, 9, 16, 19, 51, 52, 159,
    170; forms of protest 42–6; founding of
    4–6; membership growth 48;
    relationship with Earth First! 118–9;
    support for direct action 20–1
Green Party 15–16, 29, 33, 79, 82, 118;

1989 European election result 6, 25, 48;
    forms of protest 42–6; weakness of 7,
    16
Guardian 18, 27–8, 155

Habermas, Jurgen 13, 98, 195
health, effects of vehicles on 206–7
Hetherington, Kevin 13, 133, 136
hierarchy, rejection of 11, 98, 112, 114–5,
    128; by millenarian movements 95, 96
Highway Agency 167, 174
house-building 7, 47, 50, 52, 64, 75, 123,
    124, 168, 176
Hunt Saboteurs Association 86
hunting 28–31, 41, 45, 46, 64, 86

identity 65, 121, 133–50, 156; collective
    113, 130; essentialist accounts of
    136–7; and new social movement
    theory 10, 13–14; queer theory and
    137–8, 156
impacts 4, 19–21; on car culture 21; on
    government policy 20, 195–6, 199–217;
    media neutralisation 160; on political
    culture 20–1
Inglehart, Ronald 184, 190
Ireland (Republic of) 18, 74, 106
Italy 13, 64, 74

J18 9, 82, 88–9, 108, 114, 125–6, 129–30

Keele University Direct Action Conference
    45, 118

Labour Party 15, 25, 30, 49–50, 173, 190,
    194, 195
lesbian and gay movement 11, 137–9; *see
    also* queer theory
LETS 107, 124
Liberal Democrat Party 30, 190
lifestyle 13, 102–7, 115, 120, 123, 124,
    129, 138, 174, 175, 176, 178
LIFFE *see* London International Financial
    Futures Exchange
live animal exports 64, 75, 174
Liverpool dockers 75, 123
local campaigns 3, 7, 17–18, 122–4,
    167–82, 194–6; and Friends of the
    Earth 170–1; and public inquiries
    171–2, 201, 202; relationship with
    protest camps 174–9; use of the courts
    172–4

local government and opposition to the road programme 20, 209
lock-ons 68–9, 73, 74, 169
London Animal Action 127
London International Financial Futures Exchange (LIFFE) 129
luck: and congestion 207; and economic recession 212; and external factors 210–3; and policy disasters 203–5; and public health 206–7
Luddites 88

M11 9, 65–6, 67, 69, 81, 122, 152, 174, 187; as origin of RTS 143
M65 65, 66, 69, 81, 84
M77 75, 81, 120, 121, 123, 126, 152, 172, 175, 177; connection to anti-poll tax campaigns 48, 51
McAdam, Doug 63, 73
McDonald's 38, 106, 107, 108, 143, 145
McKay, George 128, 168
McLibel 106
Mail 154
Major, John, government of 17, 199–208, 211–3
Manchester airport 20, 66, 68, 70, 71, 82, 124, 152, 170, 174, 177
manufactured vulnerability 2, 52, 62–78, 85
Marshall, George 8
marxism 82, 102, 103, 128
materialism, rejection of 94, 95, 101, 102, 107
Mayday protests (2000) 19
media 1, 48, 62, 67, 71, 74, 151–66; decline in reporting of environmental protest 49; Greenpeace and 5–6; hostility to by protesters 124–5, 161–2; impact of direct action on agenda of 200, 201–3; over-reporting of violence 38–9, 44; protest as a human interest story 13, 39–40, 157; protest as spectacle 68, 70, 71; reporting of asthma 207; and the road lobby 202; as site of political struggles 2, 156–60; as source of information on protest activity 26–8; use of by protesters 62, 118, 121, 124, 141, 144; *see also* individual newspapers
Melchett, Peter 19–21
Melucci, Alberto 10, 11, 14–15, 113, 121, 158–9
millenarianism 4, 14, 94, 95–7, 107–8

Mirror 154, 158
Monsanto 19, 21, 107
MPs: and GM crops 82; and opposition to the road programme 20, 48, 208–10
multinational corporations 19, 119, 120, 126, 146–7, 174, 179
Muppet Dave 152, 155

N30 9, 19, 128
Naess, Arne 100
National Road Traffic Forecasts, 1989 203–5
National Trust 16, 131, 199, 214
Natty Trust 120
Netherlands, The 18, 74, 106
networks, as form of organisation 10, 147; in Alarm UK 8, 85–7; in anticonsumerist movements 94; Earth First! 8, 112–3, 115–6, 118; and globalisation 11–12, 141; peace movement 8; in RTS 145–6; *see also* hierarchy, rejection of
New Age travellers 35
New Left 73, 97, 160
new middle class 3, 188, 191
new social movements 9–15, 97–8, 113, 137–8; globalisation and 12–13; identity-oriented accounts of 13–14, 133–50; instrumental accounts of 13; novelty of 11–12
Newbury bypass 44, 49, 75, 81, 118, 126, 155, 176, 193; violence at 38
NIMBY 3, 50, 122, 123, 124, 138, 174–5, 181, 187–8, 214
non-violence 11, 67, 72, 128–9; *see also* NVDA
non violent direct action *see* NVDA
NOPE 174–5, 181, 187–8
normalisation 152–6, 157–8
novelty of direct action protests 3; of tactics 70–1; *see also* new social movements, tactical innovation
NSM *see* new social movements
nuclear power 5–6, 8, 15–16, 18, 19, 33, 34, 74, 82, 97, 188, 195
nuclear weapons 5, 83, 135, 195; *see also* Greenham common, peace movement
NVDA 2, 18, 62–3, 70, 73, 75, 82, 118, 128, 142, 171, 192, 193

opencast mining 9, 82, 114
organisation of protest groups *see* networks
Outsider groups 202–3

peace camps 6, 62, 72, 84
peace movement 6, 15, 72, 80, 82, 84
peat extraction 85, 114, 140
pixieing 86, 126–7; *see also* ecotage, elving
Ploughshares 84, 128
police/policing 18–19, 21, 70, 74, 120, 122, 130, 143; at the BNRR 178; costs of 192; differences between UK and other countries 18–19; infiltration of protest movements 123; at J18 129; at M11 67; surveillance of protesters 68, 178–9, 192; at Twyford Down 192, 195; violence and 38, 143
policy arenas 200–1, 214
policy disasters 200, 203–5, 214
policy image 200–1
political economy *see* anti-capitalism
political opportunity structures 16–17, 47, 48, 63, 98, 185
Pollok *see* M77
Pollok Free State 48, 120, 121, 123, 177
poll tax 15, 48, 64
post-materialism 184, 190
postmodernity 133, 134, 142, 147; and identity politics 140
predict and provide orthodoxy 204–5, 207, 208, 212, 214
Prescott, John 49, 173
Preston *see* M65
Prevention of Terrorism Bill/Act 21, 47, 131, 178
Private Finance Initiative (PFI) 173; *see also* Design, Build, Finance, Operate
private security 67, 120, 178, 187, 192
progress 15, 114, 115, 120–1, 159
protest camps 49, 62–78, 82, 123, 169; as Earth First! strategy 119; FoE support for 118; and local campaigns 174–9; at M77 48
protest cycles *see* cycles of protest
protest event analysis 18, 26–7
public inquiries 5, 6, 7, 82, 171–2, 174, 186, 195; and direct action 202
public opinion 1, 26, 27, 48, 161, 177, 195; and asthma 207; as constraint on police use of force 74; internal inconsistency of 210; and opposition to road building 209–10
punctuated equilibrium model 200–1
punk 9, 89, 102

quarries 7, 9, 82, 167; *see also* Ashton Court
queer theory 14, 133–50

radicalisation of environmentalism 6–9, 49, 127–30
Rainforest Action Group 8
rainforest destruction 8–9, 38, 75, 79, 81, 82, 83–4, 112, 114; protesters use of tripods 69
Ramblers' Association 7, 35, 43, 44
Real World Coalition 194
Reclaim the Streets (RTS) 12, 14–15, 42, 81–2, 90, 104, 121, 133, 140, 141, 146, 147, 183; Bristol party 142–3; connection to Earth First! 113; M41 action 120; outside the UK 74
religion 95–6, 99, 100–1, 107
repertoires of contention 62, 64, 79–80
Road Alert! 42, 81, 112, 118, 169, 192–3
Roads for Prosperity 20, 123, 126, 200, 208, 209, 214, 215; as policy disaster 203–5; as spur to roads protests 7–8, 9, 185
road lobby: and historical bias serving their interests 200, 201, 202–3; and loss of control of the policy process 202–3; *see also* British Road Federation
Roseneil, Sasha 72, 79–80, 120
Royal Society for the Protection of Birds (RSPB) 42–6, 199
RTS *see* Reclaim the Streets
Rucht, Dieter 3, 13, 18, 62, 115, 116

Sabatier, Paul 210
sabotage 73–4, 85–7, 119, 126, 128
SACTRA *see* Standing Advisory Committee on Trunk Roads Assessment
Sandbrook, Richard 5
satyagraha *see* Gandhi
SchNEWS 178
science: and asthma 206–7; and global warming 210–1
self-actualisation 94, 101, 102, 107–8
Shell 49, 127
Sierra Club 52, 119
Site of Special Scientific Interest (SSSI) 114, 167
Situationism 101–2
skimmingtons 80, 88–9
Snowballs 72, 80, 82–5
social ecology 94–5, 98–9, 114, 183
Solsbury Hill 152, 172, 175, 176, 177
Spain 19
spirituality 65, 114
squatts 65–6, 67, 75, 114, 123
Standing Advisory Committee on Trunk

Roads Assessment (SACTRA) 20, 205, 207–8, 214
state, the, as focus of protests 4, 21, 66, 117, 120, 122, 123, 125, 128, 144–6; and new social movements 10, 12
Stewart, John 185–6, 187–8, 209
strategy 3–4, 13, 14, 112–32, 168, 169–70, 175, 177; cost-escalation 70, 86–7, 126; court actions as 172; media in, 159, 161–2; public inquiries as 171; radical flank effect 117–9, 185
street parties 66–7, 68, 71, 81–2, 88–9, 90, 120, 142–3; *see also* Reclaim the Streets
structure *see* networks
Swampy 40, 151–60
Sweden 15, 18, 106
Switzerland 15
symbolic politics 11–12, 13, 14–15, 21, 119–21, 142, 146; media and 2, 155–6, 157–9; of protest camps 71
Szerszynski, Bronislaw 14, 133–4

tactical innovation 2, 68–72, 202
Tarrow, Sidney 63–4, 74, 79–80, 185
TEA *see* Transformation of Environmental Activism Project
temporary autonomous zones 102–3, 104, 120
Thatcher, Margaret 6, 16, 47–8, 49, 199, 214
Thatcherism 103
The Land Is Ours (TLIO) 81, 120
Tilbury Docks 8
Tilly, Charles 62–3, 79
Torrance, Jason 8, 83
Transformation of Environmental Activism project (TEA) 18, 25–61, 114
Transport 2000 7, 45, 185, 193, 199
Transport Activists Roundtable 7, 119
Treasury 200; and aim to reduce public expenditure 212–3
tree houses 2, 66, 74, 114, 121, 123, 202; *see also* walkways
trees, symbolism of 2, 66
tripods 68, 69, 71, 73, 202

tunnels 2, 65, 67, 68, 69–70, 72, 74, 114, 128, 154, 169, 178, 202; at A30 69, 151
Twyford Down 49, 67, 68, 85, 113, 114, 129, 152, 174, 185, 202, 209, 214; Alarm UK at 191–2; Donga Tribe at 65, 81, 122, 136; Earth First! at 44, 118; European Commission and 211; FoE at 20, 44, 81, 118, 170; as impetus for other roads protests 9, 192; security costs of 192
Tyme, John 6, 82, 195, 201

Undercurrents 127, 161
United States of America 8, 17, 18 52–4, 63, 68, 73, 106; establishment of FoE in 4
urban protest 104–6
urban space 65, 66–7, 95, 143
utopianism 12, 95–6, 100–1, 142

vegetarianism 28–9, 133, 136, 154
violence 3, 81, 128–30; alleged rise in 25; in animal rights protests 40–1 as false justification for police surveillance 68; media over-reporting or sensationalisation of 38–40, 125, 152; by police or security 122, 46; protesters' vulnerability to 70; rarity in environmental protests 38; *see also* police, private security

walkways 18, 65, 68, 69, 202
Women's Environmental Network 45, 106
women's movement 11, 72, 84
World Wide Fund for Nature (WWF) 7, 16, 42–6

youth: as origin of new forms of protest 48, 51, 103; as part of media construction 152–3

Zelter, Angie 83–4
Zeneca 85